LATINX CIVIL WARS

AMERICA AND THE LONG 19TH CENTURY

General Editors: David Kazanjian, Elizabeth McHenry, and Priscilla Wald

Black Frankenstein: The Making of an American Metaphor
Elizabeth Young

Neither Fugitive nor Free: Atlantic Slavery, Freedom Suits, and the Legal Culture of Travel
Edlie L. Wong

Shadowing the White Man's Burden: US Imperialism and the Problem of the Color Line
Gretchen Murphy

Bodies of Reform: The Rhetoric of Character in Gilded-Age America
James B. Salazar

Sites Unseen: Architecture, Race, and American Literature
William A. Gleason

Racial Innocence: Performing American Childhood from Slavery to Civil Rights
Robin Bernstein

American Arabesque: Arabs and Islam in the Nineteenth-Century Imaginary
Jacob Rama Berman

Racial Indigestion: Eating Bodies in the Nineteenth Century
Kyla Wazana Tompkins

Idle Threats: Men and the Limits of Productivity in Nineteenth-Century America
Andrew Lyndon Knighton

Tomorrow's Parties: Sex and the Untimely in Nineteenth-Century America
Peter Coviello

Bonds of Citizenship: Law and the Labors of Emancipation
Hoang Gia Phan

The Traumatic Colonel: The Founding Fathers, Slavery, and the Phantasmatic Aaron Burr
Michael J. Drexler and Ed White

Unsettled States: Nineteenth-Century American Literary Studies
Edited by Dana Luciano and Ivy G. Wilson

Sitting in Darkness: Mark Twain's Asia and Comparative Racialization
Hsuan L. Hsu

Picture Freedom: Remaking Black Visuality in the Early Nineteenth Century
Jasmine Nichole Cobb

Stella: A Novel of the Haitian Revolution
Émeric Bergeaud
Translated by Lesley Curtis and Christen Mucher

Racial Reconstruction: Black Inclusion, Chinese Exclusion, and the Fictions of Citizenship
Edlie L. Wong

Ethnology and Empire: Languages, Literature, and the Making of the North American Borderlands
Robert Lawrence Gunn

The Black Radical Tragic: Performance, Aesthetics, and the Unfinished Haitian Revolution
Jeremy Matthew Glick

Undisciplined: Science, Ethnography, and Personhood in the Americas, 1830–1940
Nihad M. Farooq

The Latino Nineteenth Century
Edited by Rodrigo Lazo and Jesse Alemán

Fugitive Science: Empiricism and Freedom in Early African American Culture
Britt Rusert

Before Chicano: Citizenship and the Making of Mexican American Manhood, 1848–1959
Alberto Varon

Emergent Worlds: Alternative States in Nineteenth-Century American Culture
Edward Sugden

Haiti's Paper War: Post-Independence Writing, Civil War, and the Making of the Republic, 1804–1954
Chelsea Stieber

The Unintended: Photography, Property, and the Aesthetics of Racial Capitalism
Monica Huerta

The Garden Politic: Global Plants and Botanical Nationalism in Nineteenth-Century America
Mary Kuhn

Printing Nueva York: Spanish-Language Print Culture, Media Change, and Democracy in the Late Nineteenth Century
Kelley Kreitz

Latinx Civil Wars: The Formation of Latinidad in an Age of Revolution and Rebellion
Jesse Alemán

Latinx Civil Wars

The Formation of Latinidad in an Age of Revolution and Rebellion

Jesse Alemán

NEW YORK UNIVERSITY PRESS
New York

NEW YORK UNIVERSITY PRESS
New York
www.nyupress.org

Please contact the Library of Congress for Cataloging-in-Publication data.

ISBN: 9781479837113 (hardback)
ISBN: 9781479837144 (paperback)
ISBN: 9781479837175 (library ebook)
ISBN: 9781479837168 (consumer ebook)

This book is printed on acid-free paper, and its binding materials are chosen for strength and durability. We strive to use environmentally responsible suppliers and materials to the greatest extent possible in publishing our books.

The manufacturer's authorized representative in the EU for product safety is Mare Nostrum Group B.V., Mauritskade 21D, 1091 GC Amsterdam, The Netherlands. Email: gpsr@mare-nostrum.co.uk.

Manufactured in the United States of America

10 9 8 7 6 5 4 3 2 1

Also available as an ebook

For David and Felipa Alemán, who taught me how to tell and write stories. I'm still listening.

CONTENTS

ILLUSTRATIONS

A NOTE ON SOURCE MATERIALS

Working with handwritten or early print texts in Spanish and English presents different challenges that bear their imprint in this book. The first is the issue of translation. Several Spanish vernaculars appear in the archival material, personal letters, newsprint, and other ephemera that span from California to Cuba via the Southwestern borderlands. Regional dialects, idiomatic abbreviations, and colloquialisms, alongside personal voice, ink bleeds, and shoddy paper, make consistent, accurate translation a minefield, to say the least. Unless otherwise indicated, all translations are provided by Mario Del Angel Guevara in conversation with me. On occasion, I have silently adjusted his professional translations to account for consistency in the writer's voice, odd colloquialisms, or creative license with language for which I bear the responsibility of any misusage. Second, misspellings, missing accents, omitted or illegible words, grammatical errors, or punctuation problems appear in more than a few personal letters and print pieces. I have opted not to mark these issues with *sic* in square brackets or to correct them because they indicate the struggle of literacy, English-language transition, or misrepresentation in the record that is central to my discussion about the formation of US Latinidad. Emendations are provided in brackets only when they are necessary for clarity's sake, and I have indicated in the endnotes when markers of emphasis (underlines or italics) appear in the original or are added by me. Finally, in terms of names, I follow how Latinx writers spelled their names in signatures, autobiographical writings, or self-authored bylines. However, in my reference material, I retain the spelling of names as they are listed in research databases, metadata, original publications, or official records, where Hispanophone first and last names can be misspelled, abbreviated, or transliterated from Spanish to English in the archival graveyards of US Latinidad.

Introduction

Latinx Civil War Writings and the Embattled Archive of US Latinidad

On May 7, 1865, Tejano Confederate Captain Manuel Yturri wrote to his wife, Elena, from camp outside Anderson, Texas, "Military life is the most miserable there is in this world. I'd rather be a Negro than [in the] military." While his letter makes no mention of Lee's surrender or Lincoln's assassination the month prior, he hints at the war's end with what he knows is trauma to follow: "Yes, my love, things have happened to me since I became a soldier which I never thought possible in this world. . . . When I visit with you one time, I'll tell you because the story is very long, but if my God permits me to survive this war, I'll first cut my neck than be drafted in another one." Yturri was not exactly a gung-ho greenhorn at the start of the war. As a private stationed at Camp Gillespie in the Thirty-Third Texas Calvary under Colonel James Duff, he tells his wife, "I never had been tired as much in my life as I was this time," and then a few months later, as a lieutenant in the Third Texas Regiment, he wrote from camp in Louisiana, on July 3, 1864, "What a sad life I experienced as a soldier, my darling. Almost all the soldiers in the division suffer from diahrrea." Soon, camp life gave way to the Battle at Jenkins Ferry, and the Tejano's tone turns grim: "My dear, during the battle, I wasn't frightened at all and I wasn't afraid either," he says. "I was just waiting to fall dead each minute." The battlefront had a profound effect on Yturri. He recounts how the Union dead were found on the field, many of them in possession of pictures of family members and fiancées. "I don't ask for yours," he explains to his wife, "because we might fight with the Yankees and I might be killed and they would keep your picture." The photographic *memento mori* haunts him with the losses left on the front, the depths of sorrow and grief that await those at home, and the terrible reality that he too might end up like so many of the battlefield dead. "Who knows if I'll die here from some illness because this country is very unhealthy or the Yankees will kill me," he writes from camp near Camden, Arkansas, on October 8, 1864, and then from Shreveport, Louisiana, on February 28, 1865, he shares, "I believe that if I were single and I knew that this war was going to last four years more, I would kill myself."[1]

The war ended three months later, and Yturri survived, unlike his Confederate *cuñado*, brother-in-law Captain Joseph de la Garza, a native San Antonian who wrote home from the front to his mother and his sisters, including Elena, Yturri's wife, during his two years in service. De la Garza's optimism, commitment, and enthusiasm for the cause contrast with Yturri's uneasy notes. He certainly had his dark nights, as when he confided to his sister Elena on August 20, 1862, from Little Rock, "You cannot know how troubled I am sometimes. Awful dreams will visit me once in a while," but for the most part, de la Garza's extant letters convey his growing confidence and optimism. From Camp McColluch, near Victoria, Texas, he writes to his mother on April 30, 1862, that he endured the roughly hundred-mile march from San Antonio to Victoria better than he expected. "Up to now I don't think I would like a military career," he says, "but we'll see later." Two months later, he tells his sister Carolina, "The boys in our company seem to like me well. I'm in good health." By August that same year, a growing stoicism buttressed his earlier optimism after roughly five months enlisted. Speaking of himself and two fellow Tejano Confederates, he reasons to his sister Elena, "In the course of time we will all be good soldiers. . . . It is true it takes us from home a considerable distance but we had to leave home one day or another so it does not make much of a difference after all." He reassures his mother as well: "Don't worry about me (and tell them not [to worry about] Navarro and Pedro) in the least for we are men and we are fighting for our country." De la Garza's determination did not go unnoticed. He shares with his brother-in-law Bart J. DeWitt that he was appointed the company's first lieutenant, and even as the tides of the war changed, he asserts, "When I went into service I determined that I would go through and I am of the same mind yet with the help of God." His commitment to the Confederate cause is also evident in his sentiments for the plantation South. From camp on Bayou Boeuf, near Cheneyville, Louisiana, on October 27, 1863, he writes to his mother, "Now we are retreating. The Yankees are pursuing us. . . . All the plantations are destroyed. Some appear not to have been inhabited for years. It is sad to see everything ruined. Now that the Yankees are coming they'll finish desolating everything. Don't worry about me. If you hear that they killed or wounded [me,] tell them that it's okay, he died well." De la Garza's letter proved prescient: he was killed on the field at the Battle of Mansfield (Sabine Cross Roads) during the Red River campaign in Louisiana.[2]

These caches of letters are undoubtedly unique. Most Mexican Texans in the Confederate army were not usually fluent in English and Spanish, but these two San Antonio scions attended St. Joseph College, a Jesuit institution in Bardstown, Kentucky. So, even though they were not from slaveholding families, the two Tejanos enjoyed the benefits of an educational institution established and maintained through the direct and indirect exploitation of enslaved Black people.[3] Moreover, unlike the many Tejano Confederates who filled and deserted the lower ranks, Yturri and de la Garza rose in rank, reenlisted, and received the support of their fellow Anglo and Tejano comrades. They fought because, as de la Garza put it, "we are men and we are fighting for our country." With this affirmation of martial masculinity, de la Garza raises a critical question for his Tejano compatriots and the rest of the US Latinx people who volunteered in, were conscripted into, or were otherwise complicit with the Union or the so-called Confederacy: which country is theirs, exactly? When de la Garza laments the fall of plantation life and the destruction that he's sure the Yankees will bring, he's mourning the loss of the "country" of his Kentucky schoolboy days: the slaveholding US South of the past. Yturri is more reserved about his allegiance to a Confederate nation (real or imagined), but his statement that he would "rather be a Negro than [in the] military" is a telling double-voiced declaration. On the one hand, he notes that, unlike soldiers and officers like himself, "a Negro doesn't need a pass" to leave camp, and Yturri is desperate to return home to his wife. On the other, the statement imagines a racialized inversion of power whereby Yturri, the Tejano officer who is fighting to preserve slavery, feels himself to be enslaved, so to speak, to the Confederate army while Blacks seemingly run free, coming and going as they please, as it were. Whether or not he realizes it, his is a rhetoric of the feelings of white racial disempowerment that will galvanize white power during Radical Reconstruction into widespread lynching, the rise of the Klan, and Jim Crow legislation. One Tejano Confederate laments the fall of the old slaveholding US South, the other resents the future of a new nation with free Black people, and somewhere in between is the borderlands of their US Latinidad that emerged from the theaters of the Civil War.

Latinx Civil Wars examines how the long Civil War years (1850s–1880s) exacerbated the historical situation that positioned US Latinos and Latinas like Yturri and de la Garza between internal and external battle lines in race, language, culture, gender, assimilation, and national belonging. I argue that the process of becoming Latinx in the United States is a theater of civil war fought on multiple fronts. Combining literary and cultural analysis with history and biography, I unearth how Latinx Civil War combatants and sympathizers express micro-wars of identity formation in the fog of the internecine wars besetting Mexico, the United States, and Cuba at the time. These transnational conflicts over race, slavery, independence, and empire find their counterpart expression in personalized experiences of Latinx assimilation, acculturation, and accommodation that make legible the formation of nineteenth-century Latinidad for a select body of actors in the United States whose lives and writings took shape at a time of massive upheaval. For these Latinxs, the Civil War put them at war with themselves and their sense of national belonging, shoring up Thavolia Glymph's reminder that "already embattled fault lines of race, gender, and class became more visible and brittle" with the war's outbreak.[4] The US Latinx writings of this time bear the marks of these "embattled fault lines" in personal letters, autobiographies, manifestos, essays, and other forms of expressive culture that narrate the pressures of acculturation, the fissures of disidentification, the displacement of separation, and the disorientation of dispossession that structure the lived experiences of becoming Latinx. To be sure, these writers were torn by the Civil War, but their lives and writings were also formed by it through embattled social processes that I characterize as our US Latinx civil wars.

As its title suggests, my book sits at the intersection—the crossing, if you will—of Civil War studies and nineteenth-century US Latinx literary and cultural histories, the latter formed predominately by the long-term success of the Recovering the US Hispanic Literary Heritage project and the former increasingly attentive to the US Civil War's relation to regional, transnational, and global conflicts. Over the last two decades, Civil War studies has moved away from an exclusive focus on the North-South divide in the United States to situate the war over slavery as one of several concurrent conflicts on the global stage. "The US Civil War," Donald H. Doyle explains in *American Civil Wars*, "erupted out of its own domestic political and social tensions. From the beginning, however, this conflict became enmeshed in multifarious international conflicts, imperial rivalries, and distant civil wars such that we cannot understand any one part of this crisis in isolation from the larger web of conflict and imperial ambition that pervaded the Atlantic world in the 1860s."[5] Steven Hahn further holds that the plurality of "Civil Wars" more appropriately captures the multiple, related rebellions globally and locally: "But the War of Rebellion was only the largest of many rebellions that either called into question the sovereign authority of the federal government or insisted upon their own claims to sovereignty. . . . We may, indeed, think of 'wars of rebellions' during the first seven decades of the nineteenth century."[6] Where Doyle and Hahn envision a macro approach, Andrew E. Masich makes the case for the microwars waged in the Southwestern borderlands. For Masich, the US Civil War corresponded with, exacerbated, and extended long-standing regional conflicts between Texans and New Mexicans, Anglos and Latinos, and Tejanos, Hispanos, Apache, Navajo, and other Indigenous nations. "The resulting struggles," Masich maintains, "should be viewed and understood as civil wars and transnational conflicts."[7] These and similar studies understand the Civil War relationally on the historical scene, connecting issues of slavery transnationally and drawing parallels or distinctions between revolution and rebellion; self-governance and states' rights; and abolition, independence, and emancipation as competing causes of so many social or political civil wars fought in theaters that range from the micro-regional to the global. Evan C. Rothera characterizes this comparative turn best in his description of the contemporaneous civil wars raging in the United States, Mexico, and Argentina. "Despite their differences, these three violent conflicts were nevertheless part and parcel of a much larger struggle that pitted democracy and republicanism against monarchy, aristocracy, oligarchy, conservatism, and other forces of reaction."[8]

The confluences, connections, and correlations that reverberate across Cuba, Mexico, the United States, and its Southern and Southwestern regions in part explain the pluralization of "civil war": "Civil Wars" dislodges the idea that the United States' conflict over slavery was the only internecine war at the time. Instead, the US War Between the States was one of many "American Civil Wars," as scholars often dub it, that erupted on the Western Hemispheric scene over interrelated struggles that connect disparate people, places, and practices.[9] Rebecca Scott's *Degrees of Freedom* and Megan Kate Nelson's *The Three-Cornered War*, for instance, map the parallels between Cuba and the US West, respectively, over related issues of slavery and indentured servitude to show how the US Civil War's *casus belli* reverberated on the geographical margins of the slave debate dividing the Union North and the secessionist South. Adam Arenson further maintains that, despite vast geographical distances, there exists a reciprocal relationship between different war theaters. "Fighting in New Mexico," Arenson holds, "affected fighting at Gettysburg, while the civil war in Mexico shaped the experience of the US Civil War (and vice versa)."[10] Granted, as Hahn speculates, such a position perhaps overstates the case, for by his count, the US Civil War does not occupy considerable space in the histographies of Cuba, Brazil, Latin America, or Mexico. However, "by thinking broadly of a post-war era," Gregory P. Downs and Kate Masur write, "and by asking where it is located and where it ends, we hope to discover new connections between western, southern, and northern story lines. We may find new stories altogether, in new settings and told by new characters speaking new words."[11]

Downs and Masur's optimism aside, largely missing from Civil War work are the voices of the US Latinx people who observed, experienced, or wrote about the war and its related conflicts. We gain an indirect understanding of them as they are viewed through US or CSA political records, diplomatic writings, skewed newspaper pieces, Anglo-American letters, memoirs, diaries, reports, or in the tomes of earlier Civil War scholarship from which subsequent studies derive. Yet, despite several efforts to write Mexican Americans or Cuban Americans (back) into Civil War history, comparative Civil War studies in relation to Latinx people and places tends to come to the field through established Anglo-American primary and secondary sources.[12] Even when scholars rely on US Latinx primary sources, they rarely situate those works within the greater field of Latinx lives, writings, and cultural contexts related to being Latinx in the United States. For example, scholars have made considerable use of José Agustín Quintero's diplomatic dispatches from the US-Mexico border to tell the history of the Confederacy's attempt to control cotton and conflict along the Rio Grande.[13] Rarely does such work examine the Cuban Confederate's missives in relation to his career as a poet and newspaperman, and never do historians read his letters as Latinx literary artifacts. My book does both in the spirit of what Lieutenant Colonel Robert N. Scott, the Union officer charged with compiling the archive of the Civil War, reportedly said of history and memory in an interview before his death: "There is a good deal of fiction in our war stories."[14]

The archivist's purported statement can be read on a few levels. First, it refers to the tricks of memory that comprise first-person accounts of Civil War engagement. In his humorous anecdotes, Scott recalls how military records often trump personal memory or put the lie to exaggerated accounts of battlefield action. Second, the statement more broadly characterizes the way stories of the war—personal, historical, scholarly, or political—rely on narrative forms and structures that remind us of the literary value of Civil War historiography. As with most historians, I take for granted that historiography is a nuanced combination of fabulation and fact, to simplify Hayden White's parsing of the "burden of history."[15] However, as a literary scholar, I lean more into the fictions of our civil war stories rather than leverage their facts to unearth the human dramas staged in the historical theaters of the war.[16] Finally, there's a third way of understanding Scott's use of "fiction": it can describe the misconceptions, mischaracterizations, and misunderstandings that Civil War scholarship produces when it focuses on US Latinx contested spaces, like the US West, Mexico's northern borderlands, or the Cuban revolutionary movement in the United States, without engaging with the writings by the US Latinx actors who weathered the action on these interrelated fronts.

Alan Taylor's comparative continental history, *American Civil Wars*, for example, situates the US Civil War in relation to Mexico's and Canada's respective internecine conflicts. As its title suggests, the study is part of the scholarly trend to see the war comparatively, but when it comes to Mexico, Taylor relies primarily on US and Anglo-American sources, often quoting Mexican politicians from translated secondary materials rather than relying on their available primary sources. The result is his inheritance of infelicitous biases, to say the least. He characterizes Narciso López and his Cuban Creole compatriots as "halfway revolutionaries," though their writings indicate that they were fully committed to breaking Cuba from Spain, and he inexplicably characterizes Mexican governor and borderland *caudillo* Santiago Vidaurri as "an accomplished thief," as if his effective and wily political maneuvers in the region to secure political leadership at a time of unrest were markedly different from the thieving designs Union and Confederate leadership held for the entirety of Mexico's northern border frontier. Finally, Taylor repeats an egregious error that was first introduced in *The War of the Rebellion*—and subsequently corrected in Civil War scholarship—by referring to José Agustín Quintero as "Juan."[17] Taylor retells Quintero's efficacy as a Confederate diplomat without consulting his copious letters in the CSA archive. Instead, he relies on secondary historiography that initially misidentified the celebrated Cuban poet and prominent newspaperman who served the Confederacy in a noncombat role for Juan A. Quintero, a.k.a. John A. Quintero, a Mexican Texan Confederate private in the Texas Infantry (Luckett's Regiment) who absconded on March 17, 1862, with his musket, bayonet, screwdriver, and worm.[18]

While it might not sound as such, I am less concerned with the factual error of mistaking José for Juan (a.k.a. John) Quintero as much as I'm interested in the cultural, social, and linguistic "fictions" that such an error reveals about the status and standing of Latinx subjects, identities, and peoples in the writings of and about the Civil War. To mistake José for Juan in the historical record could be an innocent one, especially if both abbreviated their first names, though it still rings with the presumed interchangeability of Spanish-language names in an Anglophone world. José, Juan: what's the difference? To confuse a Cuban Confederate diplomat with a Mexican Texan Confederate private with the same Hispanophone surname also borders on a certain kind of ethno-cultural ignorance about the considerable distinctions between Cubans and Mexicans. We're not all the same. These are what I would characterize as the social fictions in the historical record—ones that were in circulation long before Taylor's time. He didn't create them, but he inadvertently reproduced them because he relied on secondhand characterizations prejudiced by prevailing racial codes, official reports that got Hispanic names wrong, and long-standing assumptions that the Latinx peoples living in the United States at the time were little invested in the Civil War and its cause.[19] Such fictions tell the histories of struggle that Latinx people and identities experience in their fight for proper representation in the United States.

In this battle of representation, the slippage between "Juan" and "John" Quintero in the archive embodies the type of Latinx civil wars that are at the core of my study. In one muster roll service record is an entire cultural story about the war between Spanish and English translation, about attempted or forced acculturation between Mexican and American, and about Latinx agency to stick with or desert a nation divided. Within the record of the Civil War is an archive of civil war stories about Latinx identity transformations that we can tell only by recovering, contextualizing, and analyzing the lives and writings of the nineteenth-century US Latinx people whose sense of US Latinidad emerged out of the fog of war. This is an archive beset by contingencies. It's displaced, haphazard between chance and circumstance, stashed in a cache of someone else's papers, and delivered somewhere between English legibility and Spanish obscurity. These are "migrant archives," to use Rodrigo Lazo's term, that "are always at the edge of annihilation," and to recover and write these Latinx civil war stories requires what Carmen E. Lamas calls "archival juxtapositions" that cross methodologies, disciplines, and analytical modes to make sense of disparate texts and writers that emerge from different archival locales.[20]

My adoption of the revisionist notion of "civil wars," then, emerges from a distinctly Latinx methodology born out of the Recovering the US Hispanic Literary Heritage project's efforts to recover and republish writings long forgotten or lost by Hispanics living in the United States from colonial times to the 1980s. The ongoing project has reshaped US Latinx literary and cultural histories, which are often—and sometimes still are—conceived of as relatively recent arrivals (circa 1960s). This is obviously not the case, as the volumes of books, pamphlets, poems, newspapers, proclamations, manifestos, diaries, and letters archived or published by the project prove.[21] Yet, with the exception of María Amparo Ruiz de Burton, the first female Mexican American to date to write and publish two novels in English (one of which is set during the Civil War), most of the writers and writings recovered by the project find limited exposure in nineteenth-century American literary studies and historical scholarship. Early writings have even less traction in contemporary Latinx studies, which often finds little relevance in nineteenth-century writings primarily by elites in relation to present-day constructions and concerns of Latinx identities. However, more than just a repository of recovered texts, the Latinx archive opens a conceptual space to explore and theorize earlier expressions of Latinidad without necessarily having to square such forms in relation to contemporary forms of Latinx identities and expressive cultures. As Kirsten Silva Gruesz puts it in her foundational *Ambassadors of Culture*, the Latinx scholar must "deliberately risk anachronism in order to pose larger questions about how the anxiety of a Latino future drives readings of the past."[22] *Latinx Civil Wars* crosses this divide by recovering, analyzing, and mapping the formation of US Latinidad as an embattled process that took shape amidst competing cultural and transnational conflicts about race, citizenship, and belonging that continue to resonate in a divided nation.

Without understating the value that Hispanic participation in the Civil War holds for social and military historians, I maintain that the War Between the States structures a metaphor for understanding a body of mid- and late nineteenth-century Latinx writings that emerge out of the ruptures of a house divided. Taken literally, for example, Loreta Janeta Velazquez's 1876 *The Woman in Battle* is a Civil War narrative insofar as it recounts battle scenes and Velazquez's engagement in those scenes as Lieutenant Harry T. Buford. However, taken metaphorically, *The Woman in Battle* shows Velazquez to be embattled between Cuba and the Confederacy, femininity and masculinity, Spanish and English, Catholicism and Methodism, heterosexuality and queerness, rebellion and independence, making the Civil War the historical theater on which the civil wars of Velazquez's Latinx identity are waged. These are battles of authenticity, acculturation, and authorship that stage identity-making and national belonging on a transnational scene. The same can be said of Angustias de la Guerra's two Californio sons, José Antonio and Porfirio Jimeno, who underwent a process of assimilation that left them shell-shocked personally, culturally, and linguistically on the eve of secession.

They were sent to New York for a Yankee education, but their letters home, examined here for the first time in Latinx literary scholarship, lay the foundation for understanding Porfirio's embattled letters from the Union front: separated from home and family, split between Spanish and English, and educated just enough in Yankee culture in New York to return to their native California alienated, the Jimeno brothers didn't quite survive the fraught process of becoming US Latinos. Their cultural crossing into Anglo America left them crossed out in California—Latinxs of a different sort than most of their Californio contemporaries.

Of course, the Jimenos' experience is not necessarily representative collectively. Like most of the Latinxs in this study, they hail from elite circles, are bilingually literate in Spanish and English, and are culturally fluent in the Anglo-American world. Yet these very differences make even more readable their conflicted social, political, economic, and personal positions during the war years. For these Latinx writers, the long Civil War years proved transformative not only in the theaters of political governance and transnational relations but also on the stage of US Latinidad, where personal, political, and literary writings mirror the internal divisions and conflicts of the Civil War. Their English-language education, degrees of assimilation, political alienation, and sometimes their confused transnational affiliations comprise the many fronts on which these Latinxs wage their historical formation through wars of words, action, and the imagination. That they spent some years along the Atlantic coast, in the US South, or were mustered into Anglo educational or military structures is not insignificant either, for their social contact with Anglo America highlights their cultural difference from other Latinxs, on the one hand, and from Anglos on the other. They are what Gloria Anzaldúa will later characterize as "los atravesados": "the squint-eyed, the perverse, the queer, the troublesome, the mongrel, the mulato, the half-breed, the half dead; in short, those who cross over, pass over, or go through the confines of the 'normal.'"[23]

An instructive articulation of this conflict emerges from the letters between María Amparo Ruiz de Burton, who published her Latinx Civil War novel in 1872, and her longtime Californio pen pal, Mariano G. Vallejo. On at least three occasions, Ruiz de Burton reminds Vallejo of something he said to her in California sometime before 1860, initially perhaps in relation to a business venture she had planned for the lower

California borderlands. From Norwich, Vermont, she writes on June 23, 1860, "Todo está listo para comenzar la empresa de que hablé a Ud (cuando me dijo que tenía 'el alma atravesada')." (Everything's ready to start the business I spoke to you about [when you told me that I had "el alma atravesada."])[24] Then, three years later, from Newport, Delaware, she reminds him, "Se acuerda cuando me dijo que tenía yo el alma atravesada?" (Do you remember when you said that I had "el alma atravesada"?) Finally, on September 14, 1869, nearly a decade after her first letter, she writes from Staten Island, New York, in an impassioned letter about Mexico, the United States, republicanism, monarchy, Napoleon, and Baja's *frontera*: "No, Don Guadalupe, [la] división no curará a México, cuando su único remedio es la Unión. En cuanto a lo que me dice de la Baja California, yo lo veo y lo he visto por años. Cuando Ud. descubrió que yo tengo 'el alma atravesada' ya yo pensaba de esto, pero no por eso deja de serme menos repugnante." (No, Don Guadalupe, division will not heal Mexico, when its only remedy is the Union. As for what you tell me about Baja California, I see it and have seen it for years. When you discovered that I have "el alma atravesada," I had already thought about this, but that doesn't stop it from being less disgusting.)[25]

For almost a decade spanning the civil war years in Mexico and the United States, Ruiz de Burton returned to a phrase, *el alma atravesada*, that Vallejo used to describe her. Clearly, she took offense to the comment, and even after mulling it over for roughly ten years and conceding that perhaps he was right, she nonetheless finds his characterization of her off-putting. And for good reasons. While *atravesada* signals transitional movement, such as to traverse, break through, or cut across, in its immediate context, it more likely means something to the effect of having "a wounded heart" or a "pierced spirit" to describe Ruiz de Burton's deep-seated anger, despair, and disappointment over her inability to establish her business plans in California because of the concurrent civil wars in Mexico and the United States. Moreover, considering the many competing interests Ruiz de Burton had in the air, Rosaura Sánchez and Beatrice Pita's elegant translation of the phrase as having a "split and fissured sense of self and place" perfectly captures the Californiana's divided loyalties and "conflicts of interest" that put her sense of self at war at the same time that she was living on the Union front with her husband, Brevet Brigadier General Henry S. Burton.[26] Finally, the phrase carries with it a moral insult: it can refer to a person with ill feelings or evil intentions.[27] This latter meaning might explain why Ruiz de Burton resented Vallejo so much for characterizing her as such in the first place. He was perhaps passing moral judgment on her persistence for brokering business *en la frontera* and voicing her opinion about politics at a time when women were supposed to keep out of both.

My contention here and throughout the book is simply that what Vallejo characterized as Ruiz de Burton's *alma atravesada*—her wounded, crossed, and conflicted state of being—describes in miniature the Mexicans or Cubans in the United States whose lives and writings during the long Civil War years put them on the front lines of Americanization and its accompanying racial and cultural codes at a time of national division. They were fissured in their ethno-national alliances and at war with themselves and their place on the rapidly changing front of US Latinidad. María Irene Moyna and María Eugenia Martín make a similar point in their analysis of the Spanish-English conflict in Ruiz de Burton's letters. Beginning in 1859, when Ruiz de Burton moved to the northeastern United States on the eve of the Civil War, her letters increasingly code-switch between Spanish and English. In some instances, she incorporates loan words to fill in linguistic or cultural gaps, but in other cases, Moyna and Martín explain, the code-switching registers her *alma atravesada*, "actuando como marcadores de identidad, creando voces alternativas, cambios de registro y puntos de vista irónicos. Estos últimos cambios de código son evidencia de la dislocación geográfica, social y lingüística de la autora y de sus intentos de negociar una identidad doble." (Acting as identity markers, creating alternative voices, shifts in register, and ironic points of view. These latter forms of code-switching are evidence of the author's geographical, social, and linguistic dislocation and her attempts to negotiate a double identity.) These shifts in linguistic registers not only signal Ruiz de Burton's dexterity with Spanish and English, but show them to be embattled on the page, with English providing more loan words into a Spanish text than the other way around, for instance, and bringing with it language about social transformation "que require de nueva terminología para expresar estos cambios" (that requires new terminology to express those changes).[28]

Her 1859 letter of advice to Mariano's favorite son, Platón, hints at the social changes that her code-switching registers. The letter tries to strike a balance between reason and resistance when it comes to being a Californio in Anglo America, but in the end, it presents them as warring positions. "It is my most ardent wish that all the Californians may cherish for ever in their bruised hearts that loyal attachment to their *own race*," she begins. "But it should be cherished, my dear Platon, with liberality, that is, without the surliness bitter and repelling which *some* seem to think is the best proof of true patriotism; without the narrowness of view which will not see virtues in others or faults in ourselves; but with that *judicious* liberality, true magnanimity, which will grant their due to others—fully and willingly—we can keep sacred that holy feeling—'the love of our own race.'" If her note sounds stately in its optimism, it gets critical at the turn of a sentence: "It cannot be denied that the Californians have reason to complain. The Americans must feel it; their boasted liberty and equality of rights seems to stop where it meets a Californian. . . . How shameful this, in the conquering, the prosperous, the mighty nation!"[29] The young Vallejo, who by this time was heading to New York to attend medical school, must have found the advice confusing, for, according to Maddie Brown Emparan, he shared the note with his father, who subsequently admonished his Californiana *comadre* for her seemingly contradictory *consejo*.[30]

Ruiz de Burton's note is a letter at civil war: one side gives the young student guidance for weathering Anglo America as a Californio, and the other cautions him about being a Californio in Anglo America; one reminds him to preserve his sense of racial pride, and another decries the fate of Californios in the United States. She celebrates Platón's departure to New York and goes on to describe a Californio who committed suicide because of his displacement. Language too gets into the melee. She pens the serious note almost entirely in English, save for her use of the word *consejo* (advice), but she Anglicizes Platón's name, addressing him as "Plato" in a playful acknowledgment of their bilingual fluency. Their shared English fluency and impending moves to the Atlantic front—Ruiz de Burton too was on the eve of traveling east—cannot be underestimated as telling signs of their transformation into Mexican Americans. It is an embattled process of mixed messages, confused allegiances, divided alliances, and competing languages that manifest even in the smallest details of a personal letter by one who has *el alma atravesada* to another about to cross into "the confines of the 'normal,'" to recall

Anzaldúa's phrasing. The letter marks the personal, cultural, and social battles of becoming a Latinx subject during the long Civil War years—it embodies in miniature the conflicted lives and writings that I analyze throughout the book.

I characterize this body of work as Civil War writing not necessarily because it is about the Civil War but because, like Ruiz de Burton's letter to Platón, it is writing at civil war. The recovered autobiographies of Rafael Chacón and James Santiago Tafolla, for instance, stage linguistic battles between their original Spanish and their English translations and the contested emergence of early Mexican American autobiographical writing in print. Manuel Yturri and Joseph de la Garza's letters too emerged from a similar linguistic battlefield. Yturri wrote in Spanish, though he would occasionally code-switch between English and Spanish, and de la Garza penned most of his missives in English, even though he was bilingual.[31] Yet their English-only publication hides the scars, marks, and sutures of their original letters in Spanish, English, and any code-switching between the two. On a smaller scale, the letters by the Jimeno brothers show how the battle between Spanish and English leaves psychological trauma akin to post-traumatic stress disorder, and Miguel Otero's published war of words with Horace Greeley over slavery in New Mexico gives rise to the tortured rhetorical gestures the Hispano territorial representative offers to distinguish between chattel slavery in the South and Indigenous servitude in the Southwest. Meanwhile, José Agustín Quintero's diplomatic missives, which themselves could be said to constitute a Latinx *War of the Rebellion*, show him to be a keen Confederate agent with very little resemblance to his reputation as a revolutionary Cuban poet and a radical newspaperman.

Sometimes, embattled identities manifest in shifting pronouns, as when Quintero uses "our" to indicate the possessive interchangeability between Cuba and the Confederacy. Other times, nomenclature itself becomes a point of ethnolinguistic embattlement and identity transformation, as with the telling variations of de la Garza's first name. Baptized with the name José, he's listed as "Joseph" in Confederate records, is known as "Joe" in Anglo circles, and signs his personal letters as "Jos.," a strategic abbreviation that straddles the space between his Spanish-language given name and the formal English name given in military records without accepting the informal, shortened Anglicization of

"Joe." The battles over nomenclature also differentiate the experiences of Latinxs residing in the United States as ostensible citizens from the lives of exiles, émigrés, visitors, or diplomats who operated in the United States. There are considerable political and diplomatic writings about Mexico's War of Reform, the United States' Civil War, or Cuba's Ten Years' War by Mexican and Cuban nationals. We see in the voluminous writings of Matías Romero, Mexico's indefatigable diplomat to the United States, that he almost single-handedly politicked, pressured, and later conspired against the Lincoln administration to secure the Union's recognition of Juárez's government. Moreover, Mexican President Benito Juárez may have been briefly exiled to New Orleans in the 1850s, where he established his Revolutionary Mexican Committee with his liberal compatriot Melchor Ocampo, and hatched his plans for the War of Reform against Mexico's conservative regime, but even in exile, their sense of their Mexican national identity never wavered. They believed themselves to be citizens of the Mexican republic even when they were ousted from it.[32] There are also scores of newspapers, pamphlets, and other forms of writing penned by exiled Cuban nationals in the United States, but most émigrés were bent on returning to the island after reform or revolution. Not so for the Mexicans and Cubans who were living in the United States as citizens. Their national identities were more fraught with the fissures that underlie the notion of civil war: they were divided between one national identity and another; at home neither here nor there; and, in the end, as embattled internally as the nations embroiled in internecine warfare at the time. Theirs is the literary legacy that marks the wounds and scars of becoming Latinx in the United States through a process that had them proffering the discourses of independence even as they upheld slavery; lamenting racial inequality even as they invoked racial privilege; and likening the Confederate cause to Cuba's anti-imperial insurgency.

My thinking on Latinx identity formation stems in part from the work of Laura E. Gómez and John-Michael Rivera, who explain Mexican American racialization as a social process of "emergence," as Rivera describes it. Rather than understanding race as a fixed category, Gómez argues that the "making" of Mexican Americans occurred in the social and legal arenas that define race in the nineteenth century. Their work echoes what I have elsewhere called the "invention" of Mexican

America as a historical and literary process by which US Latinx subjects become racialized within prevailing racial codes and, simultaneously, can internalize, embrace, advance, or adopt the United States' racial norms in an attempt to preserve, protect, or exert their economic or social power.[33] For me, the *x* in "Latinx" carries with it the space to map these vicissitudes of the embattled identity transformations pulled by the known and unknown variables of race, gender, language, and national belonging. Admittedly, "Latinx" does not seem applicable in any real-historical sense to refer to nineteenth-century peoples who self-identified as Californios, Hispanos, Nuevomejicanos, Tejanos, Cubanos, Spano- or Spanish Americans, or members of *la raza latina*, and at times, I reserve the use of specific nomenclature to underscore regional Latinx identities.[34] However, the *x* signals the intersectionality, the contradictions, the crossings, the conflicts, the variables, and the hidden values that characterize the Latinx lives and writings that emerged from the theater of Civil War split, divided, and in some instances, reconstructed, so to speak.

These Latinx subjects might sit on the margins of Civil War scholarship, Latinx studies, and American literary history, but they invite an analysis of the complex transformations of Latinidad during the years of civil wars that connected Cuba, Mexico, and the United States. While broadly understood as "Latin-ness," "Latinidad" is a capacious and contested term that encompasses what's marked and marked out in the *x* of Latinx identity formation. It includes (among other things) race, ethnicity, language, culture, region, religion, place, and space as they intersect or diverge in the social construction of Latinx identities.[35] "Latinidad is the antithesis of uniformity," Amanda Ellen Gerke and Luisa María González Rodríguez maintain, "and a living symbol of an intercultural and linguistic dialogue, involving a blending of cultures that recreate similar, yet distinct identities, often put aside in a perpetual reconstruction of identity."[36] *Latinx Civil Wars* sets out to mark this process in the lives and writings that have, for the most part, been left for dead on the battlefield of American and Latinx literary and cultural histories.

Latinx writings about slavery underscore US Latinidad's peculiar formation during the war years. California newspaperman Francisco P. Ramírez's Spanish-language editorials against slavery in the so-called Model Republic are exceptions rather than the norm of Union-identified

US Latinx writers who remained relatively quiet on supporting abolition as a *casus belli*. None of the Union combatants included here—Porfirio Jimeno, Rafael Chacón, or Federico and Adolfo Cavada—outright voice their opposition to chattel slavery or raise their concern for the plight of Black people under it. They may have fought for the Union, but their extant writings reveal that they didn't necessarily fight against slavery, and like many Hispanos, Chacón took the opportunity to continue to practice and protect Indigenous indentured servitude with Union arms. Latinx Confederates present a more complicated case. Even though James Santiago Tafolla worked as a plantation overseer before the war, he never espoused states' rights or slavery as the reason for his joining the CSA. It's possible he threw in with the rebels either to avoid conscription or the confiscation of his landholdings if he didn't declare. However, his Mexican Texan Confederate compatriot Santos Benavides was a fugitive-slave hunter before secession; he trafficked in anti-Black scare tactics during the war to muster men into his border skirmishes; and according to Thompson, he found time during the Civil War to track down "peons who were escaping from wealthy landowners and merchants in Tamaulipas and Nuevo Leon." "The Benavides family, like most families in Texas, had no inclination toward abolition. Yet there is no evidence they ever aspired to own slaves. Through their political connections in Austin and their large landholdings, however, they tended to identify with the slaveholding planter elite in the state."[37] Cuban Confederates were likewise committed to the cause, and their identification with the slaveholding South makes legible the way the rise of Latinx whiteness emerged from personal, political, and possessive investments in preserving and protecting the racial lines of a circum-Gulf slave society.

A crucial element of understanding US Latinidad during the war years, then, is to come to grips with the way Latinx whiteness hinges on the active racialization of Black and Indigenous peoples. These US Latinx Civil War writers line up somewhere between reticence on the issue to outright support of slavery as a new world order of the circum-Gulf South that stretched from the Texas-Mexico borderlands to the Cuban-Confederate Caribbean. Because Mexico abolished slavery in 1829, the slave debate dividing the United States seemed less pressing to the Mexican American populations in California, Texas, and the New Mexico Territory, where Indigenous servitude and debt peonage had long provided the solution to coerced labor that placed elite, landholding Latinos on the white side of the labor divide. However, the parallels between slavery in the United States and slavery in Cuba undergird the peculiar formation of Confederate Latinidad. For the better part of the nineteenth century, white Cubans fretted about their fate under slavery on the island. Some called for its abolition during the early and mid-nineteenth century, but most Cubans found themselves stuck between the shackles of Spanish monarchy and the specter of a race war that Spain manufactured to keep the island's independence movements in check. "Some creoles, especially the major planters of sugar-rich western Cuba, adopted a pro-Spanish strategy because of their desire to maintain slavery and the slave trade. But others . . . paradoxically turned toward Spain because of their fear of slavery and the slave trade. For them, Spanish rule was the safest alternative to revolution and race war."[38] For some Cubans, the Confederacy promised an alternative to the Spanish crown that would protect the master class and its slave interests. While Cuban advocacy for slavery could be unequivocal, as when Ambrosio José Gonzales explains it as a necessity to the twin independence of South Carolina and Cuba, Mexican Americans often displaced the issue, as when Chacón wages Union forces against Native peoples and takes captives for indentured servitude. The greater point is that the racial codes that structure power or disenfranchisement in the United States, Cuba, Mexico, or the Confederacy shaped the construction of Latinidad for these US Latinx writers.[39] Whether they fought for the Union or to uphold slave interests, none of these writers associated with Black or Indigenous peoples as equals; at least two of them cut their teeth before the Civil War as so-called Indian killers; and one Hispano left behind a dubious record of trafficking enslaved Black people into the New Mexico Territory.

A pro-Union manifesto shores up the intersecting complications of Latinx racial formation in relation to the Civil War. In a Latinx call to arms, Hispanos Facundo Pino and J. M. Gallegos, the president of the New Mexico legislative council and the Speaker of the House, respectively, frame their January 1862 declaration to preserve the Union through an anti-Texas and anti-Indigenous position. "That a savage tribe of Indians should be your new enemies, and plunder and murder, is not a thing new or unexpected. Such has been *their* habits, since our brave ancestors first possessed the Valley of the Rio Grande. But we have another enemy less excusable than the barbarians, because he has grown in the midst of civilization, and enlightenment." Pino and Gallegos are referring to Texas and Texan Confederates whose incursion into the New Mexico Territory, they argue, threaten the Hispano way of life. The invading Texans are "our ancient enemies," the Hispanos note, reminding their readers of the Texas-led 1849 invasion of New Mexico, and this time, they bring with them "negro slaves and slavery," which are "not congenial with our history, our feelings our interests." Besides, the Texas "rebels" are "without money or credit," a point the Hispanos reiterate: "they have no Government, that can bring into our Territory one dollar of money or credit."[40]

The manifesto gives critical insight into the multiple fronts Hispanos waged in their desperate bid to be incorporated into a Union that wanted nothing to do with them. They stake a position against Texas rebels and Black enslavement because both are a threat to the territory and its long-standing practice of enslaving Indigenous peoples. Further, Hispanos stand to gain more from the Union's capitalism, with its "money and credit," than presumably they do from the South's slave economy. Finally, the successful campaign against the Texans will allow New Mexicans to turn full attention to Native peoples: "Drive off the audacious invader," Pino and Gallegos conclude, "and then the Indian marauders can be exterminated."[41] The manifesto echoes New Mexico Governor Henry Connelly's September 9, 1861, Civil War proclamation, which, Anthony Mora argues, "framed the conflict as a battle between local Mexicans and Texans" to garner Hispano support for the Union effort.[42] However, as Pino and Gallegos's address indicates, Hispanos needed no such ruse. They saw the issue as a disruption of the longer-standing civil war between Hispanos and Indigenous peoples: the Union could help tip the scales for Hispanos in their war against the surrounding Indigenous nations.

This is not to say that Latinx investment in Black enslavement was only symbolic. Quintero, Gonzales, and Velazquez—the three Cuban Confederate Latinxs in this book—supported slavery on the island, fought to preserve it in the South, and loathed so much the emancipation of Black people that they avoided Cuba's 1868–1878 civil war because revolutionary leaders proposed extending independence to the enslaved. Further, if the estimate that roughly ten to twenty-five enslaved Black people resided in the New Mexico Territory in 1860 is correct, then Hispano Rafael Armijo almost single-handedly doubled that range by 1864.[43] His first of four (extant) bills of sale show that he held a monopoly on the grim trade. In March 1864, he paid $1,100 in gold for five Black people, including two children who are described as "backwards in walking." His second recorded bill almost a year later is for a ten-year-old child named John for $200. He paid $500 for twenty-year-old Sarah. And finally, he paid $1,300 in cash for James, who was thirty-five, Rachel, who was twenty-seven, and her two children, Ann, about five, and Robert, about four years old. All transactions were with a San Antonio slave trader, and the people listed in the documents are all pronounced "slaves for life," though all the bills of sale are dated after the Emancipation Proclamation.[44] The documents put the lie to the scholarly position that the debate over Black enslavement was marginal to Mexican Americans or that Hispanos embodied some kind of "off-whiteness," as Laura Gómez calls it.[45] These bills of sale put Armijo in league with white power and privilege.

Moreover, the first bill of sale is yet another Latinx archival document at civil war. The phrase "backwards in walking" bespeaks the hidden Spanish that haunts the English-language record. Considering the physical and psychological trauma of enslavement, the phrase could refer to the medical condition of retropulsion. In the context of borderlands enslavement and indentured servitude rooted in Spanish colonial and Mexican neocolonial racial hierarchies, it also suggests the *casta* term *torna atrás* (turn backwards or around), a term used to describe a mixed-race person. However, it is more likely a literal English translation of the Spanish phrase *andar atrasado* or *andar retrasado*, the latter of which translates as "to walk backwards." Both phrases suggest a delay in walking.[46] The two enslaved children haven't learned to walk or are somehow impeded in their ability to walk. This small linguistic detail sheds light on the history of the enslaved in the Latinx archive. It suggests that the initial transaction took place in Spanish, likely between a Spanish-speaking slave trader in Texas and the Anglophone buyer, who, in turn, translated the transaction details into English for his bill of sale to the bilingual Hispano, who secured his whiteness for posterity by paying $3,100 for eleven Black people: six adults and five children.

24

Received San Antonio Texas March 17. 1864
of Rafael Armijo Eleven Hundred Dollars
in Gold in Payment for the following Negroes
to wit: Isham about thirty years old.
Maria Elisa about ~~thirty~~ twenty seven years.
Preservera about six years.
Shane about four years.
Hamp age two years.
I warrant the title to said slaves, I also warrant
them to be sound in body and mind, except
the two youngest children which are backward
in walking and I also warrant them to be
slaves for life.—
In testimony whereof I hereunto subscribe my
name and affix my seal using scrawl for seal
this Seventeenth day of March A. D. 1864.
In Presence of
F. S. Bugner.
J. G. Truehart
C. J. Atkins (seal)

Figure I.1. The bill of sale for four enslaved Black people includes two children who likely have not yet learned to walk or are delayed in their ability to walk. San Antonio, Texas. Bill of Sale to Rafael Armijo for Purchase of Four Negro Slaves, March 17, 1864, box 1, folder 24, Colonel John L. Gay Collection of Papers Pertaining to the Armijo Family, MSS 193-BC, Center for Southwest Research and Special Collections, University of New Mexico Libraries.

Latinx racialization also intersects with gender and sexuality in yet another plural reconfiguration of the Civil War. As George Rable, Catherine Clinton, Nina Sibler, and LeeAnn Whites demonstrate, the war set off gender and sexual "civil wars" in the home and on the home front. These crises disrupted and changed normative social codes about masculinity and femininity in the North and the South that found their way into popular print representation and social commentaries about race, power, defeat, and labor. Despite the relative paucity of female writers in this study, then, the collection of actors included narrate how the Civil War launched conflicted gender constructions that place Latinx manhood in the historical situation of facing feminization under the banner of assimilation, on the one hand, or racialization on the other. Adolfo Cavada's unpublished military diary, for example, could be read as his coming-to-manhood on a variety of battlefields that take him from greenhorn to grizzled combatant by the time he celebrates Independence Day after the Union victory at the Battle of Gettysburg, while his brother's prisoner-of-war narrative shores up the way cowardice and captivity plague Federico's inability to escape his feminization on the Civil War battle scene until he returns to the island. Not surprisingly, Loreta Janeta Velazquez stages just the opposite, as Velazquez escapes feminization under the island's Old World gender regimes and outfits into freedom, independence, and Confederate masculinity during the Civil War, while Ruiz de Burton laments her lot as a woman writer forced to negotiate her personal and public affairs through men, like Vallejo, who prove to be a confederacy of dunces in business savvy and venture capitalism. "Ah!, si yo fuera hombre!" (Ah! If I were a man!), Ruiz de Burton exclaims to Vallejo in a February 15, 1869, letter, echoing a common sentiment of gender conflict women often expressed in their Civil War writings.[47] "The key to this body of writing," Elizabeth Young says in reference to women's writing of the time, "is its use of the Civil War as a multivalent cultural symbol as well as a literal setting" that "employ the idea of 'civil war' as a metaphor to represent internal rebellions, conflicts, and fractures."[48]

The embattled process of becoming Latinx in the United States is akin to the Civil War, but Ruiz de Burton's copious letters aside, there's a significant erasure in the historical record that the *x* in "Latinx" also marks:

writings by women, especially their personal letters, remain lost, hidden, or unmarked. In a testament to archival power, Hattie Elliott Gonzales's letters to Ambrosio, their children, and her extended South Carolina family remain ensconced in the Elliott and Gonzáles Family Papers, an extensive collection of letters, documents, and ephemera of a slaveholding family that dates from 1701 to 1898. However, we're left only to infer the lives and writings of Latinas at this time through the letters of the men to whom they wrote. Contra to his extensive and well-preserved Confederate dispatches, Quintero's letters to Eliza Bournos, his New Orleans-born upper-middle-class wife of French descent, are lost. Manuel Yturri's missives indicate that on the home front Elena was tasked with childcare, buying and selling staples for survival, and arranging rental and lease agreements, often contrary to Yturri's directions, and while Porfirio Jimeno acknowledges the notes he receives from his female relatives, the prevailing theme in his letters is his long-standing complaint that he does not receive enough news from the women at home. Perhaps paper is scarce, mail delivery unreliable, or more likely, women's lives are embattled in so many different directions that their body of writings remains MIA on the home front of US Latinidad.

The chapters that follow move in a geographical direction that reverses the standard mapping of the Civil War as a North-South divide. The book begins in California and ends in Cuba. Along the way, it charts the scattered archives of Civil War writings that mark the diaspora of the literary graveyards left on the field of Latinx and US Civil War histories. There are personal letters displaced from family collections; official writings buried in the massive *War of the Rebellion*; newspaper missives hidden in plain sight; longer essays prominently published in white nationalist periodicals; personal and military diaries that remain unpublished; composite autobiographies published in English, though they were originally written in Spanish; photographs and artwork that capture competing conflicts; and literary texts proper in English released by major publishing houses. Moreover, as with most Latinx studies scholarship, the book's analysis assumes that identity formation occurs through social processes that are more fluid than fixed and position individuals and communities in spaces between having agency over their lives and being subjected to forms of disempowerment that shape those lives. It takes a methodological combination of history, biography, archival research, and literary and cultural studies to recover, examine, and reconstitute the lives and writings that survived the nineteenth-century Latinx civil wars that took place on the field of US Latinidad. This book is the start of that reconstruction.

1

War-Torn Californios

The Jimeno Brothers and Their Almas Atravesadas

On April 12, 1848, a US army lieutenant assigned to service duties in California during the US-Mexico War wrote a letter to Francisco de la Guerra, scion of the prominent de la Guerra family and brother to Pablo de la Guerra, soon-to-be member of California's first constitutional convention and the state's future lieutenant governor. The young officer's concern at the time was for a missing cannon believed to be in the hands of a faction headed by the de la Guerras, who, contra to their Californio counterpart, Mariano G. Vallejo, opposed California's forced annexation into the Union. With diplomatic tensions on the rise, the lieutenant pressed de la Guerra for the cannon: "That gun must be returned, and the persons who took it delivered up. . . . Unless you can do this," the lieutenant continued, "some influential men in your midst will have to suffer a penalty."[1] For his part, de la Guerra denied any knowledge of the lost gun and further questioned the officer's authority to punish Santa Barbara residents as ransom for the cannon's return.[2] The stalemate continued as accusations of Californio intrigue, insurgency, and rebellion persisted in military circles and the press. De la Guerra and his fellow Santa Barbeños, though, never gave up the names of any possible suspects, if they ever knew them, and the cannon did not turn up until a decade later, buried in the Santa Barbara sand. Nevertheless, as Louise Pubols explains, the so-called Missing Cannon Affair entrenched the local and state political power of the de la Guerra family, as the future career of Pablo de la Guerra would soon attest.[3] The incident also marked the first epistolary engagement between the elite Californio family and William Tecumseh Sherman, who saw no combat action during his US-Mexico War administrative stint, save for his letter-writing campaign against Francisco de la Guerra.

Sherman served as a commissary and staff officer and spent much of his time traversing California with fellow lieutenants and close friends Henry Halleck and Edward Ord surveying towns, mines, and resources. After the war, he continued scouting the region before returning to the Eastern Seaboard in January 1850. He also took up the responsibility of escorting to school José Antonio and Porfirio Juan de Dios Jimeno, Angustias de la Guerra's two eldest sons. Angustias was the sister of the aforementioned Francisco, and at the time, she was married to the politically prominent Manuel Jimeno Casarín. As her *testimonio* makes clear, she was at the center of Californio political and cultural life, making her a significant personage in California's history in her own right.[4] So, when their surveying took them to Monterey, Sherman, Ord, and Halleck occasionally boarded with the Californiana, and on the eve of Sherman's departure for New York, Angustias sent her two young sons with him. Sherman recalls in his *Memoirs*, "I again was welcomed by my friends, Doña Augustias [*sic*], Manuelita, and the family, and it was resolved that I should take two of the boys home with me and put them at Georgetown College for education, viz., Antonio and Porfirio, thirteen and eleven years old. The doña gave me a bag of gold-dust to pay for their passage and to deposit at the college."[5]

Aboard the *Oregon*, the group departed Monterey on January 2, 1850, touching at San Diego, Acapulco, and Panama, where the passengers disembarked, navigated the Isthmus of Panama by mule and boat, and found the *Crescent City* waiting on the other side. After a monthlong trip, the steamer arrived in New York, where the Jimeno boys were "put up at Delmonico's, on Bowling Green."[6] Their route took them in the opposite direction that many Gold Rushers from the East traveled to arrive in California during the same period, a fact made even more significant because of the bag of gold dust Angustias gave to Sherman. It must have been a hefty sack, considering Sherman paid $600 for his own passage; the 1850–1851 catalog for Georgetown lists tuition at $200; and the new Delmonico's on Bowling Green was a New York City hotspot for the cultural elite. As hotel lore exaggerated it, "Another Army officer . . . made straight for Delmonico's Hotel when he landed at New York early in 1850, bringing the first official report of the gold being scooped out of the streams of California; his name was William Tecumseh Sherman."[7] The apocryphal anecdote gets wrong the history of the Gold Rush and

Sherman's part in it, but his stop at the hotel with José Antonio and Porfirio nonetheless proved to be historically significant for the boys and the rest of their Californio kin, as it marked the beginning of their culturally conflicted transformation into Mexican Americans during the long Civil War years.[8]

While the Jimeno brothers were not the only Californios to trek east for an education, their mid-nineteenth-century experiences mark the opening salvo in their civil war of identity formation in the years between 1848, when the Treaty of Guadalupe Hidalgo ended the US-Mexico War with the acquisition of Mexico's far northern frontier, and 1861, when Southern secession from the Union to maintain a slave economy launched the Civil War. As historians agree, the US-Mexico War's resolution exacerbated the sectional crises it worked to ameliorate over the balance of free and slave states, and the war also served as the proving ground for most of the combatants on both sides of the Civil War, especially the West Point–trained officers. "The American victory over Mexico and the acquisition of the Southwest had sealed the triumph of national expansion," David M. Potter explains, "but it had also triggered the release of forces of sectional dissention."[9] It also put the Jimeno brothers in conflicted states of being. Theirs is a story of uneven cultural transformation, as they traveled from west to east, from Mexican California to the Anglo-American seaboard, from rancho ruralism to urban industrialization, from boys to young men, and from Spanish to English. Such social transitions for Latinxs—then and now—are fraught with cultural and psychological fissures that split the subject in the name of assimilation, education, and socialization. These are uneasy changes, conflicted in terms of language and belonging and vexed with personal and social struggle that, for the brothers Jimeno, left them war-torn on the geographical, social, linguistic, and cultural field of US Latinidad. The first front of the Latinx civil war, then, is not on a military battlefield but in the theater of change in the years preceding secession, when Latinxs found themselves already embattled by the time the Union split.

The War with Words

When Angustias de la Guerra sent her two sons east, her intention was to see to their Catholic education at Georgetown College, a Jesuit school neither unknown to elite Mexican and Latino families in the United States and Latin America nor unfamiliar to Angustias, whose choice of schools James and Edward Ord no doubt influenced. The Ords were alumni. Angustias described herself in her diary as "more Spanish than Mexican," and her decision to send the boys to Georgetown might have been an attempt to insulate them from the tides of secular, liberal principles rising in California and Mexico at the time, but the move also shores up her budding optimism about the prospect of Americanization to improve California, which she characterized in her *testimonio* as "on the road to utter ruin" on the eve of annexation.[10] Angustias no doubt hailed from an extended elite family. Their "race, aristocratic lineage, and relative economic wealth," María Raquél Casas explains, "placed the de la Guerras within the most privileged social, economic, and racial class."[11] In her later "Recuerdos," she describes attending a dance in honor of George Washington's birthday as "American citizens" with an American lieutenant as her companion: "His name was Sherman," she recalls.[12] Even by elite Californio standards, though, a private East Coast education for two children close in age came at a cost more than one bag of gold dust could cover. Georgetown's 1850 annual tuition was $200, including lodging and meals but excluding books, supplies, and uniform, so the prospect of educating two boys at the same time was an expensive venture, especially when Californio wealth was on the decline.[13] Angustias must have banked that an East Coast education would improve the chances for her sons to navigate California's transition into the Union. However, funds dried quickly. By 1853, Sherman wrote Angustias on the boys' behalf requesting "pocket money," and by 1856, on the eve of the boys' return to California, the president of Georgetown sent José Antonio's unpaid bill to their uncle Alfred Robinson after receiving no answer from Manuel Jimeno Casarín. They owed $876.02 for, among other things, postage, pocket money, stationery, socks, shoes, gum, cash, buttons, skates, haircuts, medical aid, and tuition and board.[14]

The boys were not the first of their extended family to go through cultural changes on the East Coast. Their aunt Anita de la Guerra Robinson moved to Boston in 1838 after she married Robinson when he arrived in California during the early 1830s. As Pubols explains, Anita's departure for New England bucked normative Californiana gender roles as she pursued her education in line with liberal, reformist thinking sweeping

Mexico and New England at the time. "In 1840, elite middle-class New England society, like that of reformers in Mexico, subscribed to the notion that women needed to be educated because raising children and overseeing their moral values fell within their domain."[15] Despite the challenges of child-rearing, Anita was steadfast in learning English as part of her transition to life in Boston and New York. Her few extant letters home characterize her fifteen years away from California as one of struggle, adaptation, and longing for her parents and her first-born, Elena, whom Anita and Alfred left to be raised by the de la Guerra grandparents. Anita characterized her choices as "sacrifices" for the sake of her education, Michele M. Brewster notes. "Despite her marriage to Robinson and to having lived on the East Coast for fifteen years," Brewster continues, "Anita remained loyal to her home country and opposed its conquest by the United States. . . . Highly educated and having access to power in both US and Californio circles, Anita adapted to, and at other times, resisted US culture."[16] Several Californio kin also joined the Jimeno brothers for different periods of time. Their cousin José Ramon followed them to Georgetown, while Francisco de la Guerra Jr. and another Santa Barbeño, Queremón Carillo, ended up with the Jimenos at the same boardinghouse.[17] Robinson dealt with the boys' schooling. He brought them into his Yankee Californio domestic sphere, where they spent holidays together, either in Boston or New York, with their *tía* Anita and her children, and he visited them in New York's Irving House in the mid-1850s. He managed their economic, educational, and religious affairs, and he placed them with Margaret Gordon Meade, who served as their tutor and caretaker in New York in preparation to attend Georgetown. She was also the sister of George Gordon Meade, a veteran of the US-Mexico War who would later be appointed general of the Army of the Potomac during the US Civil War.

For roughly four years, the Jimenos were under Margaret Meade's supervision, and their formal education gave way to a cultural one that didn't quite pay off in the dividends that Angustias might have hoped for. For instance, in 1852 the boys wrote a letter home in English, in part to practice their new language but also to challenge the translation skills of their Spanish monolingual parents. "Ayer recibí tu letras escritas en ingles," Manuel Jimeno wrote to José Antonio and Porfirio, "pero me la traduzeron y entiendo que estas bueno y mas gordo que tu mama de lo que me alegro mucho." (Yesterday I received your letters written in English, but it was translated for me and I understand that you're well and fatter than your mama, which makes me very happy.) Angustias was less enthused, for at the end of her otherwise warm postscript to Manuel's letter, she reminds the boys, "Promesa no olbidan tu idioma español." (Promise that you won't forget your Spanish language.) The warning is not just in response to the boys' English-language letter. The de la Guerra parents feared the very linguistic-cultural loss they initiated by sending their sons east for their education, a real threat that Manuel indicates in the same missive: "El hijo de Larkin, Federico, esta en Monterey solamente andande con algunos muchachos sin hablan una palabra por que no entiende la lengua Española." (Larkin's son Frederic is in Monterey spending time with some guys, without saying a word because he does not understand the Spanish language.)[18] The contrast isn't unintentional. Thomas O. Larkin, an Anglo-Californio booster who served as the only American consul to Alta California before statehood, kept a bilingual home, but when he sent his sons to New York for school, around the same time that the Jimeno boys shipped out with Sherman, Larkin feared that his sons would lose their Spanish, which seems to have happened with Frederic, though he could "speak Spanish better than English" before he left for school.[19] The boys' letter home in English understandably raised Manuel and Angustias's concern that José Antonio and Porfirio might return home like their Anglo-Californio counterpart, Frederic Larkin—aloof, bereft of his Spanish, and Anglicized to the point of social alienation. They might become *pochos*, in other words: Americanized Mexicans.

The seemingly minor language skirmish marks a major opening in the battle between Spanish and English literacies, Californio and Anglo cultures, and the shifting personal and social pressures the Jimeno boys navigated as vanguards on the front of Mexican America's first generation. "While Californio and immigrant parents struggled to speak English and learn about Atlantic American ways," David E. Hayes-Bautista says of the 1850s–1860s Latino population in California, "their United States-born children were growing up almost naturally bilingual and bicultural, at home in both English and Spanish."[20] José Antonio and Porfirio were both born before the US-Mexico War, so they were not exactly "naturally bilingual and bicultural." During their formative teen years, they lived at the center of the American colonial culture working to displace Californios like the de la Guerras. They were subjected to Robinson's paternalistic reach and his concomitant attitude toward Californios, which mixed sympathy with coloniality, as best expressed in his marriage to Anita and subsequent 1846 pro-expansionist memoir, *Life in California*, which Pablo de la Guerra deemed "quite biased."[21] To different degrees, all the Californio cousins sent to New York underwent a process of education that should be understood as nothing short of psychologically alienating insofar as the young students were taught to embrace the nation that displaced them. Attached to Francisco de la Guerra Jr.'s April 3, 1853, letter to his father, for instance, in which he sends his greetings to his extended family and insists "que estoy bueno y contento," is a note from Meade: "I send you Francisco's letter, but I am not at all pleased with the writing or spelling, he wants ambition sadly and is satisfied with the idea that he 'cannot learn' without being willing to make the effort. . . . I am determined that he *must* and *shall* learn."[22] *Tía* Anita too suffered from linguistic trauma. From Boston, she opens her short August 16, 1843, note to her brother Pablo de la Guerra with an apology that betrays her anxiety: "For years, I may say, I have been contemplating doing myself the pleasure of addressing a few lines to you in english, according to your request, but the *fear* of escposing my difficiences has prevented."[23] Perhaps her English-language lessons are to blame for her sense of linguistic self-doubt: Robinson encouraged his Californiana wife to learn English by having her read Prescott's *History of the Conquest of Mexico*.[24]

While Anita and the circle of cousins wrote home occasionally, mostly in Spanish, José Antonio's English missives from this period show him to be the writer of the bunch, especially as he navigated the sociolinguistic transition from Spanish to English. During their years on the Yankee front, he wrote on the boys' behalf, probably because he was the elder, and his extant letters cleave in two directions. While only a few of his Spanish-language missives can be found in the de la Guerra family collection, his English-language notes remain in the William T. Sherman Papers, housed among the eighteen thousand items that comprise the Civil War general's life correspondences and writings. Collectively, the letters embody the boys' historical displacement from California, their family, and the language that (dis)connects them, but the constellation of missives in the Sherman Papers by and about the Jimeno brothers underscores the concerted effort that Sherman, Father James Ryder (who officiated Sherman's marriage), their uncle Alfred Robinson, and Meade exerted to Americanize the boys through English-language literacy. Read together, the 1850s letters by and about José Antonio reveal that the "making" of Mexican Americans, to recall Laura Gómez's phrase, occurs as much in Anglo-American schools and boardinghouses as it does through the legal construction of Mexican American racial identity.[25] It's a civil war of identity formation that leaves the boys *almas atravesadas* on the field of national belonging.

The Jimenos didn't fare well almost from the start of their move. They remained at Georgetown College for about ten days—long enough to have their names transliterated on their respective directory cards from "Jimeno" to "Gimeno"—before being sent back to New York to board with Meade for care and tutoring, with the plan of their eventual return to the college better prepared. "They require the care of a female," Meade explains to Sherman, the boys having arrived to her with sores on their heads. Placed in charge of the boys' education, lodging, and adjustment to their move, Meade later explains to Sherman that Porfirio arrived unable to write, and even after learning his letters, he still seems to "have difficulty using his pen."[26] Whatever struggle he had holding the pen, Porfirio still managed to write a note to Sherman in which he characterized Meade as "the best lady I ever saw."[27] José Antonio too had some physical difficulty writing, and in his first response to Sherman's request that the boys write to him (see appendix), he explains to "Castañares," an affectionate family nickname Sherman went by while in California, why they are not in Georgetown.[28] "I hope you will not be anscous that we are not in college," José Antonio says, "but you know that we were very ignorant besides our heads are not well yet."[29] Meade explains that a doctor considers their condition "a disease of the head," implying that it's more psychological than physiological, for he opts to "wait-it-out of their system" rather than treat their physical symptoms.[30] Father Ryder further explains that the boys have sores on their heads and that it fell on Meade to shave them and treat the sores, which she did "with a mother's affection."[31]

Either way, José Antonio's letter indicates his understanding that he and his brother are in Meade's charge for more than just physical care.

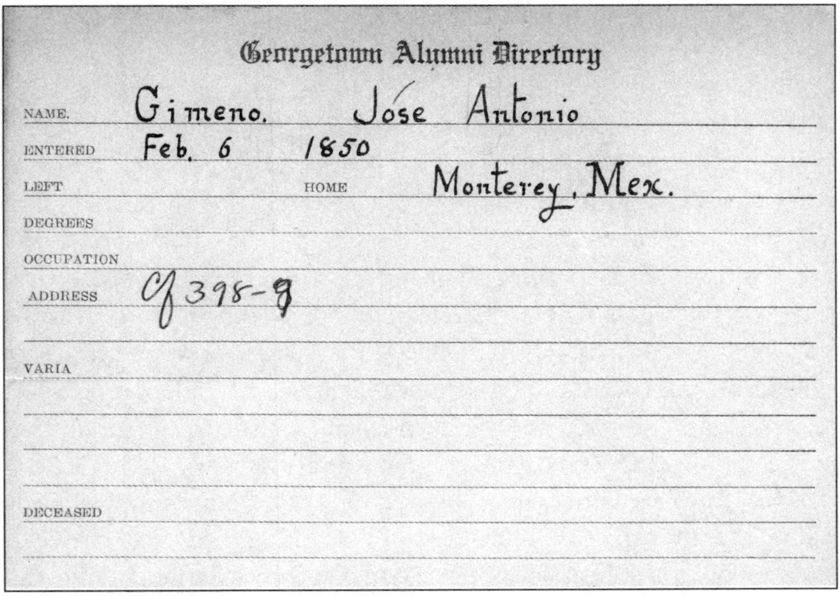

Georgetown Alumni Directory

NAME. Gimeno. José Antonio
ENTERED Feb. 6 1850
LEFT HOME Monterey, Mex.
DEGREES
OCCUPATION
ADDRESS Cf 398-9
VARIA
DECEASED

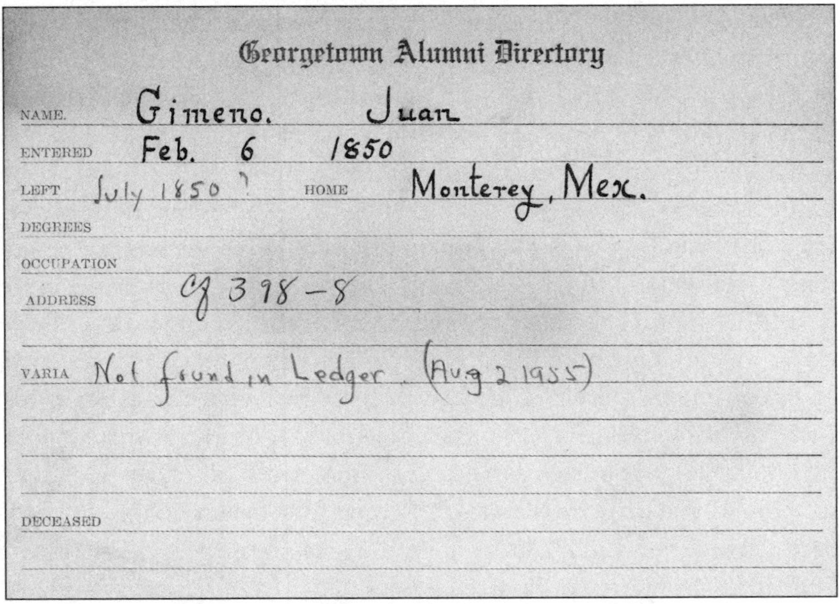

Georgetown Alumni Directory

NAME. Gimeno. Juan
ENTERED Feb. 6 1850
LEFT July 1850? HOME Monterey, Mex.
DEGREES
OCCUPATION
ADDRESS Cf 398-8
VARIA Not found in Ledger. (Aug 2 1955)
DECEASED

Figures 1.1 and 1.2. The Georgetown Alumni Directory cards transliterate José Antonio and Porfirio's surname from Jimeno to Gimeno, a change that forces their move from a Spanish-speaking to an English-speaking educational experience. The directory also lists a shortened version of Porfirio's second name, Juan de Dios, over his given name. Georgetown Alumni Directory cards, 1850, courtesy of Georgetown University Archives, Booth Family Center for Special Collections.

With his parents' blessing, they have been left with her because, as he puts it, "we require much training in many things we could not get in College." This simple phrase conceals a cycle of psychological violence that the boys have already endured at the start of their transition and that they continue to experience at the site of their letter writing. The two Californios have been taught that they are deficient—defective, even—in their new Anglo-American world. José Antonio repeats to Sherman the explanation he likely heard from either Ryder or Meade for why the boys are not attending school, and because Meade is proofreading José Antonio's letter, he has no room but to affirm the diagnosis that the two brothers are "very ignorant." No wonder the boys' "heads are not well yet." They are both being subjected to coded forms of social racialization that they risk internalizing, and José Antonio has little choice in his letter but to reaffirm what Meade and company have taught him: the boys are intellectually, socially, physically, psychologically, and linguistically sick in character and personhood. They need curing. The hazard of internalizing such racist views of themselves as Other seems to have set seed: "We hope by good conduct and hard study," José Antonio writes to Sherman, "to prove ourselves worthy of your friendship."[32]

The silence from home exacerbates José Antonio's pained process of disidentification. While he notes receiving family news in a February 15, 1851, letter, he complains to Sherman in July 1852 that he has not heard from his parents: "I feel very unhappy that, something must be the matter I think that if my father or mother are well they ought to write to us for we are so far from them, & we write to them by every mail (two or three times a month)."[33] A year later, he writes to his sisters from Boston, "Mis Queridas Hermanas Como no lo recibido ni una carta de Uds. tomo la pluma para darles a Uds unas pocos noticias. . . . No he recibido ni una carta de Mama. . . . Porque [no] me escriben?" (Since I have not received a single letter for you, I take up my pen to send you a little news. . . . I have not received a single letter from Mama. Why don't you all write to me?)[34] Finally, in 1854 he opens a more direct plea in English for communication from his uncle Pablo de la Guerra, "*Querido Tio*—This is the 3rd letter that I have written to you but I have not heard an answer from you and I think it is very strange indeed. I am sure I have not done anything to offend you. Please write to me directing your letters to Georgetown College for Mr. Robinson is going to take us next week."[35] Letters to the Jimenos—only a few of which are extant—were rarely received, despite José Antonio's repeated attempts to keep lines of communication open, and the depths of his isolation can be gauged in his persistence to get his family to write to him to explain why they do not write to him. "I think that this is very strange," he says to Sherman of not receiving letters from his parents, "[I] wrote them asking what is the cause of not writing."[36]

Lack of correspondence is a common refrain across the de la Guerra family collection, but José Antonio's repeated pleas for letters affirm his belief in the power of writing to maintain connection over geographical distance and cultural space. He's a writer of letters to a family that does not seem to respond. It's not just news that he craves but personal, familial, and cultural communion through the act of writing. William "Castañares" Sherman, as the boys called him, fills this void for José Antonio, whose growing bond to the army captain can be tracked in his writings to him. Sherman's letters to the boys are not extant, but he wrote to them regularly, presumably to encourage them to practice their English because he gave them the charge to write back. Three months after his first letter, José Antonio responds to another of Sherman's letters, reporting on his education and health: "We are studying geography, grammar, tables, cyphering, spelling, definitions, dictation, and reading. We are all very well esccept my elbow is just alike my leg, but it is almost well."[37] Meade's accompanying letter sheds more light on José Antonio's condition: "He has been suffering a great deal since you left here. The wound on his leg healed, and then his head broke out. Now his head is nearly [healed?] he had a large lump on his elbow which has been very painful for a month."[38] Young José Antonio has had a flare-up of sorts after Sherman's departure. His body attacks itself as he breaks out in sores or boils on his head, leg, and elbow—battle wounds, so to speak, that mark the trauma of his geographical, social, cultural, and familial displacement. He misses Castañares, who connects him to his Californio family during his isolated and infirm stay in New York, and bereft of communication from home, he cultivates a filial epistolary relationship with the future Civil War general.

In contrast to his formal regards for "Mrs. Sherman," for instance, José Antonio addresses Sherman as "Castañares" four times in a one-page English-language letter, as if to conjure through writing the man and the memory of Mexican California that seems to have forgotten José Antonio altogether (see appendix). No doubt the repetition of the nickname conveys his juvenile literacy—José Antonio is still learning to write, after all. It also betrays a degree of Spanish-language familiarity with which the fifteen-year-old José Antonio connects with the then thirty-one-year-old captain in the US army. As Meade puts it, "Antonio never tires for those he loves."[39] The young Californio is coming of age, and his writings to Sherman mark the process by which the captain becomes the male figure through which José Antonio matures relationally, in this case at first through an intimate family nickname but also, by the end of the letter, through a valediction that straddles the English-Spanish divide. José Antonio closes by referring to himself as Sherman's "gratefull friend and *Hermano*."[40] Besides the use of formal names and Sherman's nickname, it is the only Spanish-language word in the letter, with its capitalization announcing its significance on the field of English. His bilingual valediction announces his bond with Castañares glued by the intimacy of strategic Spanish words that retain the sounds and memory of the Californio family that seems distant to him.

Analyzing Latino *cartas* in an earlier context, Rodrigo Lazo explains that such stylized notes of intimate expression between Latinos signal "affective friendship and closeness, sometimes in homosocial ways," and these modes of "epistolary affect, whether in personal correspondence or print, spoke to the urgency of communicative attempts to touch people and change their minds so they would transform their local societies and do away with colonial rule."[41] However, this affect takes on a different expressive colonial erotic because it occurs between a younger, displaced Californio and an older, Anglo-American military man in the service of US empire. The name "Castañares" holds a special meaning for José Antonio, and its repetition in the short letter betrays his longing, his desire, for the man and the Californio coloniality his name represents. José Antonio does not express similar regard for his Yankee uncle, Alfred Robinson, for instance. While Robinson visits the boys on occasion, there is no extant indication that they wrote to each other. Rather, Robinson communicated to Ryder and Meade about the boys, and in his letters, José Antonio references Robinson only in relation to family news. In contrast, Sherman writes to the boys and instructs them to write back to him. Perhaps with the desire to "prove" himself "worthy

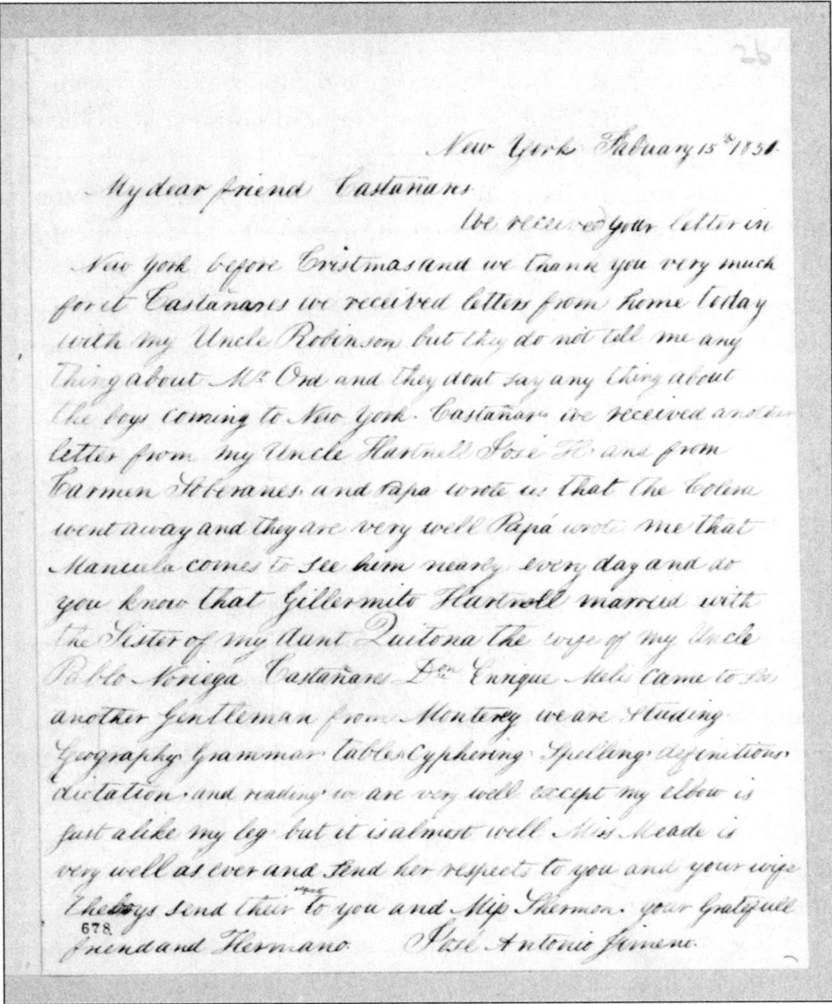

26

New York February 15th 1851

My dear friend Castañares

We received your letter in New york before Cristmas and we thank you very much for it Castañares we received letters from home today with my Uncle Robinson but they do not tell me any thing about Mr Ord and they dont say any thing about the boys coming to New York. Castañares we received another letter from my Uncle Hartnell José H. and from Carmen Hebernanes and Papa wrote us that the Colera went away and they are very well Papá wrote me that Manuela comes to see him nearly every day and do you know that Gillermito Hartnell married with the Sister of my Aunt Quitona the wife of my Uncle Pablo Noriega Castañares Dn Enrique Melis came to see another Gentleman from Monterey we are studing Geography Grammar tables Cyphering Spelling definitions dictation and reading we are very well except my elbow is just alike my leg but it is almost well Miss Meade is very well as ever and send her respects to you and your wife The boys send their regards to you and Miss Sherman your Gratefull

678

friend and Hermano José Antonio Jimeno

Figure 1.3. José Antonio Jimeno practices his English by writing to family friend William T. Sherman, whom he affectionately addresses as Castañares. José Antonio Jimeno to William T. Sherman, February 15, 1851, William T. Sherman Papers, Manuscript Division, Library of Congress.

of his friendship," as he put it, José Antonio responds with what Meade characterizes as an "effusion" of a letter.[42]

José Antonio's so-called "effusion" also marks English transcriptions of Spanish-language rhetorical structures that remain residual in his writings. "My dear friend Castañares," for instance, is a conjoined

English- and Spanish-language greeting. It combines a normal English salutation ("Dear Castañares" or "Dear friend") with what in this case would certainly be a warm, informal greeting to the family friend: "Estimado amigo." The "hidden" Spanish salutation transcribed literally into English explains the seemingly ornate greeting. The letter's opening corresponds with the linguistic battleground that marks José Antonio's cultural transition that here and elsewhere bears the scars of coming into English. The phrase "married with" echoes Spanish phrasing in an English structure: José Antonio is transcribing what would be "casaron con" (married with) instead of stating "married." In a different letter, "anxious" becomes "ancious" in a homophonic translation of the *x* that puts it under erasure, while details across his writings—such as "alike" for "like"—serve as reminders that the transition from Spanish to English is neither seamless nor smooth linguistically, personally, and culturally. José Antonio's formal salutations and valedictions further map his sociolinguistic transition from Spanish- to English-language fluency and its related cultural codes. In his first letter to Sherman, on November 9, 1850, he opens with "My dear friend Castañares" and ends with an ornate complimentary closing: "and received the heart of your friend who never forgets you." By February 15, 1851, he addresses Sherman similarly but closes as "your gratefull friend and *Hermano*," but by July 11, 1852, he greets Sherman as "My Dear brother" and signs with "Your affectionate Brother" and "very truly Brother" to the postscript. He also uses "Castañares" twice in his last four-page missive written two and a half years after his first note.[43]

While not likely rooted in "Enlightenment concepts of brotherhood and friendship," as Lazo describes early *cartas* between Latinos, José Antonio's discursive filiation for Sherman through English facilitates his affective affiliation with the United States as his national body politic.[44] Regarding Henry Clay's death on June 29, José Antonio writes, "We had up a flag dressed in mourning so you see how much the people of America loved him, and I hope that they will do the same in St. Louis and all the places his body will be carried to. The paper says that his body is in Cincinnati, and I suppose they will take it to St. Louis." At this time, José Antonio remains with Margaret Meade, whose brother, George Gordon Meade, was married to Margaretta Sergeant, the daughter of Clay's 1832 presidential running mate, John Sergeant. The young

Californio is boarding in a house shrouded in US national mourning. His tone is also strikingly different from his previous extant letters, especially in the topic he takes up with Sherman, as his missive marks a confluence between noting "how much the people of America loved [Clay]" and how much José Antonio himself is moved by the statesman's death: "I hope you will have the pleasure of seeing his body or funeral," he says. As he imagines himself a member of "the people of America," José Antonio's reading and writing interpellate him into the scene of national mourning for the statesman who opposed the US-Mexico War but also balked at the incorporation of Mexicans into the Union.[45] In the belly of the beast, José Antonio reads about Clay's death, must have been in conversational circles about it, lives in a house publicly mourning him, and seems to have been moved by it to the point that he recounts to Sherman Clay's reported death scene, where Clay "escpired like an infant," José Antonio writes. By way of the Anglophone press and its imagined community, José Antonio's linguistic and cultural literacies all but cross out the *x* of his Latinx alphabet, even as his persistent spelling of words like "ancious" and "escpired" remain telltale markings of the very ethnolinguistic erasure that he has endured.[46]

The extent of José Antonio's cultural transformation can be summed up in a long letter that Margaret Meade writes to Sherman on July 17, 1852, a few days after José Antonio's note above:

> Porfirio is very much amused at your idea of his being a Priest. Why the boy's head is full of the Army, and a drum excites him to a degree too amusing. I will be glad if he does go to West Point (after graduating at Georgetown) for the discipline will bring him all right. This is all he wants, but he would be a daring "head over heels" fellow if I did not curb his disposition to ride over his brother. Antonio has become as gentle and refined as a lady, he is the admiration of everyone.[47]

Porfirio's purported reluctance to write, his so-called laziness, as Meade first characterized it, has left him rough in temperament and disposition, traits that will manifest more fully in the tone and sentiment of some of his Civil War letters from camp. However, José Antonio, the writer, newspaper reader, and "friend and brother" who set out to prove himself worthy of Sherman's admiration, has become "as gentle and refined as a lady." In a snippet, Meade's note reveals the violence that undergirds the concerted efforts to Americanize the Californio boys. Their bodies, minds, letters, and lives have been subjected to the disciplining of Meade's gaze, Father Ryder's authority, Alfred Robinson's presumption of parental proxy, and the weight of Sherman's absent presence—all with the approval of the boys' parents and in the seeming absence of correspondence from California. The note describes the concerted efforts to socialize the Jimeno brothers, to bring them of age through a process of acculturation through letters, language, and literacies to make the two elite Mexican boys more racially and culturally legible to Anglo America. Theirs has been a battlefield of racialized formation, from their ostensible "ignorance," as José Antonio once characterized it, to their budding acculturation, but their educational process is also a gendered one that took unevenly. While Porfirio requires more "discipline," José Antonio's "refined manners," acculturation, literacy, and expressive gestures—all taught to him under Meade's care, perhaps in an effort to transform him into a version of her Spanish-born brother George—feminize him within Anglo culture.[48] Two years of education in New York have left José Antonio an "effeminate man," which, as Travis M. Foster explains, was "unlike other nineteenth-century manifestations of male femininity, such as the dandy," because "the effeminate man was understood a priori as white—as, indeed, an effect of white supremacy itself."[49] Much to the "admiration of everyone," José Antonio could be read as Americanized.

The War with Home

Sometime in 1856, José Antonio and Porfirio returned to California, leaving behind a cache of unclaimed letters held in the Boston post office.[50] While neither of the boys completed their formal educations, they underwent a cultural schooling in the US Northeast that left them the worse for wear. To compound their problems, they also returned to a new domestic arrangement. Three years a widow by 1856, Angustias married James Ord, the assistant surgeon who had arrived with his brother, Edward Ord, Halleck, and Sherman aboard the *Lexington* in January 1847. The marriage marked Angustias's own transition to a domestic cultural broker between Mexican and Anglo California in the heady years after statehood.[51] While the boys were in New York, the marriage between Manuel and Angustias was on the decline, which might explain why they did not write more often, and after the warring parents separated in 1852, they pulled José Antonio and Porfirio into their domestic battle. Having left for Mexico to look into the rights to a plot of land, Manuel wanted the boys to join him, but Robinson, perhaps a little reluctant to cross Angustias or his father-in-law, balked at the request. The brothers were torn between following their father's orders and respecting their mother's wishes. They opted for the latter. The squabble was short-lived, however, because Manuel died in 1853 while still in Mexico, leaving the land dispute he was investigating unresolved and the boys firmly under Robinson's control for the remaining three years that they stayed on the East Coast.[52] When they returned home, they had a new Anglo-American stepfather, a Georgetown alumnus who arrived with the invading army and made himself at home in California after its annexation. They left one Yankee front to come home to another.

The personal impact of the boys' East Coast cultural education, combined with the psychological effect of their new domestic arrangement in California, should not be underestimated. To put it into perspective, while the boys were undergoing their socialization into dominant culture, they were also the unwitting collateral damage of divorce. The fact that their father ordered them to Mexico but their mother (via Robinson) controlled the fiscal ability to travel underscores their relative lack of agency as minors in the domestic skirmish. To compound the situation, their father died unexpectedly of natural causes during the thick of the dispute in what the boys must have felt as a painful dissolution of their already divided house. The two brothers could not have known that, when they left for school with Sherman, they would never see their father again. Finally, in a *coup de grâce*, the boys returned home to their mother's new marriage, which, as with similar Californio arrangements at the time, brokered through the sexual-marriage matrix the lopsided power relations under the new Anglo-American regime. "The American takeover" of California, Mirosilva Chávez-García explains, "irrevocably altered gender relations and family patterns and created opportunities for women to contest power relations in marriage and the family."[53] It is of course difficult to divine the depth of the effects that these transformations had on the boys socially and psychologically, but there's no

Figure 1.4. Doña Angustias de la Guerra, circa 1856, in mourning wrap, flanked by perhaps her two sons, José Antonio and Porfirio Jimeno, on their return from New York. Maria de las Angustias Josefa Antonia Bernabe or Doña Angustias de la Guerra (1815–1890), daughter of José de la Guerra y Noriega, de la Guerra Family Photographs, BANC PIC 1984.062:03—PIC, Bancroft Library, University of California, Berkeley.

doubt that they felt the weight of the war at home, if for no other reason than that they returned to the very colonial culture they endured on the East Coast.

The California to which they returned was also undergoing a tumultuous time that proved to be especially transformative for its Latino populations. "Hispanophobia reached a peak" in the late 1850s, Leonard Pitt explains, as the state saw widespread racial violence in the streets and in its canons of law, and even as elite Californios struggled to keep their decline at bay, the state's Latino population became increasingly diverse.[54] People from Mexico and greater Latin America converged on the state and began to establish a political culture through print production and *juntas* that pulled Californio regionalism into transnational debates about liberalism, republicanism, and the place US Latinos were going to occupy between the United States and Mexico. "From 1769 to 1848," Hayes-Bautista explains, "Spanish-speaking residents of California developed a regional variant of Mexican identity and society. After being annexed by the United States in 1848, they—and especially their children—developed a society that was neither simply a variant of Mexican society nor an exact replica of Atlantic American society. It was something new and different."[55] It was decidedly US Latino and formed, as Hayes-Bautista argues, within a transnational crucible of civil wars that put these new Latinx subjects on multiple front lines: they weathered war at home against Anglo oppression; staged support for Juárez's liberalism and, later, against the French occupation of Mexico; and as with the rest of the nation at the time, they were divided on the question of slavery and the problem it posed for the Union.

These divisions found expression in California's newspapers, and in the southern part of the state, Francisco P. Ramírez epitomized this new Latino voice as it emerged in the Spanish-language press. As a teenager, the California-born trilingual autodidact apprenticed as a printer for the bilingual *Los Angeles Star/La Estrella de Los Angeles*, and in June 1855, the eighteen-year-old became the editor of Los Angeles's first Spanish-language newspaper, *El Clamor Público*. The paper was a one-man show, with Ramírez writing, setting, and printing a weekly that one of his Anglophone competitors, the *Southern Vineyard*, characterized as "a seditious and anti-American organ."[56] In its early runs, the paper was liberal.

Ramírez staked clear anti-slavery and anti-racist positions anchored in his belief in racial equality, inalienable human rights, and an inviolable social contract with just government and laws, including freedom of the press, freedom of speech, and the right to vote. He placed such a high premium on the power of the latter that he would in some instances leverage the former to admonish California's Mexican population for not mobilizing as a united voting bloc against American laws, pro-slavery party systems, and vigilante violence that disproportionately targeted Mexicans. His liberal positions ran counter to those of the elite Californio conservatives of Los Angeles County, many of whom, contra to their northern California counterparts, sided with Southern-sympathizing political groups, such as the Know-Nothing Party and the so-called Chivalry Party, in an effort to maintain a vestige of their economic, racial, and cultural clout in the rapidly changing region. Ramírez did not shy away from conflict and used his paper to expose and critique the forms of Anglo-American structural racism he saw emerging in California under the new US colonial regime. *Clamor* and its editor "achieved a level of social and political analysis," Nicolás Kanellos explains, "that was well beyond the years of its young editor and even beyond what Hispanic intellectuals in Texas, the eastern seaboard, and much of Spanish America were concluding at this time."[57]

As Kanellos and others have maintained, Ramírez's *Clamor* waged a war of words against the rhetoric of American exceptionalism when it came to issues of race, governance, rule of law, and Enlightenment liberal ideals. It challenged the notion of the United States as a "model republic," pointing to its upholding of slavery, its colonial expansion, and its displacement, dispossession, and disenfranchisement of California's Mexican peoples as proof positive that the hypocrisy of widespread racism put the lie to the United States' founding ideals. However, Ramírez's point of critique stemmed from his belief in those ideals and the failure of the United States and Anglo-American governance, laws, and practices to live up to them. This, in part, explains why *Clamór* at times "challenged and perpetuated the ideology of white supremacy in its coverage of other nonwhite groups," as José Luis Benavides has it, but it also underscores how Ramírez envisioned uniting a Hispanophone community around the issues of shared rights, privileges, and power.[58] “In the course of publishing *El Clamor Público*,” Kanellos notes, “Ramírez continuously broadened his view to recognize the conditions that Californios shared with Hispanic immigrants—made up principally of Mexicans, Chileans, Peruvians, and Nicaraguans—and to evolve an understanding and an ideological posture that was more representative of colonial resistance to expanding imperial power.”[59] Even though *Clamor* cultivated a pan-Latino, anti-colonial sensibility, Ramírez had little luck mobilizing southern California's diverse Latino population and less support from its landed California elite, leaving *Clamor* to end its run on the eve of the Civil War after three and a half years of print. Yet the short-lived Spanish-language periodical epitomized the tumultuous decade in California that pulled the state's Latinos into the transnational debates dividing the Union and threatening the Mexican republic.

While some Californio elites tended toward Southern sympathy and the protection of slavery, there was also a large contingent of California Latinos who were invested in preserving the Union under the presumption that an undivided United States provided the best protection against the establishment of monarchy in Mexico. Among those on the Union muster rolls was the twenty-two-year-old Porfirio Jimeno, who served as second lieutenant of Company C under his uncle, Captain Antonio de la Guerra, until 1865, when Porfirio was promoted to captain of the same company. In January 1863 the War Department approved State Senator Romualdo Pacheco's suggestion that volunteers from the state's Mexican American population should be enlisted and armed with lances in homage to their Mexican martial history. The department gave “authorization to raise a four-company battalion of ‘native cavalry’ in and around Los Angeles.”[60] The so-called Californio lancers weren't comprised entirely of Californios or Mexican Americans. It enjoyed a roster of volunteers as diverse as the state, but with the initial commission of Andrés Pico as the cavalry's commanding officer (a position the fifty-three-year-old Californio declined) and the later commission of Salvador Vallejo as a major in the battalion, the First Battalion of Native Cavalry was Latino in spirit if not in corpus. Company C “was very much a family business. Its two lieutenants, Santiago de la Guerra and Porfirio Jimeno, were the captain's nephews. Juan José de la Guerra, age nineteen, was among the ranks along with more than a few other nephews and cousins."[61] Such kinship companies tended to keep loyalty to the chain of command, but in Porfirio's case, they didn't provide the individual familial support he craved.

Porfirio's Civil War letters are housed in the de la Guerra family papers, and they betray a gendered divide between Spanish and English. With one extant exception, his letters to his female family members are in Spanish, but when he wrote to his uncle Pablo de la Guerra and to his stepfather, James Ord, he moved between Spanish and English. The difference, of course, shores up who does and does not have access to the cultural power that English-language fluency might bring to Spanish-speaking Californios. However, the longer Porfirio stayed on the front, the more embattled he became with home, Spanish, and his sense of national belonging. Three prevailing themes characterize his letters. The first is that he finds camp and military life sad; the second is that no one seems to respond to his letters; and the third is the sociolinguistic slippage his writings betray. As might be expected of any letters from camp, his missives have their share of commonplace complaints—boredom, deplorable conditions, intolerable weather, and, in Porfirio's case, lack of good cigars. However, "Captain Jimeno," Tom Prezelski explains, "was by far the best educated of the Native Cavalry's officers but was also clearly a man of two worlds."[62] Recall that he rarely wrote under Meade's instruction (she characterized him as "lazy"), but he nonetheless gained English-language literacy in the same theater as his older brother.[63] In this light, his writings detail a different civil war, one waged with himself, camp life, and the frustrating feeling that his entire family has forgotten him on the front between the "two worlds" he straddled.

From the start of his service, Porfirio felt it hard. After a "horrible and terrible trip," he writes to his aunt Josefa María de la Guerra, he arrived in San Francisco "solo y muy triste, sin ningun amigo, y demasiado aflijido" (alone and very sad, without any friends and too distressed).[64] Three years later, he repeats the sentiment: "Esta vida es muy triste" (This is a very sad life), and more, he finds camp life stationed at Drum Barracks the same—"triste y feo" (sad and ugly). He closes by reflecting, "Jamas pensaba que era tan triste la vida de un militar pero tengo que aguantar." (I never thought a soldier's life can be so sad but I have to endure.)[65] A month later, he seems to have resigned himself to his lot, as he repeats to his aunt, "La vida de un militar es muy triste, pero que vamos a hacer?" (A soldier's life is very sad, but what can we do?)[66] By October 1865, five months after the end of the Civil War, he seems to have had his fill with service. Writing from Fort Mason, Arizona, where the Native Cavalry was dispatched to patrol the borderlands from Apache incursions, on the one hand, and from French imperialist forces in Mexico on the other, Porfirio laments, "Esta es un pais triste, feo, y casi sin gente civilizada. Lo que se habla nomas, es Apaches, Apaches. De fiebre, casi cada dia muere uno. Deberas hasta rabia da." (This country is sad, ugly, and almost without civilized people. One speaks of nothing but Apaches, Apaches. Someone dies almost each day of the fever. Truly it makes one angry.) Porfirio does not extend the same sympathy in this letter to the three Native people he casually reports killed on this expedition, including the one by his own hand.[67]

Prezelski is no doubt correct that Jimeno "spoke for most of the men at Fort Mason" in his frustration with their camp conditions, especially considering that their duty on the border kept them in service well after the Civil War ended.[68] But his sadness and frustration might have less to do with his service and more to do with the isolation he felt from his family, who rarely responded to his letters. Over the four years he wrote home, his frustration about the lack of correspondence becomes a rising tide of sadness, confusion, anger, and the growing concern that his entire family has forgotten him. Beginning in September 1864, he writes, "Le escribé a mi mama, a José Antonio, y Carolina pero no me han contestado." (I wrote to mama, José Antonio, and Carolina but they haven't responded to me.) The next month, he opens, "Hace cuatro dilijencias que les escribe a Francisca a Elena . . . y estraño que no me han contestado." (There's been four stage coaches [carrying mail] since I wrote to you, to Francisca, to Elena . . . and I find it strange that you have not written back to me.) The next week, he adds the postscript, "No se olvide de escribime pronto, y no se olvide de su sobrino." (Don't forget to write me soon, and don't forget your nephew.) Eventually, his ire begins to get the better of him, for by the week's end, he writes again, "Le escribi a Francisca y a J. y tambien a Clotilde y nadie me ha contestado—Así se acuerdan de sus primos." (I wrote to Francisca and to J. and also to Clotilde and none of them replied. This is how they remember their cousins.) Finally, after a year of relative silence from home, Porfirio pens an uncharacteristically vicious note from Fort Yuma, Arizona, that betrays the extent to which his emotions—his sadness, loneliness, and stress on the front—boiled over into a one-sided war of words with his aunts:

> Queridas tias—
> Si no fueran tan flojas les escribiera mas, pero les he escritó dos cartas a las dos, y ni una han contestado, y poreso no quiero escribirles mas largo. Ya saben como derijir mis cartas, conque si quierian escriban y sino "vayanse" al choris, cochinas, algun dia me la va a pagar—Adios—Adios, Saludes a todos.
>
> (Dear aunts: If you weren't so lazy, I'd write to you more often, but I've written two letters to each of you, and you have not written back even once, and so I don't want to write to you any longer. You already know where to send my letters, if you want to write and if not go screw yourself, filthy women, one day you'll pay for this.—Adios— Adios. Give my regards to all.)[69]

Like his older brother, Porfirio is a persistent writer, a militant one, in fact, who relies on letters to maintain a sense of family connection from camp. He writes often to share information about the company's movement, to describe camp conditions and his surroundings, to lament his loneliness, but most often, he writes to complain about not receiving letters from his extended family. It seems odd that he feels so much isolation from family when he's surrounded by Californio kin—he's enlisted in a company comprised of his extended male family, after all. His uncle is the company's captain and several of his cousins are on the muster rolls. However, military manhood does not seem to suit Porfirio. Most of his extant letters are written to the women in his family. It's their company he desires through writing, and it's their lack of correspondence that leaves Porfirio facing erasure between the gendered spheres of camp life and the domestic front. If "Mexican American women actively constructed manhood in order to express an array of social positions and to intervene in developing forms of citizenship," as Alberto Varon puts it, then Porfirio's sense of masculinity—and its concomitant concept of citizenship—is in a discursive vacuum at best because the women he writes to do not respond.[70] His letter from Drum Barracks to his younger half-sister Rebecca captures his troubled sense of masculinity through his tenderness, melancholy, and anxiety that his entire immediate family will forget him:

> Dear little Sister.
> I wish you a merry Christmas, and on Christmas day give "papa grande" a kiss, another to papa one to mama, one to José Antonio one to Carry, also to Santiago and Henry, and tell them that the poor soldier tu hermanito has nothing more to send them, but a kiss through his hermanita Rebecca. Good bye sister and never forget in your prayers your brother who loves you.[71]

Even though Porfirio wrote to his aunt Josefa exclusively in Spanish, his letter to his sister Rebecca shifts between Spanish and English, seamlessly, abruptly even, as if both languages work simultaneously—rather than bilingually, as it were—in his modes of expression. Perhaps Rebecca, the only daughter between James Ord and Angustias, does not read Spanish, which might explain why Porfirio reserves Spanish only for intimate diminutive phrases ("hermanito" and "hermanita") that do not require translation to be understood. Yet the touching note also marks the way English and Spanish compete for the field of emotional expression. A similar linguistic civil war comes into full display in a letter detailing his march from Drum Barracks to Carisso Creek en route to Fort Yuma along the Colorado River. Captain Jimeno writes to his uncle Pablo de la Guerra, "Hemos tenido un lindo viaje de Drum Barracks a este punto [We had a lovely trip from Drum Barracks to this place], *'via hell' alias 'Carisso Creek.'* For heaven's sake never come out this way if you can help it, you will surely melt.—Thermometer, every day in the shade 112 to 116,—wind—none—Scorpions thick as molasses, flies, still worse, and when we want to drink cool water we have to boil it and drink it immediately or else it will get hotter. Es imposible dar una descripción de este punto [It's impossible to describe this place]."[72] As it moves from Spanish to English, the letter retains Jimeno's humorous, ironic tone that walks a fine line between real and feigned outrage at the desert heat, but there's also a discursive battle at play here. The letter's fluent bilingual code-switching puts English and Spanish at war with each other, for after perfectly describing Fort Yuma, Arizona, in English,

Porfirio concludes in Spanish that the place is impossible to describe. His languages do battle on the contested terrain of representation.

Porfirio's linguistic civil wars and his war with home were one-sided skirmishes, for there is no record that his family members responded harshly to his written salvos. Judging from his growing frustration, they didn't respond at all. Yet the letters embody the interiority of his split subjectivity. Linguistically, his letter about the march to Drum Barracks, for instance, moves along a bilingual front that wages a war of representation, with his English offering the description of the trip that his Spanish proclaims cannot be represented. Here is Walt Whitman's "unwritten" Civil War, written, as it were, as a war between English and Spanish vying for the field of Porfirio's letter to his reluctant English-language literate uncle, Pablo de la Guerra.[73] Moreover, Porfirio's missives home comprise a veritable war of words with unwitting family combatants. Whether it be the vitriol with which he shells his *tías* or the melancholic Christmas note he sends his half-sister, Porfirio's letters betray his embattlement with home and family: he's torn between loving them and berating them; missing them and wanting nothing to do with them; remembering them and fearing that they've forgotten him altogether. While this frustration might be characteristic of many war letters from the front, it takes on added significance in Porfirio's case because he's surrounded by a company of Latino kin whose martial masculinity has no place for the younger Jimeno's emotive outbursts.

Not surprisingly, at the war's end, Porfirio did not return home. Instead, after turning down a commission in the regular army, he headed to another front—Mexico, which was, by his April 1867 arrival, seeing the tumultuous end to the French interregnum and Maximilian's rule. As Prezelski notes, he didn't arrive to join the republican cause but rather headed south to purchase the land that his father set out to settle fourteen years prior, when Porfirio was still in New York.[74] "Now that Max is clearing out," Porfirio writes to his stepfather, "the value of property is ascending. I hope so, at least after fourteen years of waiting we ought to get something, don't you think so?" What's striking about the letter is the investment opportunity Porfirio sees in Mexico's regime change. Much of his letter assesses Mexico's quality of life and economic potential, and both come up wanting through his now Americanized eyes. He says of Mazatlán that it's "truly Mexican" (verdaderament mexicano):

"la temperatura buena, pero al medio dia mucha calor, en fine dicen que desde las onze hasta las tres en las calles no le ve mas de [The weather is good but very hot at noon, anyways, they say that between eleven until three you will only see] 'Beggars and dogs.' I of course don't go out between those hours." He continues, in English, "Tell uncle Miguel that if he wishes to speculate on horseflesh he had better not come here because everybody rides on 'burros.' I have not seen a horse since my arrival. They have many fruit trees here, cocoa-nut, banana, etc. I hardly taste it because I don't think they are healthy." And finally, even as he notes that "there is no empire nowadays" in the city, he complains about the restriction of his movement under a liberal civil government:

> This is a free country here, if you want to cross the city limits you have to get your name recorded and get a "Passport," with about 20 signatures, but the worse part is a person has to pay for it. So I don't go out of the limits and don't think I will until I have to start.[75]

Put bluntly, Porfirio sounds like a Yankee expansionist weighing Mexico's worth in investment, quality of life, and governance, and he finds the country lacking on all counts. His audience might be in part to blame, as he is writing to his Anglo stepfather, who was complicit with colonial boosterism in California and seems to have bankrolled Porfirio's trip to Mazatlán. Porfirio isn't writing to his mother, for instance, but to her husband to tell him, "I made it!"[76] His bilingual letter betrays his larger bicultural rifts, a split sensibility by which the young boy who launched off for New York with Sherman for an education has returned, quite literally, to his father's land but sees it through the alienating gaze of Yankee eyes. To be fair, Porfirio complains pervasively about his travels and locations. Recall that he characterized his initial trip to San Francisco as "horrible and terrible"; he had nothing good to say of trekking through the desert to Arizona either; and he described Fort Mason as "ugly and full of fleas." His caustic ethnographic eye for place tends to extend to its peoples, as with his characterizations of Apache people as uncivilized or his complete disregard for mentioning the unnamed servant who accompanied him at camp.[77] Unlike the melancholy and sadness that might explain his letters from camp, however, Porfirio's missive from Mazatlán seems to linger on one central issue: Mexico is simply too

Mexican for him. "Digale a mi 'Nana,'" he says, "que this city is what we call in California: 'a la moda del País'" (Tell my Nana [?] that this city is what we call in California: 'the Country's style"), sarcastically suggesting that Mazatlán is the best Mexico has to offer.[78]

Porfirio didn't return from Mexico. He died in Mexico City in 1870, and if he wrote any more letters from there, which he probably did, they're fugitive, as are any responses he might have received from family, who hardly wrote to him even when he was stateside. He is ironically remembered less in the annals of the Californios and his famous de la Guerra family as he is remembered for his stint in Company C of the First Battalion of the Native Cavalry. *El Nuevo Mundo* sang Porfirio's praises after Company C disbanded. On his arrival in San Francisco, the *Mundo* described him as "one of the first young sons of California who, upon the south's rebellion breaking out offered his services to the United States government. His honorable conduct, his affable manners, earned him a well-deserved popularity among his superiors and the respect of his subordinates."[79] Neither earned him much posterity, perhaps because he fell somewhere in between the "superiors" of US military brass and its racialized "subordinates"—not quite the former but neither the latter either, as was the case when he left for New York that fateful day in January 1850 with that bag of gold dust under Sherman's watch, en route to becoming a split Latinx subject.

José Antonio fared no better. Soon after his 1856 return to California, he again found himself under the care of Sherman, who was living in San Francisco as a banker. He loaned José Antonio fifty dollars on his arrival from Boston.[80] A few months later, José Antonio indicated in his March 20, 1857, letter to Ord that he was setting new type for the recently sold *True Californian*, which is "now a simple commercial newspaper" that he's running on smaller type.[81] Before its March 16, 1857, sale, the *True Californian* supported San Francisco's 1856 Vigilance Committee, which staged a veritable civil war of its own in the streets and in the press between the Vigilance group and the Law and Order faction, the latter of which Sherman headed for a short spell. The future Union general pleaded in an open letter, "Civil war, or the array of armed citizen against citizen, is too horrible in its consequences to be spoken of, and it is to be hoped that all good citizens will, forthwith, return to their business, and cease any display of force or resistance to the regular operations of our courts of law."[82] José Antonio's interest in newspaper work, which started with his literacy lessons in New York, no doubt put him on the front lines of the heated wars in the press about the Vigilance Committee and placed him in the thick of San Francisco's Anglophone print community, but his extant letters make no mention of these rifts. Instead, he seems to have taken great pride in his trade, as he explains the new, smaller type to his stepfather. He also shared his work with Pablo de la Guerra: "Have you received the newspapers I've sent you? How do you like this style, etc. etc?" Rewarding as it was, print work was not a paying proposition, as he also asked his uncle to send money for board and another twenty-five dollars for a new Sunday suit.[83] By the early 1860s, he left the print world altogether to manage a family ranch in Santa Barbara, where he briefly served as an inspector of the electoral board and became embroiled in local election politics as they related to the growing national divide. However, unlike his younger brother, the male members of his extended family, and Sherman, he did not enlist, serve, or otherwise volunteer for any kind of military duty when the war broke out. He was likely not physically fit for duty. He wrote to his uncle in September 1863 that he was ill again and suffering from chronic debilitation: "Sigo malo y grandes dolores. Narcoticos ya no me hacen efecto para dormir." (I continue to be ill and in great pain. Drugs no longer have an effect on me to let me sleep.)[84]

Nevertheless, from his sickbed, he mustered the energy to pen a feverish open letter to Porfirio's company of native Californios to admonish them to cast their vote for Lincoln. The call to voting arms brings José Antonio's transition full circle, as the once displaced Californio in New York returned to California, reconnected with Californios, and passionately supported Union and Lincoln's second term. He addressed the letter to the entire company, presumably to have his brother read it out loud, and the piece straddles a pro-Lincoln and pro-Union position that centers on José Antonio's body in pain:

> Entre mi sufrimiento pensé en mi Patria adoptiva y doblemente sufri, pensé en sus hijos, y en vosotros pensé. Veo a esa Protectora Nuestra, abatida por el cumulo de infamias de sus mas queridos hijos, que, rompiendo los vinculos de gratitud y humanidad, y hollando la autoridad de ella; no contentos en verla sangrienta por sus crueles heridas, intentan

rasgar su vestidura, y desnuda abandonarla a la mofa del Mundo. Mil brazos se estíenden a defenderla del fratricida y tantos y mas cadáveres fueron victimas del encono del Traidor.

(During my suffering I thought of my adoptive Nation and suffered twice as much, I thought of the children and I thought of you all. I see our Protector, beaten down by the large number of insults from her most beloved sons, who, breaking the links of gratitude and humanity, and trampling her authority; not content in seeing her bloody from their cruel wounds, they try to rip off her clothing, and abandon her naked to the mockery of the World. A thousand arms extended to defend her from fratricide and many more dead bodies were victims of the bitterness of the Traitor.)[85]

For José Antonio, the suffering of the United States is his suffering, just as he felt the national mourning of Clay as his own mourning for the statesman. He suffers "doubly," raising the gender trouble that left him "as gentle and refined as a lady," as Meade put it. To a company of men, he likens his prostate body to the feminized national politic ravaged, rent asunder, and left naked by "la Rebelde Fiereza" (the Rebel Ferocity). His letter registers his passionate concern for Union through the language that echoes his educational experience of dis-union from Mexican California and incorporation into Anglo America. He continues, "Vosotros Californios, sed tambien heroes en esta gloriosa Causa, siendo agradecidos a ese pais a quien debeis, despues de Dios, todo vuestro bien, porq. cuando os vio tristes y desamparados os atrajo a su seno, cubriendoós en su manto real de azul y estrellas, y os dotó con el derecho de Ciudadanos Americanos." (You Californians, must also be heroes in this glorious Cause, being grateful to that country to which you owe, only after God, all your good fortune, because when she saw that you were helpless and sad, she brought you to her breast, covering you in her royal cloak of blue and stars, and bequeathed you with the right of being American Citizens.)[86] To be sure, José Antonio is describing the historical process of Californio displacement, and at the same time, he's describing his own process of departure, acculturation, and return to California as a Mexican American with a tenuous cultural belonging, registered here in his deep investment in the second-class citizenship the United States extended to Mexicans after 1848, the debt of gratitude Californios ostensibly owe the United States, though in fact it was the US laws of the land that left them "tristes y descamparados."

While José Antonio practiced English in his early letters to Sherman, his only extant Civil War letter to Company C might at first appear to be a return to his Hispanophone community, proof positive that he did not forget Spanish after all, as his mother once feared. Yet Meade's hand is here too. "I have engaged a Spanish teacher for them," she says to Sherman of José Antonio and Porfirio, "and will endeavor to have them *properly* taught their own language."[87] The Spanish-language lessons show: he addresses the Native Californio Cavalry, which is comprised of elite Californios, Mexican volunteers, impressed Indigenous people, and non-Latinos, with the formal *vosotros* form, which is more associated with Spain than Mexico or Mexican American everyday usage in the later nineteenth-century California. In a pained attempt to connect with the company of Californios, José Antonio's Spanish also marks his social, cultural, class, and linguistic separation from them. Instead, his education on the Yankee front cultivated such a deep allegiance to the United States that he takes its violent disunion physically, and as with other times of stress, dispossession, and anxiety, José Antonio's "disease of the head," as the doctor once put it, has taken hold at the height of the Civil War. His body is the nation's body—pulled apart and at war with itself. Wounded in the theater of his acculturation that William "Castañares" Sherman, Alfred Robinson, and Margaret Meade directed years before, José Antonio's process of becoming a Mexican American has left him bedridden, feverish, and on painkillers that no longer have effect. By January 1866, he was dead—a civil war casualty of a different sort who, along with his younger brother, was left war-torn on the field of US Latinidad.[88]

2

Southwestern Microwars

Rafael Chacón, Santiago Tafolla, and the Borderlands Front

While forays to the Eastern Seaboard left the Californio elite war-torn on the eve of secession, the Southwestern theater staged multiple civil wars of its own that were unique to the region, its colonial histories, populations, and territorial status. Here, the Civil War layered over regional conflicts already in circulation. It was one between the Union and the self-proclaimed Confederacy, but it also reignited the tensions between New Mexicans and Texans, which the latter initiated years earlier with an ill-fated invasion of New Mexico in an attempt to extend the borders of the young Texas Republic. Moreover, as Union and Confederate Mexicans of the region well knew, the war gave cover to the long-standing engagements with Native peoples such as the Navajo, Apache, and Comanche, who mobilized across different fronts throughout the Southwest during the US Civil War. Much of the military action for the New Mexico Volunteers involved chasing, quelling, and ostensibly preempting Native salvos rather than lining up against Confederates, and the CSA too tended to order its Mexican Texan soldiers to track, scout, and wage war against Indigenous forces rather than serve on its front lines against the Union.[1] Theirs was a civil war within the Civil War as campaigns against Indigenous groups made up the majority of military action in the region. Finally, the animosities and resentments stemming from as far back as Texas's 1835 bid for independence, the 1846–1848 US-Mexico War, and the US occupation of New Mexico that followed, combined with a general anti-Mexican sentiment of the time, assured that life in the ranks of the federal or CSA armies for US Latinxs would include skirmishes over language, race, religion, and national belonging that often turned uncivil if not outright racist. As Andrew E. Masich concludes, "The American Civil War created the conditions that resulted in or expanded violent conflict between and among peoples of different communities (bands, tribes, races, ethnicities, and nations) and led to multiple concurrent civil wars in the Southwest Borderlands between 1861 and 1867."[2]

When we recall that the New Mexico Volunteers were fighting for the Union even though New Mexico was not a state in the Union, and the majority of Texas's Mexican Confederates might have had little to gain politically or economically by throwing in with pro-slavery rebels, Mexican America's service in the Union or CSA armies must be understood with critical, cultural nuance. An estimated 9,990 Mexican Americans enlisted to uphold the Union or Confederate cause, and Jerry D. Thompson surmises that they "joined the conflict for reasons less to do with states' rights or slavery and more with class and economics."[3] Conscription aside, this is not always the case, as we saw with Joseph de la Garza's letters, and as Omar S. Valerio-Jiménez points out, such historical "interpretations discount the ability of Tejanos to understand political issues in the United States as well as the reality that many Mexican Texans acted on such beliefs. . . . Mexican Texans chose to participate in the sectional conflict because they understood the reasons over which the Civil War was fought."[4] They also understood how the outcome of those reasons might threaten their sense of belonging in their respective homelands. New Mexicans and Mexican Texans, for instance, were not foreigners in the same way as the scores of German, Irish, and French immigrants in the ranks, but they nonetheless faced a tenuous status as second-class participants in both armies. Colonel Canby's May 10, 1862, General Order 44 reorganizing the New Mexico Volunteers betrays such an ambivalence: "In the organization of companies the enrolled men of native and foreign birth will be kept distinct except that in the New Mexican companies one or more officers and one-fourth of the noncommissioned officers shall be persons who understand and speak both the English and the Spanish languages." The order further instructed that four of the newly formed E Companies would be outfitted specifically "for service in the Indian country in suppressing the banditti and marauders who infest certain localities of the Territory."[5]

The understandable necessity to convey military commands in English notwithstanding, Canby's order demonstrates the confusion with which Anglo America understood Mexican Americans and, in turn, the ambivalent status they held in the ranks. For Canby, most of the

Hispano New Mexico Volunteers may have been of "foreign birth," having been born in Mexico's far northern frontier before it became the US Southwest after 1848; even so, their birth in the region made them native to it, contra to the Kentucky-born Union colonel. The de facto segregation of companies based on native and foreign birth likewise instituted an arbitrary identity affiliation based not so much on origin but on language fluency. As the order further makes clear, the segregation of companies may not have anything to do with language or birthplace after all, but with using both as a pretext for assigning specific companies, in this case, the Spanish-speaking Hispano E Companies, to so-called Indian campaigns, almost as if to segregate the combatants along two fronts: Anglo-Americans fighting each other in the Civil War while Mexicans on both sides mustered into microwars against Indigenous groups, Anglo America, and its institutionalized racism in the Union and CSA ranks.

It's within these intersectional racial conflicts that I take up the life and writings of Rafael Chacón, a Union man with the New Mexico Volunteers, and James Santiago Tafolla, a Santa Fe-born Texas Confederate, who joined the ranks as a bugler and ended up on the front lines of a mini-rebellion against the Texas rebels. There are plenty of other Mexican American Union and Confederate soldiers who penned letters, brief battle accounts, and official reports and correspondences, such as Captain J. Francisco Chaves of the New Mexico Volunteers or Captains Joseph Rafael de la Garza and Manuel Yturri of the Texas CSA.[6] However, Chacón and Tafolla are unique in so far as they both produced postbellum autobiographies that recount the embattled process of becoming Mexican American during the war years. Both narratives can be considered Civil War stories in the sense that they each offer a first-person account of the war, but they also narrate the internal conflicts and competing identities that put the self at civil war in the racialized process of becoming Mexican American behind Union or Confederate lines. Moreover, they each give expression to the microwars—the civil wars within the Civil War—that characterize the region's ambivalent place as a Civil War front. Theirs are a series of skirmishes that pit competing racial, religious, linguistic, national, and regional categories against each other in a series of battlefronts that force the "emergence" of Chacón and Tafolla as Mexican Americans whose autobiographies represent their internal civil wars in the context of their participation in the Civil War's trans-Mississippi theater.[7]

The Southwest Slave Debate

Chacón's and Tafolla's Civil War narratives must first be understood in the context of the debates over slavery in the greater Southwest, where the question took on the peculiar racial fault lines already fissuring the region. "In the west," Adam Arenson reminds us, "both Civil War battlefields and Civil War politics engaged a wider range of ethnic and racial distinctions."[8] With a mixed attitude toward Black enslavement, New Mexico was more strategic as a gateway to California than it was a stronghold of either Union or Confederate sympathies, making the *casus belli* for the region's native-born more murky than it was along the Eastern theater.[9] After all, Mexico had abolished slavery throughout its republic in 1829, and even though the newly formed Texas Republic endorsed slavery after 1836, Tejano land, labor, and economic practices generally relied on a *patrón-peón* arrangement rather than enslaved Black labor.[10] Historical systems of peonage, indentured servitude, and Indigenous enslavement were more familiar across the borderlands during the Spanish colonial, Mexican republic, and American neocolonial periods as forms of labor that structured kinship, cultural exchange, racial intermixing, and caste hierarchies that organized social arrangements in the home and across the homeland. For many pro- and anti-slavery pundits, regional forms of labor fueled or extinguished the chattel slavery debate. Pro-slavery advocates viewed the legacy of peonage and servitude as a culture of impressed labor analogous to slavery; anti-slavery advocates saw the system as one that would make Black enslavement redundant in the Southwest. "As pro-statehood and pro-territorial political factions contended between 1848 and 1850," James F. Brooks explains, "neither side felt it necessary to make public comment on the slavery controversy nor to meddle with customary systems of bondage in the region, which provided cheap labor that rendered the importation of black slaves impractical and unnecessary."[11]

Miguel Antonio Otero's politicking for the New Mexico Territory is instructive of the region's ambivalence over the slavery question and the way it situated US Latinxs in a tenuous position within a US national debate that didn't necessarily include them in the first place. The territory's Democratic congressional delegate from 1856 to 1861, Otero might perhaps be one of the most politically visible and vocal Hispanos in the days leading up to the Civil War. He had a hand in creating, advancing, and justifying the New Mexico Territory's 1859 Slave Code, a series of laws that didn't so much protect slavery in New Mexico, for there were very few enslaved Blacks in the territory, as invite slavery with the promise of its protection.[12] In Washington, he was the political face attached to the code, which Horace Greeley lambasted in his *New York Tribune*:

> The most insidious and systematic efforts have been made to plant Slavery there [Territory of New Mexico], and not without success. Zealous Slavery Propagandists fill all the important Federal offices. . . . A Slave Code of signal atrocity and inhumanity has been put through the Territorial Legislature, and is now in full force. . . . In time, everything conspires to make New-Mexico, if now admitted, a Slave State.[13]

In his response, first published in the *Washington Constitution* and then reprinted in the *Santa Fe Weekly Gazette*, Otero lambasts Greeley and explains the Slave Code as a humane set of laws:

> Recognising the right of the citizens of the different States to take with them into the common domain of the people of the United States every lawful species of property, and there enjoy the same as fully and uninterruptedly as they were accustomed to do in the State from which they respectively came, the people of New Mexico, through their legislature, enacted a code for the protection of property. Although I have none of that kind of property to demand protection, I commend the wisdom and applaud the patriotism that prompted the enactment of such a code; and I denounce as false and malevolent the allegation that said code is one of signal atrocity and inhumanity. Its purposes are just and its provisions humane. It aims to protect the slave corporeally and morally, that his usefulness to his master and his own sobriety, morality, and happiness may be in the highest degree attained.[14]

Without conceding that treating people as property is itself inhumane, Otero manages to muster an argument for property rights in general rather than slavery in particular, drawing a duplicitous description of the New Mexico Territory as neither for nor against slavery but patriotic in its commitment to protect property of all kinds brought into the region. Greeley wasn't convinced. In a follow-up to the debate, published later in his history of the Civil War, he characterized Otero's open letter, presumably the one circulated in the *Constitution* and *Gazette*, as "intended to disaffect them [the people of New Mexico] toward the Union, and incite them to favor the Rebellion."[15] Otero claimed nothing of the sort. In a November 8, 1860, letter published a month later in the *Gazette*, he declared, "I can be nothing else but a Union man."[16] The fact that South Carolina participated in a national election but was unhappy with the results is not enough, in Otero's eyes, to warrant secession and is a bit disingenuous. "It looks too much like a man who takes a hand in a game of cards," Otero further explains in the letter, "with the previous determination that if he win he will be satisfied but if he lose he intends to break upon the game and ruin everybody."[17] On the eve of secession, he expressed his reluctance to dissolve the Union and to advocate for Civil War for the sake of "the accursed negro": "God forbid that this fair land should be stained with fratricidal blood, and that the freest and best government on earth should be changed for anarchy and ruin and despotism."[18]

As Laura E. Gómez argues, Otero's support of the territory's Slave Code, along with his articulation of the history of Spanish and Mexican colonial legacies in the region, bolsters a very deliberate effort to distinguish Mexican American elites as higher on the racial ladder than Native and African Americans within the new Anglo-American colonial regime. Gómez describes the rhetorical conundrum Otero crafts in his response to Greeley: "The ability of Mexican Americans to at times succeed in claiming whiteness led them into a perverse trap," Gómez explains. "To solidify their classification as white, they had to act like whites, especially with respect to non-white groups. Mexican American elites, in particular, acted in ways that shored up their whiteness, at the expense of every non-white group below them. Intentionally or not, they became agents in the reproduction of racial subordination and contributed to the consolidation of a new version of white supremacy in the Southwest."[19] Gómez's characterization of the "off-white" status of Mexican Americans corresponds to what I've been advancing as the split subject position of US Latinxs during the war years. "Mexican Americans came to occupy a position in the American racial hierarchy," Gómez explains, "that was between white and non-white."[20] I suggest that their in-between position embattled them both politically and personally not only across enemy lines but also within their own home fronts.

For instance, the debate over slavery and the territory's Slave Code turned on two interrelated questions: statehood and the racial composition of New Mexico's Hispano population. Greeley's initial editorial maintained that New Mexico should not be admitted as a state because its standing Slave Code, along with what Greeley characterized as rabid secessionist leaders, would result in the admission of a slave state. He further maintained that New Mexico's population was unfit for racial and national US citizenship: "The mass of the people are Mexicans—a hybrid race of Spanish and Indian origin. They are ignorant and degraded, demoralized and priest-ridden. The debasing Mexican system of Peonage—a modified Slavery—is still maintained there. . . . Slavery rules all."[21] This wasn't the first time anti-slavery pundits linked the question of statehood and slavery in the territory to the New Mexican population. At the second session of the thirty-sixth Congress, the senator from Ohio, John Sherman, similarly raised the question, "Shall New Mexico be free or slave?" With Otero on the congressional floor, Sherman answered his own question with a sentiment similar to Greeley's: "The question is, whether New Mexico, with its peons, with its wild lands, with its half-breeds and Mexicans, its mixed populations shall be free or slaveholding Territory." The senator and brother to William T. Sherman rejected the idea of bringing the territory into the Union, but not before Otero voiced his objection in the congressional record: "The gentleman should yield to reply against so infamous and malicious a libel against the character of the people I represent," Otero interjected to no avail. Sherman did not yield the floor.[22]

Otero's rebuttal on the congressional floor and in the press took much more offense at the racism heaped on Hispanos than on the question of slavery and statehood that framed it. The "half-breed hidalgo," as another Greeley affiliate characterized Otero in the *Tribune*,[23] responded to Greeley with a keen understanding—if not justification—of the territory's position in between the region's long-standing cultural practices and its newfound place in national politics. First, Otero worked to disentangle the region's history of peonage from the national question of slavery.

> I deny that peonage, as it exists in New Mexico, is a modified slavery, or any slavery at all. It is merely a system of apprenticeship or temporary voluntary servitude, whereby a man is enabled to borrow money, or otherwise create a debt, and to give his personal service, at a stipulated rate of hire, as security for the payment thereof. . . . I deny that there is anything debasing in this system. The social and political status of an individual is not effected by his entering into the condition of a peon. . . . This system has none of the elements or attributes of slavery.[24]

In much the same way that Otero's advocacy for the protection of property upheld the logic of the Slave Code and, by extension, slavery, his argument for peonage maintains it as a fair and equitable transaction of debt and service that just happens to traffic in human labor power. His distinction between the two practices, though, shores up the way Spanish colonial and Mexican neocolonial cultural practices resonated in the New Mexico Territory even as the region changed hands to Anglo America. The appearance of an act amending the Law Relative to Contracts between Masters and Servants in the same New Mexico Territorial Legislation that printed the Slave Code makes it even more compelling that both policies were related even if their practices, according to Otero, were distinct.[25]

But what was the greater concern in national politics was the lesser one in Otero's foray into the national debate, as he tended to proffer ambivalent arguments around the issue of slavery but impassioned ones against the racist sentiments heaped on New Mexico's Mexican American population. The positions were, for Otero and many Hispanos invested in statehood at the time, two sides of the battle, for on the one hand, the slavery question dominated and determined the road into the Union for the territory gained by the Treaty of Guadalupe Hidalgo, and on the other, the conundrum of Mexican America's racial composition tended to obfuscate the path to US citizenship that statehood promised. The historical explanation that Otero offers Greeley is so instructive and so fraught with homologous anxieties encoding the question of slavery and the presence of African America that it's worth quoting at length:

> The attempt to disparage the Territory of New Mexico, by branding her people as a hybrid race of a Spanish and Indian origin will meet a prompt refutation and rebuke from every mind that is familiar with the history of that portion of our country. Ever since the conquest and colonization of the valley of the Rio del Norte, under the prowess of Don Juan de Onate in the latter part of the seventeenth century, the Spaniards and the aborigines, or Indians, have been separated and distinct from each other, and have so remained up to this day. The conquest of New Mexico by the Spaniards reduced the aborigines, or Indians, to a state of abject but sullen and reluctant slavery. In that relation they continued—socially separate and distinct races—until a servile insurrection of the aborigines drove the Spaniards from the land. At the close of the seventeenth century the country was reconquered by the Spaniards; and from that time to the present day the Indians within the settlements have occupied pueblos or towns exclusively set apart for them, and they have scrupulously refrained from intercourse with the Spanish population excepting so far as became necessary for the ordinary transaction of business. They have their own exclusive and peculiar government, their own places of worship, their amusements; their social intercourse is exclusively amongst themselves; they never intermarry with the Spanish people, and are to all intents and purposes separate and distinct from them. The two races never have amalgamated; and although the Spanish blood has sometimes manifested itself on the aboriginal race, and the Indian blood less frequently on the Spanish race, those instances are of rare occurrence—so rare as to render the sweeping allegation that the mass of the people of New Mexico are a hybrid race, of a Spanish and Indian origin, grossly defamatory and shamefully mendacious.[26]

With the promise of statehood lingering, Otero makes a case for Hispano racial purity, despite substantial proof to the contrary, as a way of leveraging Mexican America into the regime of Anglo-American social, political, and economic power. Ironically, though, the presence of Indigenous slavery in the region undermines the logic of Otero's idea of blood and cultural purity, for the history of capture, peonage, and servitude structured domestic kinship bonds and systems of cultural exchange that fostered and fueled hybridity of all sorts.[27] If the future of statehood hung in the balance between servitude and slavery, then it also put into play two competing models of labor systems that would determine Mexican America's ambivalent place in the new economic state. That is, the slavery question impacted the long-term regional practice of peonage that, regardless of the slippery description Otero gives to it, served as a racialized labor arrangement designed to keep Mexican American elites in power, socially, structurally, domestically, and ethno-racially. It's not so much that Otero and his Hispano compatriots were invested in the practice of chattel slavery, Estévan Rael-Gálvez explains, as that they were concerned with protecting its kin labor system—peonage—as well as the analogous regional practice of taking Native peoples as *cautivos*. "The fact remained that this servitude, however different from the form of slavery in the US south, was an underlying element of paternalism, based upon racism and class exploitation," Rael-Gálvez concludes.[28]

Yet, for Otero, the enslavement of Black people was intimately familiar to him. It was familial to him, in fact. He married into a white South Carolina family of enslavers and likely helped to broker New Mexico's Slave Code because enslavement and indenture ensured the marriage between the South and the Southwest at a time of national dis-Union. In effect, his "off-whiteness" put him between Union and Confederacy, free and slave, and white and Black, even though the Southwest in general and Hispano regional identities in particular belied such clear-cut battle lines. A photo from the Blackwood family collection captures with stunning clarity the triangulation of racial power that seated Otero's whiteness askew (if not askance) in relation to the frontal pose of Mary Blackwood, who looks directly into the camera in a gesture of power over the staged and visual space, and an unnamed enslaved girl whose downward gaze averts her face even as she occupies the center of the picture's visual plane. In this one picture is the proximity and complicity of Hispanos with slave society in the US South. Latinx racial whiteness is here captured in a set of social relations, an equation, so to speak, in which the unknown variable stands at the center, obscured by the camera, staged almost like a prop of the portrait studio picture, and left without a formal name other than "enslaved girl" in the archive's metadata. Serving as the backdrop to Otero's tortured arguments for Hispano

Figure 2.1. A studio portrait from around 1860 captures the triangulation of racial formation and the uneven power dynamics between Anglo, Hispano, and Black people. Miguel Otero, Mary Blackwood Otero, and enslaved girl, M16–30 Alexander Melvorne Jackson Papers, Historical Manuscripts and Photographs Repository, Special Collections, University Libraries, University of Southern Mississippi.

whiteness, the unnamed Black girl is also a haunting reminder that, despite the Southwest's long-standing racial conflicts and related labor practices between Hispano and Indigenous groups, the enslavement of Black people pulled the region into the nation's Civil War, with the lines between the South and the Southwest fuzzy but familiar.

The Microwars of Chacón's *Legacy of Honor*

Written between 1906 and 1912 but posthumously published in 1986 with significant editorial alterations, Rafael Chacón's autobiography is an embattled text. He penned his memoirs longhand over the course of six years, in part to leave the story for his family but also propelled by the impulse to write his history of life experiences in the region during the Civil War. Family history tells that Chacón wrote his narrative longhand in Spanish. As he completed chapters, his son, Eusebio, a lawyer and literary aspirant, would send portions to Chacón's nephew, Felipe, who would read portions to his family after dinner and then return the text to Chacón, with comments. When Chacón completed the manuscript in 1912, Eusebio had the script typed, copied, and bound. He kept the longhand manuscript and one copy of the typescript; Chacón's daughter, Gumecinda, received another copy; and Chacón's wife, Juanita, gave Felipe the third copy after Chacón's funeral in 1925. With time, family members lost track of the original memoir, and two of the three typescript copies were also lost, leaving Felipe's typescript copy extant in the family's hands.[29] The University of Colorado Historical Collection holds portions of the manuscript, translated by Eusebio with the seeming intention of publication, but the entire narrative remained in private hands until historian Jacqueline Dorgan Meketa arranged with the Chacón heirs to gain access to the typescript copy and a family translation of it by Felipe's daughter for republication. At first, Meketa explains, she planned to directly reprint the memoir, but as she worked through it, she decided to supplement it with other textual documentation, Chacón letters, military records, and ephemera related to the events covered in the narrative, to round out the story, corroborate details, or correct Chacón's memory of events.[30] In the process, she also reorganized certain passages; inserted paragraph breaks; deleted chapter headings, correspondences, and military orders; embedded her own commentary and historical research at specific points in the narrative; added photos; and produced her own translation of the typescript Spanish memoir. As a result, she published *Legacy of Honor: The Life of Rafael Chacón, a Nineteenth-Century New Mexican*, despite qualms expressed by one manuscript reviewer for the publisher, who objected to the heavy editorial hand in the making of *Legacy*.[31]

As Genaro Padilla argues, Meketa produced a troubling edition, for while she made available an important narrative, one of the earliest Mexican American autobiographies, she also hijacked it, sublimating Chacón's voice not so much through translation, for Meketa's rendition of the text is generally accurate, but through editorial intrusion that displaces Chacón's voice for Meketa's authority. At times, Meketa's historical corroboration proves helpful, as when she supplements Chacón's narrative with other documents or materials produced by or directly related to Chacón, such as letters or general orders that he didn't include in his narrative. Yet this gesture tends to speak for Chacón, to make his memoir express what he chose not to express in his own retelling of his life. "In supplementing Chacón's memoirs," Padilla maintains, "Meketa gives us a version of Rafael Chacón that in the process of thickening the biographical subject, eventually so disperses Chacón's own narrative that the autobiographer himself is displaced."[32] The only extant copy of Chacón's typeset narrative, a copy of the family's copy given to Meketa for use and available in the Meketa Papers, bears the scars of its dismemberment. It's mostly intact, but it's also missing pages in the places where Meketa decided to supplement Chacón's voice, leaving the only available copy of the Spanish-language typescript of Chacón's original memoir marked with missing parts here and there—a symbolic testament to the memoir's embattled process of coming to light nearly eighty years after Chacón sat down to write it.

Nevertheless, *Legacy of Honor* is the only accessible version of Chacón's life story in lieu of the original or the butchered copy of the family's copy of the Spanish typewritten narrative in the Meketa Papers. Its linguistic and textual history serves as the first front in the battle for Mexican American self-expression and identity formation during the Civil War. For instance, while Chacón was literate in Spanish, his facility with English was more limited. Up until his service with the Union, he spoke only Spanish, but once he was named captain of Company

K of the First Regiment of the New Mexico Volunteers, he picked up enough English to give commands, do paperwork to draw rations, and file reports, even though almost all of Company K consisted of Spanish speakers—many of whom were Chacón's family and friends.[33] However, his staff transcribed and translated most of his military letters and orders. His is a Hispanophone world, with all its cultural trappings, at a time when English and Anglo America were encroaching on the entire Southwest. This civil war between Spanish and English languages later repeats itself with the textual history of his memoirs: Chacón writes them in Spanish; his son types and copies the original document in Spanish, titled "Memorias de Rafael Chacón," but the narrative doesn't see light until Meketa translates, alters, and republishes it in English as *Legacy of Honor*.[34]

The point is not so much to question the translation's accuracy as to highlight that the process of becoming Mexican American in Anglo America is one that involves, first and foremost, a battle of languages and literacies that are not as seamless as a final product, such as *The Legacy of Honor*, might otherwise indicate. The process involves linguistic and textual violence of expression that gives double meaning to the idea of Civil War writing. Not only does Chacón write about his participation in the Civil War in the New Mexico Territory, but his very writing about it in a Spanish-language memoir that must enter the English-language world before it can be published, circulated, and made accessible is itself a battle that pits his Spanish-language memoirs against the English-language text attributed to him. His "memorias" and Meketa's *Legacy of Honor*, in other words, discursively stage the embattled transformation between being Mexican and becoming Mexican American: it involves a violent dispossession of the Spanish language; the dismemberment of agency and self-representation; and the re-presenting of the ethnic subject into an identity more palatable—more readable—for Anglo consumption. This process splits the difference between Latinx Civil War writings and writings that embody the civil war of becoming a US Latinx subject.

We can understand Chacón's narrative, then, as indicative of multiple microwars. First, *Legacy* proves to be an embattled text in its publication as it undergoes the sociolinguistic violence Meketa puts it through to publish it in English. This process of textual appropriation and acculturation mirrors Chacón's Civil War narrative proper, which recounts his service to the Union and the way that service didn't guarantee him and his fellow Hispanos equal treatment and inclusion into the Union. In this regard, his Civil War narrative expresses Chacón's internal conflict as a subject split between his service to the Union and his growing disillusionment with its promise of equality. The longer he fought for the Union, the more he warred against its institutionalized racism and Anglo America's open hostility toward Hispanos. The narrative also expresses the fault lines of Chacón's expectations of racial equality. His war against Indigenous sovereignty shores up his vested interest in maintaining the Spanish colonial and Mexican neocolonial presumption of Hispano whiteness, privilege, and power in the region, in league with Anglo America, over what he calls their "common savage foe."[35] *Legacy of Honor*, in other words, is Chacón's record of the wars of Mexican American identity that the relatively short-lived Civil War in the Southwest forged and fissured.

A former cadet with military training and brief experience in the US-Mexico War, Chacón doesn't make mention of his interest to join the Union war effort. He is making good money and doing good business at the time as a freighter, so when he gets word that he's being considered for a captain's commission, his mind is unresolved: "I did not know what to decide," he says about accepting an invitation from Colonel St. Vrain to become a captain of New Mexico Volunteers.[36] However, "when the colonel returned to Santa Fe he brought me the notice of my commission as captain, which obliged me to deliver myself to Fort Union. . . . This forced me to abandon the idea of becoming a freighter, and on August 13, 1861, I presented myself at Fort Union with my company and we were received into the volunteer services of the United States, in the bloody war which was called the Rebellion of the South, or the Civil War."[37] Chacón expresses his enlistment as reluctant at best and involuntary at worst in his memoirs, which runs counter to the explanation he gives General James Carleton in his October 1, 1863, letter of resignation: "Desde el momento en que estalló la Rebelion del Sur, penetrado del mas sincero patriotismo por la causa de la Union, me presente inmediatamente a la voz del Gobernador del Territorio, que llamaba alos ciudadanos del, para apoyar la justa causa." (From the moment in which began the Rebellion of the South, filled with the most sincere patriotism for the Cause of the Union I presented myself immediately at the call of the Governor of the Territory which summoned the citizens thereof to sustain The Just Cause.)[38] The competing explanations highlight Chacón's rhetorical dexterity and mark a difference in sentiment between his 1863 letter and his later, postwar reflections. Something has changed his feelings about his Union service, and one indication might be the disparity between his Spanish letter and its English translation in his service record. The official translation does battle with Chacón's original Spanish, with simple differences, such as the translation of "estalló" as "began" rather than "broke out," "burst," or "exploded," to a more deliberate mischaracterization with the capitalization of "The Just Cause" to Chacón's "la justa causa." From his service record to his autobiography, Spanish and English wage war to tell Chacón's life story on two fronts: one on which he's the agent of his Hispano identity and the other in which his Hispano identity is subject to the Union cause. His commission letter further demonstrates the divided service Chacón faces: "Know you that we, having confidence and faith in your patriotism, bravery, conduct, and loyalty, have commissioned you Captain of a Company of Volunteers. . . . For which, you shall carefully and diligently dispense with the duties of this office, performing and executing all matters that pertain to you, according to the laws of the United States and this Territory, and according to military rules and discipline."[39] As his record will prove, Chacón followed the letter of his commission to the point that he exposed its lie—he was not treated with the same due diligence the United States expected of him, though he enforced military discipline with a keen sense of racial equality.

His first narrated encounter as a captain, for instance, involves him tolerating Lieutenant A. P. Damours's racism. Proffering his bilingual services, Damours appealed to Chacón for an officer's commission as first lieutenant, but no sooner had he joined Company K, than he "would begin to talk against the Mexicans."[40] More, during drills, he "would prick the soldiers' thighs with his sword," "put a stick on their neck in order to straighten up," and "always mistreated and insulted the Mexicans." His animosity extended to Chacón himself when Damours, in an act of insubordination, expressed to the soldiers—mostly Chacón's friends, family, and comrades—that "he should be the captain because the one they now had was no good."[41] At first, Chacón reports holding his tongue, but after suffering the challenge to his leadership, he confronts Damours "the next time he began with his jokes once again at the table." Chacón asserts, "Until now I have suffered and allowed you to talk of my race, but from now and henceforth I will not allow you to return to denigrating them in my presence."[42] The ensuing fight is played off for comic effect, with Chacón losing his temper but also besting Damours to the point that he runs out of the mess hall, "dragging his sword," in an actual and symbolic gesture of his deflated ego. In the end, Chacón comes off well, in his narrative and with his commanding colonel, who had seen Damours running outside "dragging his sword with no respect, and that [the colonel] was only waiting for [Chacón] to bring charges against Damours for conduct unbecoming an officer and gentleman."[43] As Padilla maintains, "Episodes of this kind . . . adopt an accent of comic detachment from experiences that might just as easily have been remembered in bitterness or brooding self-righteousness. Chacón maintains a rhetorical mask that transforms repressed anger into comic dismissal of an old adversary."[44]

While Chacón masks his bitterness, as Padilla has it, he also unveils the first in a series of articulations about race that, up until his participation in the Civil War, remained muted. It is the first time in his narrative that he identifies "his race" as Mexican and the first time he labels Mexican as a race. To be sure, it's assumed beforehand that Mexican is a racial category imagined differently from Native America, as is evident in the narrative events that precede the Civil War, but it's neither the so-called Indian wars nor the US-Mexico War that give rise to Chacón's use of Mexican as "his race"—"mi raza" in the original Spanish typescript.[45] Rather, the Civil War and Chacón's experience in it give cause to his racial consciousness to articulate an identity that operated unconsciously, so to speak—an assumed identity category in contradistinction to Indigenous people rather than a contested one among Anglo America. One might even say that his confrontation with Anglo-American racism pressures Chacón to give expression to his sense of racial pride and, by extension, to articulate a sense of Latinidad forged out of the Civil War and the civil wars he encountered in the Union ranks.

He elaborates further after detailing the end of his Union service. Noting that he "had the honor to exchange the first shots with the enemy Confederates" and "the honor to discharge the last shots on the enemy . . . at the end of the Texas invasion," Chacón closes with a telling reflection on his sense of racial pride:

> Before going into the details of our campaigns in the Navajo country against that tribe, a sentiment of pride for my race makes me note a reflection on their martial character. Since the Spanish colonization this nation of New Mexico endured an unequal struggle against the savage nations that surrounded it, without rudiments, without resources, without assistance of any kind from capitals of the ruling countries. They have fought and died, always with the faith that it was necessary for them to defend their hearths. Obliged by circumstances always to defend themselves with weapons, in the country and in the villages, like the Roman populace in primitive times, they soon raised among their sons a populace of soldiers by nature intelligent, intrepid, valiant, and lovers of their country and of their liberty. The New Mexicans, raised in the use of arms from their childhood, did not know what fear was and God grant that those in whose hands our destiny has fallen will begin someday to appreciate their beautiful qualities and their temperaments.[46]

Chacón's "final words on the Civil War," Padilla writes, "are unsettling, divided by deep regard for his people's topographic identity and his recognition of their unfortunate subordination in a country that exploited the Nuevomexicanos during its wars."[47] But his passage also indicates how Nuevomexicano identity emerged out of a civil war that forced Hispanos to articulate their sense of racial dis-identification as Mexican Americans so as not to be mistaken for Indigenous people nor misunderstood by Anglo-Americans. In the above passage, for instance, Meketa's translation is uncharacteristically imprecise. Chacón's typescript reads, "este pueblo de Nuevo México," which Meketa translates as "this nation of New Mexico," but it should more accurately—in terms of translation and sentiment—read "the people of New Mexico," with "pueblo" in usage as "people," especially considering that Chacón reserves "naciones" in his phrase "naciones salvajes" to indicate "savage nations" and refers to New Mexicans further as "un pueblo de soldados," which Meketa has accurately but inelegantly translated as "populace of soldiers." He's using "pueblo" to refer to "a people" in the singular. Further, he writes "sin auxilio ninguno de la metrópoli," which Meketa translates, inexplicably, as "without assistance of any kind from capitals of the ruling countries." Chacón's statement is in the singular, however, most likely indicating that, in this context, he's referring to the lack of support from Mexico City. Finally, Chacón concludes his statement with a singular usage to characterize the New Mexican people as he did with "pueblo": "El Nuevo Mexicano," he writes. However, Meketa translates it as "The New Mexicans." The difference is significant, for by using the singular to describe plural persons, Chacón invokes one racial group with a shared collective history: "The New Mexican" refers to the imagined community that Chacón hails to at the start of the passage as his "race," "el Nuevo Mexicano."[48]

In much the same way that Otero made a dubious claim for Hispano racial purity, Chacón articulates a regionally specific racial identity that may be framed by the statehood debate but was forged out of the Civil War conflicts. "Symbolically," Phillip B. Gonzales explains, "it was off the statehood issue that Nuevomexicanos began to elaborate what would become a compelling public identity. The terms of this identity stressed the fact that the Spanish speakers of New Mexico were native to New Mexico, their roots going back two centuries before the United States conquered the Southwest. . . . A principal utility of claiming *nativo* roots was to emphasize birth rights precisely as New Mexico was rapidly moving toward becoming a state, and . . . as Hispanos faced attempts to exclude them from the rights and privileges of statehood."[49] Chacón's notion of Nuevomexicano identity, then, emerges from the lingering social tensions the Civil War ignited across the territorial Southwest. The first, as Gonzales notes, is the quest for statehood that dominated post–Civil War discourse for Hispanos, but the second is the Civil War itself, which increasingly pitted Anglos against Mexican Americans within the Union ranks and afterwards, when the cultural memory of the war colored Latino service. No doubt, Chacón is writing against the lopsided accounts of Civil War history, correcting it in a subtle war of words that aims to restore his name and, literally, the names of other, loyal Latino volunteers, which explains why he goes to great lengths to list his entire Company K, "since in everything they showed valor." Equally important, his roster, from captain down to private, "[omits] those who deserted, who were few, as a remembrance and a recollection for their posterity."[50] His is a subtle sentence construction in Spanish, and its translation, "remembrance and a recollection for their posterity," refers both to the soldiers he names and the deserters he omits. He preserves both for posterity as much by their presence on the list as by their absence from it. He names only one absconder on his muster role: "Lieutenant Damours deserted the army."[51] The aforementioned Damours, who took to insulting Mexicans in the ranks, is in turn insulted by being the only deserter named following a list of almost ninety loyal Spanish-surnamed volunteers in Company K, including Pedro Leyba, the peon Chacón held in indentured servitude. Such a gesture maintains Padilla's point that Chacón's "Memorias" should be read for his "tight-lipped" rhetorical subtlety that doesn't require Meketa's voice and supplementary material to speak for him.[52] Chacón is capable of waging his own war of words.

His narrative makes clear that he articulates a Nuevomexicano identity not so much because of the statehood question during which he's writing but because his armed service for the Union didn't ensure any rights and privileges for him or his fellow Nuevomexicano compatriots in the Anglo-American social system put into play with the Civil War's outbreak. His might be the condition of all drafted and enlisted combatants who feel disillusioned by the end of their tour. However, Chacón's service to the same colonial power that disenfranchised him, his family, and Hispanos after the US-Mexico War leaves him conflicted between being Mexican and becoming American. "Chacón's is the common predicament of the colonial subject," Padilla concludes, "whose loyalties are split by conquest."[53] He no doubt recalls the dispossession the American invasion brought to the region in 1846, but he also remembers the disenfranchisement he and his fellow New Mexico Volunteers faced and felt in the service of the same army that dispossessed Hispanos in the first place. In his fight for the Union, he realizes that, like the New Mexico Territory, he won't be equally incorporated into the Union. Even with rank, the regulars treat him as a second-class captain, while the brass keep him in that status by deferring his promotion up the ranks. He's obviously proud of his service but not so proud of the way the nation he served treated him.[54]

However, as with the territory itself, Chacón embodies layers of colonialisms that divide him, and his service as a so-called Indian fighter before, during, and after the war position him across competing colonial practices that reaffirm the confluence between the custom of Indigenous servitude in New Mexico and the brewing debate over slavery, which Chacón never mentions. Along with Captain Kit Carson, Chacón engages in warfare against the Apache people that results in, among other things, one soldier scalping and castrating an Apache. "We also took several women and children prisoners," Chacón continues. "At Ponil, after having killed several Indians, we captured fifty squaws and their little ones. From that point the main force under Colonel St. Vrain went to Fort Union with the captives."[55] Characterizing the long-held *cautivo* practice, Brooks writes, "In the Southwest Borderlands, two powerful social impulses, inclusion and exclusion, met on the historical terrain of colonialism and resolved themselves in forms of slavery that were at once particular and mutual. Diverse traditions of capture, servitude, and kinship met and meshed to accommodate both the community-forming impulse of assimilation and the community-preserving impulse of alienation."[56] Borderland slavery, Brooks elaborates, emerged through twin practices of intertribal capture before colonial contact and Spanish captivity culture in the New World that stemmed back to Muslim-Christian conflict in the Old World. "Both branches of borderland slavery could interact because they grew from shared patriarchal structures of power and patrimony that contrast sharply with the racial divisiveness and labor exploitation around which the more familiar forms of Euroamerican enslavement of Africans function."[57]

Recall that Otero went to great lengths to distinguish between servitude and slavery, while Greeley saw very little difference between the two. But Chacón does not seem fazed by the debate. Given the region's politics and Chacón's characteristic rhetorical reticence, it's not surprising that he makes no mention of the enslavement of Black people—it wasn't necessarily fueling the battle over the New Mexico Territory in the first place. More telling is the way Chacón benefits from the region's labor practices and engages in campaigns that result in capturing Native people, who were held as *cautivos*, incorporated into Hispano homes, hired out for labor, and sometimes sold as forms of labor power. On one scouting expedition, Chacón recalls "four little girl Indians and one boy, about four, eight, and twelve years old, crowded together holding [his] horse. . . . One of the little Indian girls," Chacón continues, "I took home with me and she later died in Peñasco. Her name was Maria. This Indian girl I took care to have instructed in the Catholic faith in order to be baptized."[58] Later, he estimates that sixty women and children were taken captive, along with their sheep and horses. His warfare in and out of Union uniform against Indigenous groups nets captives who ended up as servants under Spanish colonial and Mexican neocolonial labor practices that were factually illegal but culturally tolerated in the region. Moreover, on his Indian campaigns and Civil War service, Chacón enjoys the labor of Pedro Leyba, a peon who accompanies the Nuevomexicano on his trading ventures and Native campaigns. Leyba even enlists in Chacón's company. At least according to New Mexico custom and its Law Relative to Contracts Between Masters and Servants, Chacón is Pedro Leyba's "master" throughout the time they both fought for the Union.

This might explain why Chacón makes no mention of slavery as a *casus belli*: his investment in the Union is to protect the territory from Texans and to win the war against the region's Indigenous nations in an effort to preserve the cultural practices, including indentured servitude, that Hispanos enjoyed before the Civil War. In this instance, Chacón's and Leyba's service contradicts Thompson's thesis that New Mexicans fought "to escape the ruthless peonage system."[59] Leyba likely served by Chacón's command, and Chacón fought in part to preserve the peonage system. His rationale for fighting lines up more with Pino and Gallegos's manifesto, which called Hispanos to arms against Texas Confederates so that they can get back to the business of waging war against Indigenous peoples.[60] Chacón's resignation letter signals such a subtle rhetorical position when he characterizes his Union service as one "contra el enemigo común salvage" (against a common savage enemy), which, for the Hispano and his Union leadership, could refer to Texas Confederates and the greater Southwest's Native nations.

Chacón's narrative can thus be understood as civil war on multiple fronts. It's embattled linguistically and rhetorically with Meketa's publication of his "memorias," and it tells the story of his internal struggle and disillusionment with the embattled process of becoming Mexican American under Union service. It's also a Civil War narrative proper that provides a history of the conflict in the region, recounts skirmishes and military movements, and serves as a record of Hispano service. The narrative also spends as much time narrating the other civil war in the region—the war against Indigenous sovereignty. Before the outbreak of the Civil War, Chacón enlists as a first sergeant in the campaign of 1855, during which he recounts participating in the killing raids of Apache and Ute, the latter of which "did not make much resistance," and though they were in retreat, Chacón goes in active pursuit to kill or capture them.[61] He orders men under his command to fire on retreating Mescalero Apache during a post–Civil War expedition that left a grisly scene: "I ordered the men to shoot at them and they fled, running, and on the slope where they had run down to the bottom of the canyon could be seen the blood mixed with the dirt." During this skirmish, Chacón also allows the company doctor to keep a grim trophy of a particular corpse: "The dead Indian was of gigantic stature, six and a half feet tall. The doctor asked permission to dissect him and save the skeleton, and permission was granted. He put some balsam on it, took out the entrails, and put it in a cart wrapped in a blanket."[62]

Such details—and there are many of them in his narrative—curtail any celebratory sentiment commemorating Chacón's service in the Union ranks before, during, or after the Civil War. He was an Indian killer working in the service of colonial cultural practices of warfare waged in the name of preserving Hispano racial power over Indigenous groups in the region; that his service in the US army involved sustained and strategic assaults on Native groups only speaks to the degree to which the Hispano and Anglo-American colonial projects overlapped when it came to Indigenous people. They waged concerted civil wars against Native America. Many of these encounters, including a few led by Chacón, left a wake of Indigenous people killed, captured, terrorized, or chased across the region. The warfare was mutual, but Hispanos had the military backing of the Union, so much so that their encounters were recorded as Union operations in the official record. In fact, Hispanos gained more unequivocal regard for their service as so-called Indian killers than they did for their service against Confederates. In his report on Southwestern military operations, Assistant Adjutant General Ben C. Cutler writes,

> The alacrity with which citizens of New Mexico have taken the field to pursue and encounter the Indians is worth all praise. Many of them have been conspicuous for their courage; and all have shown a settled

> determination to assist the military in their efforts to rid the country of the fierce and brutal robbers and murderers who for nearly two centuries have brought poverty to its inhabitants and mourning and desolation to nearly every hearth throughout the Territory.[63]

Yet Chacón finds that his Civil War service also situates him as impressed racialized labor in much the same way the *cautivo* culture positioned Pedro Leyba under Chacón's charge. He is compelled to enlist for minimal pay, for instance; he's situated in a marginal status between the Union brass, army regulars, and his contingent of volunteers; he's charged with perilous campaigns against Indigenous groups without much Union support in terms of munitions, supplies, or manpower; and his letters for promotion or resignation have little effect on the status of his commission. He makes this point all the more compelling when, after completing his service time and receiving an honorable discharge, he writes to Judge R. C. McCormick, one of the civilians on the Arizona Expedition, "Forgive me for not having thanked you before, but my time has not been my own."[64] As it turns out, his service didn't elevate him to whiteness and its attendant legal and social status within the Union. Instead, the Civil War put Chacón at war with his Anglo counterparts because of his dark skin and against the Spanish-Mexican regional practices that, until the Rebellion, upheld Chacón's elite status despite his complexion. It put him at war between two colonialisms—one that bolstered his cultural privilege and another that assaulted the racial power that accompanied his cultural privilege. He fought for the latter in a war to lose the former. "On writing these memoirs," Chacón closes, "I have nothing, but, nevertheless, in what seems like a paradox, I lack nothing. The God, who has watched over me since I was a child on *foreign soil* and who later allowed me to come out of combat unharmed, watches over me."[65] In the Spanish typescript, Chacón uses the phrase "suelo extraño," which Meketa translates as "foreign soil," but it should read as "strange land" not only to echo Chacón's biblical reference (to be a stranger in a strange land) but also to register a specific Nuevomexicano deterritorialized nostalgia. For the aged Chacón, "suelo extraño" is more allegorical than literal. Writing from Colorado on the eve of New Mexico statehood, the displaced and dispossessed

Chacón turns to self-writing to assert his only possession to emerge out of the Civil War: his "clean and honorable name," already marred by his legacy of violence against Indigenous America.[66]

From *Extraño* to *Desconocido*: Tafolla's Transnational Transformations

As with *Legacy of Honor*, the history of James Santiago Tafolla's manuscript proves to be a textual and linguistic battleground waged by the Tafolla family. Originally penned by Tafolla in Spanish in 1908, the manuscript, which he wanted to title "Beyond the End of the Trail" or "A Spark Ignited in Old Santa Fe," remained in a box until Tafolla's grandson, Fidel, transcribed the original Spanish document for family members and produced an English-language translation of it in 1970 with the hope of publishing it as "the true life story of a self-made man."[67] Fidel titled the manuscript "Nearing the End of the Trail: The Autobiography of Rev. James Tafolla, Sr. A Texas Pioneer, 1837–1911." His preface description imagines his grandfather's tale as quintessentially American, which might explain why he suggested naming it "The Autobiography of James Santiago Tafolla," in homage to Benjamin Franklin. Fidel's English translation, however, did not get published. Instead, it ended up in the Nettie Lee Benson Archive at the University of Texas–Austin, while the original 1908 Spanish text remained in a box until Tafolla's great-granddaughters, Carmen Tafolla and her cousin Laura Tafolla (Fidel's daughter), rediscovered the original and republished it in 2010 as a bilingual edition titled *A Life Crossing Borders: Memoir of a Mexican-American Confederate/Las memorias de un mexicoamericano en la Confederación.*

The genealogy of Tafolla's narrative spans the original 1908 Spanish manuscript, Fidel's 1970 English translation of it, and then a new translation of the 1908 text in 2010, with careful attention to the original and its first translation, along with a transcription of Tafolla's original Spanish text, with minor corrections. Carmen Tafolla, perhaps unwittingly, explains this textual history in language reminiscent of civil war: "The editing of the English translation," she writes, "followed two loyalties: one, that it be loyal to Santiago's original document . . . and two, that where discrepancies with the original text do not arise, that it be kept as close to Fidel's original translation as possible."[68] In effect, Tafolla's narrative set off a linguistic house divided between "two [family] loyalties": two versions of Tafolla's text (his original, handwritten copy and the transcripted Spanish-language version the coeditors produce) and two translated versions (Fidel's translation of the original and the reproduction of that translation, with silent corrections, that the coeditors present). As a result, the coeditors published a bilingual edition with an updated English translation and a different title, thus creating an internally fissured fifth text that further compounds the narrative's fractures. Even without such a vexed textual history, the author's name alone tellingly displays the autobiography's divided subject: James is an English version of Santiago. Literally, his name is redundant, but it's also an indication of how language transition from Spanish to English splits Tafolla and his narrative, a fissure that the family coeditors attempt to suture by attributing their 2010 bilingual edition to Santiago Tafolla, sans the English-language version of his name, though the problem of nomenclature plays a crucial role in his autobiographical identity formation.

The narrative is also embattled at the level of genre. It is an autobiography that presents Tafolla's life as a conversion narrative on multiple levels: his religious conversion from Catholicism to Methodism structures his autobiography, while he also recounts his movement from Spanish to English languages and, by correlation, from Mexican to Mexican American. He tells a coming-of-age story, a picaresque narrative, an adventure tale, a travel account, a military memoir, and a family history. He even opens with a framework reminiscent of nineteenth-century slave narratives as he recounts his escape from family servitude in his brother's house. Seven years after their father has died and soon after his mother's 1844 death, Tafolla goes to live with Lorenzo, who "always had three or four peones who worked the fields, and he made me work right along with them," Tafolla recalls.[69] To make matters worse, the peones treat Tafolla poorly: "If they got angry with me, they would kick me and knock me down," and while the peones were able to return home after collecting wood, Tafolla had to sell the wood before he could return to Lorenzo's house, only to run more errands for his brother. As he recalls, "my older brother was so cruel that he would tie me up, take off my shirt, and whip my back with a horsewhip until the blood flowed. The welts this caused would remain for a long time and were so painful that I could not lie on my back."[70]

This scene of peonage *cum* slavery structures many of the narrative's genre lines. It serves as a bleak family history, for instance, as he records for posterity the experience of being raised by Lorenzo, whom Tafolla presents as a hypocritical Catholic gambler who "would always commend himself to the Virgin of Guadalupe in order to win. Sometimes when he lost, he would get drunk with his own sadness. On such occasions, he would come home in the middle of the night, beating on doors, shouting and cursing. And as soon as we heard him, we began trembling with fear. For on these nights, he didn't remember his religion, and he didn't remember the Virgin of Guadalupe."[71] Also, because he's recounting here his life between the years of seven through eleven, the moment marks the beginning of his coming-of-age story, especially in the sense that he grows from a waif watching over the burros for the peones to a skilled cavalryman with a special affinity for horses by the narrative's end. Finally, the scene launches an ironic reversal as he escapes domestic bondage as a child and later will escape the CSA army for similar reasons. Tafolla's experiences in Lorenzo's house, in other words, set the stage for his first rebellion, so not surprisingly, by the time he's eleven, he decides to run away, seceding, so to speak, from his family, Catholicism, and the Old World Mexican cultural practices that keep him *cautivo* in Santa Fe.

His foray away from home brings him to the front lines of a cultural and linguistic battle of national, racial, and gendered identity formation. Along with his cousin, the young Santiago escapes to Las Vegas, New Mexico, in September 1848, a year after Mexico City fell to the invading US army and eight months after the Treaty of Guadalupe Hidalgo. On the road, the runaways encounter a wagon returning to Independence, Missouri, after dropping off munitions and supplies to the occupying US army. "Muchacho," Mr. Matthews, one of the wagon passengers, says to the boys, "quiero vamos Estados Unidos?" Tafolla takes this as an invitation and responds, "Si, yo quiero," while his cousin decides to stay behind.[72] It's not clear whether Matthews is inviting Tafolla to go with him to the United States, or if Matthews is stating that he and the two other wagon passengers want to go to the United States. A direct translation of his "poor Spanish," as Tafolla calls it, is "Boy, I want we go to the United States?" This might mean, "I want us to go to the United States" or "Do you want to go with us to the United States?" Either way, Tafolla hears in Matthews's poor Spanish a clear invitation to leave New Mexico, and he jumps at the opportunity to light out east, toward the aptly named Independence in what must be recognized as a Mexican reversal of the Anglo adage for young men to go west, attributed to Horace Greeley but perhaps made most famous by Huck Finn's decision to "light out for the Territories" at the end of Twain's 1885 novel.

Tafolla's move puts him on the linguistic battleground between Spanish and English, and he quickly learns that the Anglophone world also situates him on the bulwarks of Anglo America's racial codes. In St. Louis, Missouri, for instance, after marveling at the steamships along the banks of the Mississippi, Tafolla cannot find his way back to his hotel, so he stops at a barbershop, "where," he writes, "I saw a negro man who was a quadroon [*cuaterón* in the Spanish original]. He looked like a Mexican, so I spoke to him in Spanish, but he didn't understand me. However, he took me . . . to a house where there was a Mexican woman. . . . And . . . she advised me not to associate with Negroes."[73] And after living and working in Washington, DC, for about a year, Tafolla follows Matthews to Talbatton, Georgia, where among other things, he undergoes a religious conversion, learns to read the New Testament in English (a testimony to just how far he's moved away from his Spanish Catholicism), and finds himself ambiguously situated within Anglo America. "When the townspeople heard there was a Mexican boy in town," Tafolla remembers, "they came to see me out of curiosity and everyone was talking about 'the Mexican boy.'" Folks begin to talk about "Mexican Jim," as he's dubbed by the Talbatton residents: "He is nearly White," one resident explains, "while others would say, 'He's as white as anybody.'" As Tafolla explains it,

> Since there was still slavery at that time, the Whites would not associate at all with the Blacks and considered it a degradation to even sympathize with Negros. I remember that Mrs. Matthews' daughter asked her mother one day, "Mama, is Mexican Jim sure enough White?" and her mother answered, "Daughter, James' blood is as free from Negro blood as yours or mine."[74]

Mrs. Matthews's un-assuring response aside, the discussion of Tafolla's whiteness elaborates the precarious "off-whiteness," to recall Gómez, that he occupies. The minor episode also demonstrates how different identity categories scaffold around the appearance of a racial identity. As Tafolla recounts it, he's initially referred to as the "Mexican boy." He's roughly fourteen or fifteen years old at the time, so the appellation "boy" might be accurate but nonetheless resonates with the racist practice of referring to Black men, free or enslaved, as "boys," despite their age. "Mexican boy" signals an attempt to situate Tafolla within the South's preexisting racial paradigm around the masculinity of men of color. The process is further advanced and compounded when he is referred to as "Mexican Jim," insofar as he gains a name, Jim, which is at once a diminutive of the English version of his Spanish name, but as Twain's aforementioned novel memorialized, it too resonates with the diminutives that circulate with slave naming. In both cases, "Mexican" buttresses his name as if to wedge one racialized identity into another set of racial codes. Finally, Tafolla gains a name, James, affirming by association his whiteness, manhood, and, in the erasure of "Mexican," an assumption of his acceptance as American after all. The brief but complex naming process charts how Tafolla's gendered and national coming of age from boy to man, from "the Mexican boy" to James, hinges on his racial passing as "white" within the US South's racial logics under slavery, a transformation that, among other things, replaces his Spanish forename, Santiago, with its Anglicized equivalent, James. As Neil Foley puts it, "Southern necessity required that Tafolla become a white person"; soon thereafter, he's hired as a plantation overseer, making him "perhaps history's only Mexican overseer of a slave plantation in the antebellum south."[75]

One can argue that at this stage Tafolla has passed or "assimilated" into Anglo-American whiteness, but his Americanization is tenuous at best. On the one hand, it is framed in opposition to African America, but on the other, Tafolla is never fully at home in Washington, DC, and the South, especially after meeting José Sena, a twenty-year-old Santa Fean who knew Tafolla's family and was in Washington attending college. He traveled with Don Juan Manuel Gallegos, the priest-turned-politician who coauthored with Facundo Pino the "Address of the Legislative Assembly" call-to-arms manifesto and held a seat in Congress until Miguel Otero displaced him in a contested election.[76] Gallegos and Sena put the idea in Tafolla's head to return home, but since he did not have enough money to make the trip, and knew he "would have to repay [a loan from them] by working for them," he decided instead to answer a recruitment ad in the *Baltimore Sun* to serve as a soldier rather than return to the same status in the New Mexico that he escaped—domestic servitude. After meeting with then Secretary of War Jefferson Davis and gaining permission from Matthews, as guardian, the seventeen-year-old Tafolla enlisted as a bugler in the US army in April 1855, so that he could "return to the place of my birth," as he puts it.[77]

Tafolla's service in the US army is troubled from the start, as he soon discovers that whatever prestige he held as "white" in the South did not extend any kind of power or equality in the military ranks, especially once Tafolla returned to the Southwest as chief bugler in the Second Calvary Regiment, stationed in Texas and commanded by Colonel A. S. Johnston and Lieutenant Colonel Robert E. Lee. At Camp Verde, northwest of San Antonio between Kerrville and Bandera, Tafolla is tasked with running the long and dangerous mail route between Fredericksburg and San Antonio, hardly the duties of a bugler. "Those were dangerous times, for the Indians would come and go on their raids, stealing horses and killing everyone they encountered. I do not know why he chose me for the job."[78] But after making the perilous run often, "during the heat of summer" and at night, Tafolla begins to understand why Captain Palmer selected him for the job: "I believe he did it because I was *mexicano*."[79] Tafolla comes to this conclusion after being sent on frivolous errands that put him at grave risk with rugged terrain, harsh weather, sparse provisions, warring Natives, and hostile Anglo servicemen. "This is how he always used me on similar occasions," Tafolla concludes, citing Matthew 8:9 for further emphasis.[80] As Foley explains it, "Once back in Texas 'Mexican Jim' thus reverted to being the Mexican Santiago Tafolla, for in Texas, unlike antebellum Georgia, Mexicans were still 'Mexicans.'"[81] However, the difference from Foley's point in this case is that Tafolla identifies himself as *mexicano*, a self-identified category that he uses to describe his second-class social status. He's not referred to as "Mexican" or "Mexican Jim," as he was in the South; rather, he refers to himself as *mexicano* in response to the way he's treated in south Texas. His cultural education in Anglo America, in free and slaveholding regions, fissures him from Mexican to American, but his understanding of the United States' process of social racialization pressures the critical emergence of his self-identification as *mexicano* rather than Mexican or

American. As with Chacón, the crucible of the Civil War gives rise to Tafolla's sense of his racial identity in Anglo America.

It's worth noting that Tafolla's experiences with racism in the US Army are not unique. Recall that Chacón too felt ill-used during his Union service when he was sent on harsh duty without adequate provisions, munitions, horses, or men. In a November 26, 1861, letter, Lieutenant Colonel J. Francisco Chaves, also of the New Mexico Volunteers, linked the mistreatment and poor housing of Hispano soldiers and laborers to racial inequality, to which the commanding officer at Fort Union, New Mexico, Lieutenant Colonel William Chapman, offered his own racist reply:

> You say in your letter "That you have not spoken to your brother officers upon the subject of your Complaints," but that you venture to say they feel as you do, "*that they are slighted in nearly every respect.*" I have yet to learn that you and your officers *have been slighted in any respect whatever* by any officer of the US Army stationed at this post. . . . You also speak of insulting language having been used by the regular soldiers towards the Volunteer officers. Your letter gives me the first information upon that subject also, and I have only to say that the officers to whom the language was addressed, *grossly* neglected their duty in not arresting and confining the officers, and reporting the fact to me, that the guilty regulars might have been brought to trial and punishment. . . . I venture to say that the volunteer soldiers of your command have never been so well fed, clothed and quartered as at present, and never will be again after they leave the Service for the U. States.[82]

Itself a mini civil war of words, Chapman's response to Chaves reveals that Anglo officers and soldiers viewed their Mexican American compatriots with skepticism, disdain, and animosity based on racial, religious, or linguistic differences, and Mexican Americans felt the sting of personal and institutional racism too much to warrant perilous service. Many deserted, resigned, or went missing in action rather than continue to put their life and livelihood on the line for men, a cause, or a nation that treated them so poorly. "There seems little doubt that prejudice against natives in both the Union and Confederate armies was common and in some instances disgraceful," Jerry D. Thompson explains.

"Mexican-Americans often went without food and clothing for months, even to a greater degree than soldiers of other nationalities. The weapons supplied . . . were old and outdated."[83]

In Tafolla's case, though, he experiences this disillusionment before the Civil War, when he's still in the service of the US army, which might be the unstated reason why, a year after his honorable discharge in April 1860 from the army, he throws in with the Confederacy. It is never explicit in the narrative why Tafolla fights for the CSA. Although he benefited from the institution of slavery during his younger days as "Mexican Jim" in the South, Tafolla never says that he supports states' rights or slavery as reasons to go to war. Rather, the year before the Rebellion, he marries, claims a 160-acre homestead plot for Texas citizens, and loses money and property on a land investment deal that goes bust when Texas secedes. At the war's outbreak, he initially takes a job at Camp Verde, caring for the few remaining camels that comprised the experimental US Camel Corps, and then in the fall of 1862, he enlists with Duff's Partisan Rangers, a San Antonio volunteer unit that later comprised part of the CSA's Thirty-Third Texas Cavalry. He possibly joined to protect his own interests, family, and property—all of which would be in jeopardy of reprisal and confiscation if he didn't declare with the Confederacy. Tafolla also suited up a few months after the Confederacy's April 1862 Conscription Law, which went into effect in Texas shortly after its passage and was extended to include all white men up to the age of forty-five around the time Tafolla enlists, suggesting that either he was conscripted or he joined before he was drafted into service.[84] The fact that he was already working at Camp Verde as a laborer suggests that he also could have enlisted for the pay, especially considering the loss he took on a land deal, and it's just as likely that he served the CSA army out of a sense of martial duty—he was a five-year veteran in the US army, after all. Either way, his experience in the Confederacy completes Tafolla's embattled Mexicanization, for once he enters the War of Rebellion, he and other soldiers of "Mexican extraction," as he calls them, struggle against racist rebels who would much rather see Mexicans lynched than linked to the Confederate cause. A far cry from "Mexican Jim," Tafolla and his Mexican compatriots are threatened with violence, sent on the most dangerous missions, and accused of being Mexican spies for the Union. True to Thompson's characterization that the Rio Grande theater "had become a civil war within a civil war" for Tejano Confederates, Tafolla and three other *mexicanos* decide to secede from the secessionists.[85] They desert the Confederacy, vowing to wage war against it before opting instead to cross the river to Mexico.

In February 1865, Tafolla, Jose Casillas, Jose Garza, and Francisco Martínez desert the Confederate Army by escaping (back?) to Mexico, though Tafolla admits earlier in his narrative that "none of them had ever been on Mexican soil":[86]

> We got to the very edge of the water. . . . I took off all my clothes, and picked up a stick to use as a staff. It was February, and the water was very cold. The current was very swift and almost swept me away, but I fought it till I got to an island in the middle of the river. I crossed the island, and got to the river branch on the other side. But it occurred to me that my companions might not be safe, considering that a squad of soldiers might come by since they patrolled the river day and night. I went back and helped them cross to the island, and then I went to check the depth on the other side. It was just as deep and just as strong a current, but when I got to the other side . . . I went back and brought my companions. . . . As soon as the last man had crossed, I shouted "Qué viva México!"[87]

Tafolla has come full circle, of sorts. He traverses the Santa Fe Trail in reverse and comes of age in Washington, DC, and the US South; he joins the Confederacy and in the process transitions from Spanish to English languages, Catholic to Methodist, orphan to husband and father, waif to landholder, and, eventually, from sinner to preacher. But when Tafolla says that he had never "been on Mexican soil," some kind of historical amnesia and identity transformation has occurred between the time he jumps a wagon from Santa Fe to Washington, DC, in 1848, and the time he deserts the Confederacy for Mexico in 1865. He was *born* in Mexico, after all—in Santa Fe in 1837. A profound, deterritorialized transformation has forced Tafolla to forget that he was born a Mexican national, an estrangement most apparent when Tafolla and his *mexicano* confederates escape to Mexico and meet the mayor of old Monclova, who happens to be a relative of Tafolla's wife. They must surrender their guns, the mayor tells them, because "no *foreigners* were allowed to carry weapons."[88] In the original Spanish, Tafolla uses the word "desconocida," which the Tafolla editors translate as "foreigner," but *desconocida* here is more like "stranger": in a person, someone unknown or someone much changed (i.e., unrecognizable or not their usual self); something strange about someone who was once familiar. In this sense, Tafolla's narrative charts the embattled, internecine process of Mexican Americanization that has made him *desconocido* in Mexico, returned estranged, unfamiliar, *pocho* we might say—a Mexican American whose house of identity is divided between one nation and another at civil war.

In a telling moment earlier in his narrative, Tafolla meets a Mexican at a hotel in Independence, Missouri. The Mexican asks Tafolla how he likes the aptly named town, and the Santa Fe waif replies that he likes it considerably, to which the Mexican replies, "Don't become enchanted, young man, this is nothing compared to Mexico."[89] Not counting his runaway cousin, this is the first in a series of doppelgänger encounters that give credence to his statement that "during the journey, I witnessed many strange sights and experienced a number of adventures."[90] Not long after leaving Independence, for example, he meets the Mexican woman in St. Louis, who warns him not to associate with Blacks. As an errand boy in Washington, DC's National Hotel, he meets the plenipotentiary minister of Mexico, who, along with some Mexican students, treats Tafolla well, calling him "el Nuevo Mexico because I was from New Mexico," while the minister of Spain, Tafolla recalls, received him cordially on a visit but then asked "if I was visiting him to obtain something from him," as if to get rid of the New World waif.[91] José Sena, the fellow Santa Fean whom Tafolla meets while working in DC, puts the idea in Tafolla's head to return to New Mexico, and while serving the US Army, he recalls another Mexican encounter with a captive named Encarnación, who, like Tafolla, operates between linguistic and racial cultures.[92] On another occasion, Tafolla, who himself is beginning to feel imprisoned by his Confederate service, recounts how a Mexican prisoner gets out of his shackles and escapes for freedom.[93] Finally, fearing that a compatriot, Colonel Juan Mercado, had been hanged for desertion, Tafolla and his fellow *mexicanos* are wary of absconding at first, but once they cross the border, they discover that Mercado had in fact made it to Mexico, where "he went crazy, and in a state of depression, took his own life."[94] In time, Tafolla would marry Mercado's widow in a symbolic culmination of identity transformations that live up to the warning he received in Independence—he's been "enchanted" after all by his freedom, changed so much from his boyhood that he's *desconocido*, unrecognizable after his experiences.

The Civil War left the United States *desconocido* too, and the nation's social transformation extended to US Latinxs in what can only be described as literal and symbolic dispossession. The end of the war didn't bring statehood to New Mexico, and despite declaring for the Confederacy to protect their livelihoods, Tejanos found themselves politically and economically disenfranchised anyway in the postwar years. For Chacón, Tafolla, and their Mexican American compatriots on both sides of the line, the war brought profound changes to their social, political, and racial standing in the United States, leaving them fissured, second-class subjects of their former selves, like the so many diasporic doppelgängers Tafolla encountered on his strange adventure of becoming Mexican American, for in the end, whether they fought for the Union or the CSA, Mexican Americans like Chacón and Tafolla were brown in Anglo America's Civil War.

3

Confederate *Letrado*

José Agustín Quintero's Record of Rebellion

"Without a literature of our own, we can have neither dignity, self-respect or any security of rights," wrote José Agustín Quintero, the celebrated Cuban poet, lawyer, newspaperman, and member of the Latinx literati. His understanding of literature as personally and politically emancipatory rings with the revolutionary sentiment that propelled him into Cuba's mid-nineteenth-century independence movement and placed him alongside a constellation of Cuban poets in the groundbreaking 1858 collection *El laúd del desterrado*. He was by then a known man of letters, having published juvenilia on the island, carried on a bilingual correspondence with Henry Wadsworth Longfellow during the latter half of the 1850s, and offered poetic proclamations, like his ode to Cuban heroes, at the gathering commemorating the third anniversary of Narciso López's death. The *Times-Picayune* reported that, following fellow filibuster Gaspar Betancourt's discourse on the "Philosophy of the Cuban Revolution" at the memorial, "Mr. J. A. Quintero then read an ode in Spanish entitled 'The Heroes,' which was very warmly received by the Cuban portion of the audience, who evinced their approval of the young poet by the most rapturous approbation." His call for literary independence also echoed similar mid-nineteenth-century appeals for an American literature separate from British cultural production. Margaret Fuller put the problem best in characterizing "all attempts to construct a national literature" as "abortions like the monster of Frankenstein, things with forms, and the instincts of forms, but soulless, and therefore revolting" in their mimicry of British and European works. Quintero's short phrase advances his similar belief that literature, especially poetry, possessed the expressive power of national liberation, and while his position is understandable in relation to Cuba's independence movement, his argument for a "literature of our own" here does not refer to the island's literature. He was calling for a literature of the slaveholding US South.[1]

José Agustín Quintero y Woodville was born in Havana to a Cuban-born father who owned a tobacco plantation and a Cuban-born mother whose British father built the Woodville family wealth by trafficking and trading enslaved peoples across Africa, Haiti, and Cuba.[2] A member of the Club de La Habana, a *junta* that advocated US annexation as the avenue to secure Cuba's independence from Spain without abolishing slavery, Quintero earned a four-year prison sentence for his contributions to a Cuban revolutionary newspaper. He was later pardoned, and by the early 1850s, he moved to the United States, where he founded, contributed to, or edited Spanish- and English-language newspapers in New Orleans, Texas, and New York. The inclusion of three of his poems in the 1858 *El laúd* put him at the vanguard of Cuban American literary history. His correspondence with Longfellow, alongside his loose connection to Harvard, where the young poet visited in 1841 but never attended, also placed him on the cusp of New England's antebellum literary scene. He "had been from the outset," Kirsten Silva Gruesz says, "perhaps the most deeply engaged of his generation of Caribbean letrados in New England sensibilities." He translated Longfellow's poems for publication, and as Silva Gruesz shows, their correspondence gave Quintero occasion to express his poetics for the island's liberation through "displays of male sentimentalism" that channeled individual suffering into the fight for political freedom.[3] He saw Southern secession as a similar struggle, and "despite the protests and warnings of his Northern friends," the *Picayune* reported, "he cast in his lot with the Southern people" as a Confederate agent assigned to the contested Texas-Mexico border zone.[4] "There probably could have been found no one in the entire Southern nation to rival Quintero's education, language skills, literary attainments and political connections as justification for a delicate Mexican assignment," Darryl E. Brock concludes, echoing the regard the Cuban enjoys for his borderlands service and the efficacy with which he managed to mobilize *caudillos* and cotton in the Confederacy's favor. After the war, he returned to New Orleans, where he resumed his work with the press, served as a notary public, and held the post of US Costa Rican consul. He also killed a man in a bar brawl, published an edition of a code book on dueling, and kept his distance from Cuba's 1868–1878 bid for independence. On his 1885 death, the *Picayune* remembered "Joseph A. Quintero" as a man who "was devotedly attached to the South."[5]

Pro-slavery sentiments fire the personal, political, and literary calls for independence that characterize Quintero as a Cuban liberation poet and a Confederate agent. He envisioned such freedoms to be the natural rights of the slaveholding class. His was a position held by many mid-nineteenth-century Cuban revolutionaries. "The specter of slave rebellion in Cuba dampened planters' enthusiasm for an independent nation, especially one without adequate resources to suppress the dreaded slave uprisings," Louis A Pérez Jr. explains.[6] Cuban revolutionary exiles in the United States faced the added challenge of seeking support for the island's independence from a nation increasingly divided over its own reliance on enslaved peoples and equally suspect of Cuban racial identities. The possibility of a consolidated circum-Gulf Southern slave society hinged on the translatability of Cuban whiteness, and here, language played a critical role. Quintero's mastery of English and German alongside Spanish buttressed his racial whiteness with the cultural capital that allowed him to enter Anglo social, linguistic, literary, and rhetorical spaces of power in the United States in ways that his monolingual counterparts, such as Narciso López, never quite enjoyed. English proved to be the *lingua franca* of slavery in the US South, granting Quintero, like his fellow Cuban Confederate Ambrosio José Gonzales, the cultural literacy to read and write his way into the US South's bulwark of slaveholding white power and privilege as a diplomat for the self-proclaimed Confederate States of America.

During the war years, the Cuban *letrado* turned away from poetry and print culture, making his unpublished diplomatic dispatches the main form of writing he produced between 1861 and 1864. They are instrumental for an understanding of his full-throated commitment as a Latinx Confederate. His letters to CSA leadership show the foundational role he played in imagining the US South and Mexico's northern *frontera* as an independent, confederated slavocracy of the kind he once envisioned for Cuba. It's in this sense that his communiqués are part of a Latinx *letrado* "continuum," to recall Carmen E. Lamas's word to characterize the connectedness of Latino literary history over time and space.[7] Traditionally, the *letrado* produced legal, colonial, and diplomatic texts that, while not always literary in nature, survived historical change because of their imprimatur of empire. "The *letrados* were the keepers of writing in the colonial period," Roberto González Echevarría explains, "not only in their official capacity as rhetoricians and scribes, but also as men of letters—lettered men, men of the letter, who lived by and of the letter."[8] As such, the *letrado* holds a foundational position in studies of early Latinx print cultures, with Raúl Coronado making the case that the history of Latino textuality can be traced back to the *letrado*. Silva Gruesz too called for a similar understanding of men of letters—those Latino ambassadors of culture whose poems, newspapers, and diplomatic dispatches form the bedrock of Latino literary history.[9] Moreover, as Rodrigo Lazo reminds us, early Latino literature can be traced to published and unpublished letters, *cartas*, that staged hemispheric moves for independence through personal and intimate rhetorical forms of epistolary writings. For the early trans-American Latino elite, as Lazo calls them, "letters (cartas) provided . . . writers a way to comprehend the transmission of ideas and conceptions of changing social structures." Between *cartas*, letters, and *letras*, Lazo adds, "is a lettered terrain of analysis as well as a range of epistolary connections" that map the contours of the early Latino literature that emerged in connection to a specific place—Filadelfia, in Lazo's case.[10]

As a Confederate *letrado*, Quintero penned dispatches; produced reports; transcribed and translated documents; made duplicates of his own letters, transcriptions, and translations; attached proclamations, newspapers, and official Mexican bulletins; and conveyed rumors and hearsay as credible news from the front. Indispensable to historians of the borderlands, his unpublished Confederate letters might at first seem less obvious as Latinx literary artifacts, but as so much "lettered terrain," to recall Lazo, they are littered with ambivalence, discursive dissonance, and epistolary moments when reported facts take a figurative nature.[11] They dissemble when they describe; they do rhetorical battle with Confederate leadership; and sometimes they betray martial motivation for literary inspiration. Much like the cipher he created to communicate to the CSA secretary of state, Quintero's diplomatic writings unfold through layers of meaning, interrelated communication circuits, rhetorical displacements, and a context of transnational conflicts raging in a region best characterized by one of the cipher's control words: "war." As his key terms suggest, Quintero occupied the interstitial sociolinguistic space in the borderlands between English and Spanish; enslavement and indentured servitude; and Southern nationalism and white Latinidad. Deciphering his letters and the archive that holds them thus requires attention to their "literary rhetoric" and the way the Cuban poet sublimated his calls for literary liberation into his Confederate dispatches.[12] They are on the same Latinx continuum as his poetry, journalism, translations, and literary essays, and their internal contradictions, figurative flights of fancy, and embattled discursive pieces make the Confederate *letrado*'s archive a Latinx Civil War literature of our own.

The Slavery of the Printing Press

Quintero's early belief in a poetics of liberation, as he understood it, helps to explain the connection the revolutionary Cuban felt for the Confederate cause. What I am characterizing as his "poetics of liberation" should not elide Quintero's unwavering commitment to the enslavement of Black people. He believed that literary production, especially poetry, could bring about national independence. However, he never once in his writings extended this belief to the emancipation of the enslaved in Cuba and the United States.[13] A genealogy of his poetics might explain why. While his inclusion in the 1858 *El laúd* cemented Quintero's place in Cuban American literary history, the publication of Mirabeau B. Lamar's *Verse Memorials* flamed his Southern sympathies. A year prior to *El laúd*'s publication, Quintero's friend, benefactor, and the former president of the short-lived Texas Republic released a collection of poems he had written over the previous two decades. Both books were published in New York, but contra to *El laúd*, *Verse Memorials* does not sing of national independence, anti-coloniality, the fettered republic, or thinly veiled love allegories for freedom, homeland, or political sovereignty. Instead, Lamar writes of love, death, joy, beauty, sadness, and more love. He dedicates poems to his first wife and their daughter, Rebecca Ann, both deceased; to his sisters; to the poet Ann S. Stephens and the writer Fannie Fern; and to legions of named and unnamed women to whom he sends his sweet verses, including one to Carmelita of Monterey, another to Isabel of Matamoros, two long cantos for Sally Riley, and a poem for his second wife at the time, Henrietta Moffit. One fire-eating poem

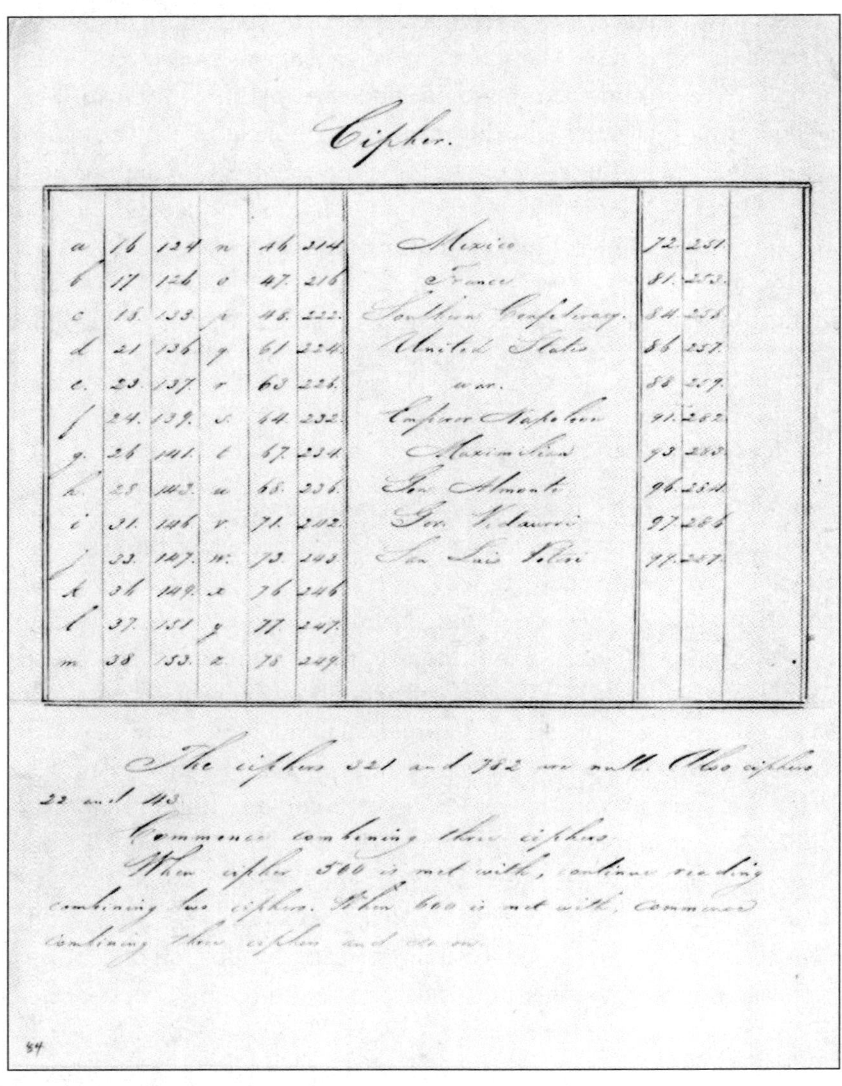

Cipher.

a	16	124	n	46	214	Mexico	72	251.
b	17	126	o	47.	216	France	81.	253.
c	18.	133.	p	48.	222.	Southern Confederacy.	84	255
d	21	136	q	61	224.	United States	86	257.
e.	23.	137.	r	63	226.	war.	88	259.
f	24.	139.	s.	64.	232.	Emperor Napoleon	91.	262.
g.	26	141.	t	67.	234.	Maximilian	93	263.
h.	28	143.	u	68.	236.	Gen Almonte	96.	264
i	31.	146	v.	71.	242.	Gov. Vidaurri	97.	266
j	33.	147.	w.	73.	243	San Luis Potosi	99.	267.
k	36	149.	x	76	246			
l	37.	151	y	77.	247.			
m	38	153.	z.	78	249.			

The ciphers 321 and 782 are null. Also ciphers 22 and 43.

Commence combining three ciphers.

When cipher 500 is met with, continue reading combining two ciphers. When 600 is met with, commence combining three ciphers and so on.

84

Figure 3.1. José Agustín Quintero created a cipher to communicate in code from his post along the Texas-Mexico border. Confederate States of America, *Confederate States of America Records*, microfilm reel 8, Manuscript Division, Library of Congress.

stands out among the precious pieces. Written in Columbus, Georgia, in 1833, "Arm for the Southern Land" captures the pre-secessionist sentiments sweeping Georgia and South Carolina during the nullification crisis, which tested the power of Southern states to reject federal authority over the passage of the 1832 Tariff Bill.[14] "Arm for the Southern land," the opening lines declare, "All fear of death disdaining; / Low lay the tyrant hand / Our sacred rights profaning! / Each hero draws / In Freedom's cause, / And meets the foe with bravery; / The servile race, / And tory base, / May safety seek in slavery." The three-part ode is a love song for violent uprising in the name of states' rights. Lamar insists in his preface that his poems were not written for the public, but the form and structure of the ode, which is set to the tune of Thomas Moore's doleful musical ballad "Oft in the Steely Night," suggest that it was meant to be sung as a parlor room rallying cry for the preservation of the idea of Southern sovereignty: "Stand by your injured State, / And let no feuds divide you; / On tyrants pour your hate, / And common vengeance guide you. / Our foes should feel / Proud freeman's steel, / For freeman's rights contending; / Where'er they die, / There let them lie, / To dust in scorn descending."[15]

The poem likely resonated with Quintero, whose 1857 praise of *Verse Memorials* makes the case for Lamar as a poet and the point that the dearth of critical reception of Lamar's book speaks to the greater marginalization of Southern literature. "So long as we acknowledge the superiority of our enemies in intellectual pursuits," Quintero says of the Northern literary and print culture scene, "and do not blush at our dependence upon them for whatever refines our tastes, develops genius and elevates the soul, so long shall we be their social inferiors and political dependents." The review, which does not appear to have been printed at the time, could be considered Quintero's declaration of Southern independence in its belief that the newspapers suppress Southern literary "works of genius."[16] Not surprised by the "neglect" from Northern journalists, he directs his ire at Southern papers, especially the Georgia press, for ignoring Lamar's poetry. Though Lamar is a Georgia native, the Cuban cries, his home state newspapers are "filled with the production of foreign writers, not of the first rank, but bearing the endorsement of *Harper's Magazine* and other similar publications." The slight is a call to Southern arms for Quintero, who understood the power of print to inspire feelings of national belonging and champion the voices of the dispossessed. After all, in 1856 he established *El Ranchero*, a saucy Spanish-language San Antonio Democratic organ he leveraged to critique the Know-Nothing Party and its anti-Mexican sentiments. "For Quintero," Coronado explains, "newspapers are not mere neutral observers; they are, instead, the defenders of their community of readers and listeners. They serve to shape that community rather than merely reflect its interests."[17] As Coronado shows, Quintero critiqued the San Antonio newspaper *El Bejareño* for its anti-Mexican sentiments in 1856. A year later, the Cuban leveled similar accusations against the Anglophone press for what he characterized as its biased treatment of Southern literary and cultural value, with the exception of one stalwart state, South Carolina: "She is the Bulwark and protector of the American Constitution—the bold, consistent and uncorrupted defender of its original and unperverted principles; and at the same time she is almost the only State of the South which has manifested any disposition to protect her own literature—to emancipate herself from the dogmatism of the North, and to build up a character of her own." Roughly three years before South Carolina declared to secede, Quintero called for his own literary secession with rhetoric that had its poetic echo in *El laúd*. "If we would maintain political equality in this Union," the poet concluded, "it is indispensable to establish social and mental equality. Without the arts, sciences and literature, there can be neither permanent prosperity nor security for liberty."[18]

Seven years prior, Quintero had penned a more reserved assessment of Cuban poetry. In his "Lyric Poetry in Cuba," another unpublished manuscript written around the early 1850s, he opens, "Before expressing our opinions of lyric poetry in Cuba, we ought to promise that it is not our intention to communicate dogmas, or to create theories, but to relate, with all possible clearness and impartiality, what we have observed." He of course goes on to present a brief theory on the state of Cuban poetry, claiming "the slavery of the printing press," an "indolence" of spirit, and the nascence of what he calls Cuban "civilization" as reasons for the paucity of lyric poetry on the island: "Poetry is a part of our literature; literature is a part of our civilization: the history of our civilization begins to be born. . . . How long have we yet to wait!" His statement closes with an exclamation rather than a question, indicating that his is a poetics of liberation waiting for Cuba to become a nation. Still, the Cuban affirms the three pillars of his literary theory: "Every one knows that Poetry has three great inspirations," he explains, "love to the Divinity, love to country, and love to women. . . . Kindled with these holy themes, Poetry has crowns of flowers for woman, laurels for his native land, and soars on golden and chrystaline wings to Heaven." Only a few of Quintero's fellow Cubans rise to the poetic occasion; among them he includes himself, "without humility," but he nonetheless remains speculative in his essay.[19] For him, the future of Cuban literature awaits the arrival of civilization, by which he seems to mean individual and political enlightenment through *belles lettres*. He conveyed a similar theory to Longfellow in 1855 that poetry would bring "civilization" to the island and its independence from Spain. Voicing the same speculative optimism that great poetry, especially Longfellow's, can liberate Cuba, Quintero explains that he understands poetry as "un órgano de la civilización, bien inteligible, poderosa, y más que todo progresista e innovador" (an organ of civilization, highly intelligible, powerful, and above all progressive and innovative).[20]

During the heady 1850s, then, the Cuban viewed poetry as a vehicle of social enlightenment, personal freedom, and literary liberation—the building blocks of an independent national homeland. The gist of Quintero's essay—that Cuban poetry will someday bring about the island's independence—put him at the crossroads of the larger transformations of modernity that Cuba and Cubans were facing. "New fissures appeared within an already deeply fractured social system," Louis A. Pérez Jr. says of mid-nineteenth-century Cuba, "riven by tension produced between those pushing forward to advance modernity and those pushing back to defend tradition."[21] Quintero understood this battle to be leveraged by the control of print because he understood the power of the press. So long as Cuba and the slaveholding US South labored under the "slavery of the printing press," as he called it, Quintero believed that their respective ruling class of whites would never achieve literary and political independence. Drawing on a language already familiar to mid-nineteenth-century Cuban revolutionaries and Southern secessionists alike, Quintero fancied that Spanish and Northern control of the press enslaved Cuban Creoles and Southern whites intellectually and politically. The fact that chattel slavery bolstered the entire global south is not so much lost on him as it is indicative of his presumption that Blacks do not possess the same natural rights of personal freedom and political independence as whites. Rather, his poetics of liberation presupposes enslavement as the *sine qua non* condition for Black people, so for whites to feel subjected to "the slavery of the press," as he calls it, is anathema not because it impinges on the liberal notion of a free press but because it symbolically situates whites on par with the presumed condition of Black people. His phrase captures the anti-Black connection between the Cuban independence movement and Southern secession: both maintain enslavement as the defining social and racial condition of being Black. His twisted racial sentiment is not unique—it's the hobgoblin of white liberation rhetorics that emerge from slave societies that cannot or will not conceptualize the emancipation of the enslaved as integral to national, political, and personal independence. The United States' Declaration of Independence shows this contradictory truth to be self-evident.

Yet the familiar contradiction explains why Quintero championed Lamar's verses. Even though he lamented to Longfellow in July 26, 1855, that Texas was "destitute of literary taste," he had changed his position by his 1857 poetry review, which he opens with the same poetic tenets he ascribed to Cuban lyrical verse: "Poetry has three great inspirations—love of God,—love to country—and love to woman. Kindled with these holy themes, it soars on golden wings to Heaven, gives laurels to the patriot and wreathes perennial garlands for Beauty."[22] For Quintero, Lamar's poetry lives up to the poetics that Cuban lyrics can only aspire to, which seems an odd position for the Cuban to stake at the moment *El laúd* cemented his poems "en la república de las letras cubanas," as the editor of *El laúd* put it in his preface.[23] By then, the poet seems to have left the republic of Cuban letters for the confederacy of Southern literature with the gusto of a fire-eating secessionist. "Our religion is uncorrupted," he writes about the South, "our patriotism fervid and our love for the beautiful and good is excessive and romantic."[24] With his review of Lamar's poetry, the Cuban comes out as a secessionist Southerner—he "identifies wholly with the society of the South," Jorge A. Marbán says; "he's one of them."[25] Echoing his "Lyric Poetry" essay, Quintero's use of "our" makes apparent the personal and political filiation between the Cuban independence movement and the language of Southern secession. They both mean to preserve and protect white power structures through writing and war.

The Confederate *Letrado*'s Civil War Archive

From June 1861, when he took up his mission to serve as a Confederate confidential agent, to December 1864, when his last letter appears in his diplomatic archive, Quintero wrote almost exclusively about the Confederacy's fate and fortune on *la frontera*. In September 1861, he was appointed the CSA's confidential agent, and his main Confederate correspondents were Secretary of State R. M. T. Hunter, Assistant Secretary of State William M. Browne, and, beginning in 1862, the new Confederate Secretary of State, Judah P. Benjamin. He penned over sixty missives to Benjamin, producing roughly four hundred pages of writing, excluding the transcriptions and translations he attached as addenda. His reports also included original letters from Mexican officials, bulletins from across the border, and copies of newspapers or clippings from the Spanish- and English-language press. Combined, his epic archive nears eight hundred pages in microfilm reel 8 of the Confederate States of America record. To compound matters, many of his messages, attachments, translations, and transcriptions are duplicated in reel 32 of the CSA archive.[26] Most of these duplications are done by different hands (as is evident by the penmanship and signature), but on more than a few occasions, he penned his own copies of his original letters or enclosures, adding to the labor of writing he performed in his official capacity. He wrote so frequently that, at the start of their correspondence, Judah Benjamin admonished the *letrado* to number his letters in sequence for more accurate recordkeeping.[27] He dated his letters, noted from where he was writing, often referred to the dates of his previous dispatches, and lettered any enclosures, but he didn't number his missives as instructed. They're numbered in the archive by a separate hand.

Tasked with the mission of opening friendly lines of communication between Governor Santiago Vidaurri and the Confederacy to secure commerce, trade, and access across the lower Rio Grande Valley's Texas-Mexico border and Mexico's Matamoros port, Quintero spent much of his time stationed in Monterrey, Mexico, where he trafficked in information as effectively as he kept cotton, goods, and supplies in transit for the Confederacy. He had a difficult diplomatic task because of the region's shifting political terrain. Following John Pickett's disastrous, short-lived service as the Confederacy's diplomat in Mexico City, the CSA realized that Mexico's northern states were not only more significant strategically for the movement of goods and supplies but also loosely tied to Mexico's liberal-leaning capital. In the wake of its own civil war (La Reforma of 1857–1860), Juárez's government held little control of its far northern frontier, where Governor Vidaurri, who aided Juárez during La Reforma, maintained a firm grip on Nuevo León y Coahuila, the two consolidated states he governed. He also held considerable sway over Chihuahua and Durango, and by 1862, he secured power over the state of Tamaulipas as well, "giving him more control over the northern frontier of Mexico than any man had exercised for decades."[28] His grip on the region, however, was tenuous. While he had designs for an independent Republic of Sierra Madre, the *caudillo* contended often with neighboring military governors, Mexican filibusters backed by American Texans, border fighters such as Juan Nepomuceno Cortina, armed Indigenous resistance, and the growing divide in Mexico between Juárez's liberal government and the invading French empire. Mexico's northern states may have held promise for the movement of goods and supplies, especially via the mouth of the Rio Grande, but they also presented considerable pitfalls that Quintero managed as "one of the most skillful and successful [agents] in the entire Confederate diplomatic corps."[29]

While not exactly a "border *letrado*" in Yolanda Padilla's use of the term, Quintero nonetheless penned letters from "a site of knowledge production" that he referred to as the Rio Grande line, the frontier, or *la frontera*.[30] Latinx scholars readily recognize the region as the borderlands—that zone of contact and crossings that Gloria Anzaldúa theorized as a third space. Established in 1749 as Nuevo Santander under the Spanish colonial project, the lower Rio Grande Valley has long been the site of regional and transnational contact and conflict. For Coronado, "it was here that the modern crucible of Texas emerged, that discursive-physical location where nation-states came and went within decades, building hopes as quickly as they were snatched away."[31] It is also the region that characterizes the border conflict and cultural production that, if we follow Américo Paredes, are foundational to Mexican American folklore, music, and Chicanx literary history. Geographically far from Mexico's capital and culturally distant too from the United States, the denizens of the lower Rio Grande Valley "experienced the borderlands as a relatively coherent in-between region, a third space separate in many ways from Mexico and the United States," explains Ramón Saldívar.[32] As the meticulous map Quintero produced for the Confederate record indicates, the borderlands opened an uncharted imaginative space for the Cuban between Mexico, Texas, the United States, and the Confederacy. While he likely crafted the map to indicate routes for the movement of troops, supplies, or cotton, the drawing also performs an intriguing cartographic erasure. It indicates Coahuila, New Leon, and Tamaulipas, the three Mexican states, but it does not identify Texas as a bordering state. It remains an unnamed space on the map. Confederate leadership would likely presume the area to be Texas, but its indeterminate status reflects the mapmaker's imaginative Latinx "third space." His cartographic consciousness left open the possibility for a borderlands Confederacy, an independent nation-in-the-making, where north points to the US South in an "illusion of empire," to recall William S. Kiser's elegant understanding of the competing nationalist projects in the region during the long Civil War years.[33] Quintero's map leaves unnamed a Southern Confederate "third space," as if its future in the region remains to be discovered.

Such subtle details, rhetorical ruptures, internal contradictions, and fissures of figurative meanings characterize the Cuban's record not so much as a Civil War archive but an archive at civil war.[34] It is filled with diplomatic dispatches disrupted by their poetics of literary liberation. For instance, in a June 1, 1863, letter to Secretary Benjamin, Quintero notes the capture of Puebla, a significant turn of events in the French military operations against Juárez's liberal government. "The city of Puebla was taken by the French on the 17th [of May]," his letter opens. "Most of the Mexican Army is captured. Its Commander in Chief Gonzales Ortega and all the Generals and officers of the 'Army of the East' are prisoners. It is believed that General Forey will now advance on the capital." As is often the case, Quintero's missive conveys information through a combination of sources that echo a journalistic tradition of attribution. He seems to glean from newspaper reports by the way he details events occurring three and a half weeks prior and roughly 650 miles south of the border. He also cites a proclamation issued by Juárez; anonymous "letters received here yesterday from the city of Mexico"; and one of his favorite sources, the word of Governor Vidaurri, who pumped Quintero with official and unofficial military and political information,

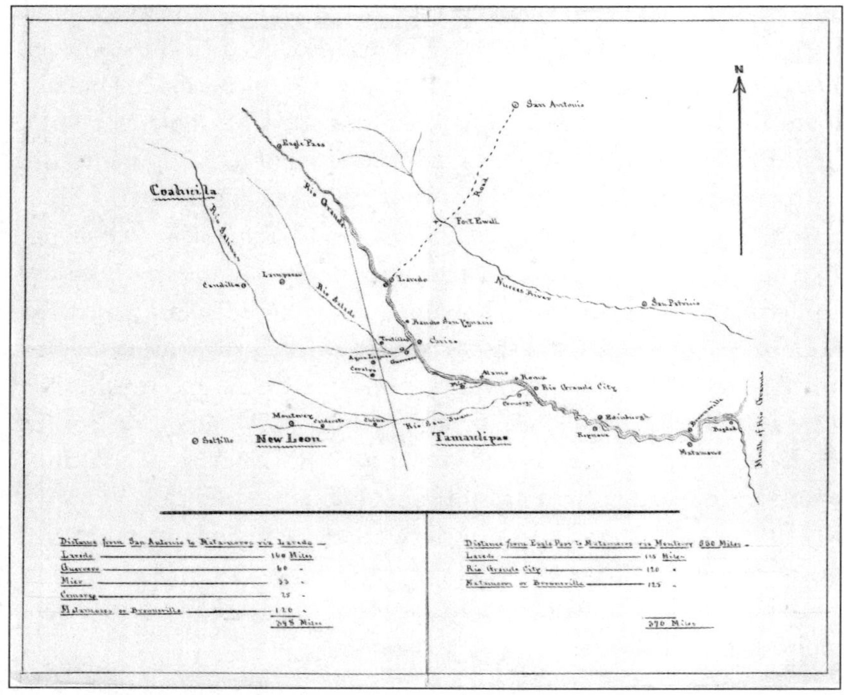

Figure 3.2. Quintero's map of the Texas-Mexico border leaves much of the northern part of the border to the imagination. Map of New Leon, Confederate States of America, *Confederate States of America Records*, microfilm reel 8, Manuscript Division, Library of Congress.

sprinkled with gossip and his vexed relationship with Mexico's central government under Juárez. The pastiche of discursive registers blends information with speculation to convey a narrative about the capture of Puebla as a potential victory for the Confederacy. "The *liberal* party is fast dying away and it is not improbable if there shall be seen a complete change in the form of Government of this country. I look forward to the day when the US will be drawn into the contest," he closed to Benjamin, observing with faint optimism that the French occupation of Mexico would divide the United States' interests between the war to preserve the Union against the Confederacy and a battle to protect the Monroe Doctrine against the French occupation of Mexico.[35]

This is one of several duplicate letters by Quintero's hand included in reel 32 of the CSA archive. He copied his original and addressed them both to Benjamin, with the second one marked "duplicate." It is a true and accurate transcription of the original except for one sentence he added to the duplicate's final paragraph: "I look forward to the day when the US will be drawn into the contest. *Great events are soon to take place.*"[36] The last sentence marks his understanding of the magnitude of the rapid changes occurring in Mexico and the potential for those shifts to better the outcome of the Confederacy's campaign. It also echoes the speculative optimism he held out for Cuba's liberation through poetry—that someday political transformation on a grand scale would unfold with such historic tectonics that new nations would be formed. "How long have we yet to wait!" he had declared in his "Lyric Poetry" essay. For Quintero, the capture of Puebla signals a moment of arrival. The fall of the Juárez government and the likelihood of Mexico under a French monarchy raised the possibility of a border nation sympathetic to the South and possibly annexed into the Confederacy, which would provide the Confederate States with the economic, geographical, and international power to turn the tide of the Civil War. "Gov. Vidaurri told me yesterday that in case that the war continued some of the Mexican States would resume their sovereignty and that New Leon and Coahuila would be one of the first to do so," Quintero explained in the letter.[37]

To recall the terms in his cipher, the Cuban understood war in the region relationally between Mexico, France, the Southern Confederacy, and the United States, so the fall of Puebla signaled the opportunity for the Southern Confederacy, as he called it, to incorporate Mexico's northern border states. After all, it was during their first diplomatic meeting that Vidaurri had proposed annexing New Leon and Coahuila into the Confederacy, a proposition that Jefferson Davis declined. The Confederacy had eyed Mexico's northern states for annexation through invasion or occupation, but the idea was short-lived because of the military and political complications the confederation would create.[38] However, for Quintero, with Puebla's fall, the possible secession of Mexico's northeastern states under Governor Vidaurri held out renewed promise for the Confederacy's control of the region, and in his only extant use of his cipher, he conveyed as much to Benjamin in a follow-up missive: "Gov. Vidaurri favors France. Gov. Almonte is to send him arms."[39]

It might be only one sentence, but "Great events are soon to take place" encodes a discursive rupture in his missive. Sitting, perhaps, with the original he had just written next to him, the Confederate *letrado* set out to copy verbatim his official correspondence, and at the final point of closing his four-page duplicate, the writer found inspiration in his own words and turned his letter into literature. Such forms of "archival excess," to adapt Alberto Varon's phrase, document moments of Quintero's subjectivity making and marking its presence in his diplomatic dispatches.[40] Its sheer volume and diversity of documents, combined with the duplicates made by his hands and others, gives credence to an "archival excess" that makes his Civil War writings impossible to ignore as part of a Latinx literary and cultural heritage. Moreover, his single sentence also expresses excess of a different kind—it registers his exuberance, his excitement at the historical events unfolding, and the momentary intrusion of the autobiographical subject in his otherwise depersonalized dispatches. It is his self-expressive excess that puts the two letters (the original and the duplicate) as well as their respective archival locations (reel 8 and reel 32) at civil war over historical accuracy, representational authority, and Quintero's struggle between reporting events about the fall of Mexico and imagining the future of the Confederacy's rise.

His epistolary excess is not the only form of self-expression. His letters also betray the *letrado*'s keen command of his rhetorical situation, as when he responds to Secretary Browne on receiving the orders for his first mission: "Having as a Cuban born, and disconnected with the civil strifes of Mexico, been fortunate enough to render some personal services to Gov. Vidaurri, . . . I feel that I fully comprehend the spirit of my instructions, and the great importance of maintaining friendly relations during the present crisis of the Confederate States, (a government to which I accord my full allegiance) and the neighboring States of Mexico, and I beg to assure the Department that I feel humbled by its confidence."[41] Quintero was clearly aware of the prejudice his appointment would trigger. For instance, John Pickett, the disgraced diplomat whose racist belligerence cost him his Confederate appointment in Mexico City, cautioned Jefferson Davis against assigning "a foreigner by birth and one of the Latin race—in short a Spanish American—to represent *us near his* kindred people."[42] However, by declaring for the Confederacy, disclosing his Cuban heritage, and disassociating from Mexico, Quintero set out to dispel any question of his loyalty or prejudicial presumptions of racial affiliation with Mexico and Mexicans. He may have been

Cuban born, he assures, but he's Confederate made. His letter reinforces this position by establishing his command of the region's information systems. He reports receiving his commission from "my esteemed friend Gen. McLeod"; he regrets missing Bishop Odin in Galveston, who Quintero notes has been named archbishop of New Orleans; he assures that he can nonetheless secure letters of introduction from the new head of Galveston's Catholic clergy; and he lets it be known that he did Governor Vidaurri a favor when he visited Austin a few years prior. He emphasizes his credentials throughout his missive by way of detailing his personal networks. He is well connected, his letter suggests, and his brief asides indicate that he already has knowledge about the movement of local people and positions. He might "feel humbled" by the appointment, but his letter establishes that he believes himself to be more than qualified for the mission.[43]

Two months later, the agent feigns similar humility in his report to Browne on the state of goods, supplies, and natural resources and the availability of arms from Governor Vidaurri. After noting that his previous communiqué indicated the Mexican governor was unable to supply munitions, he provides a list of all the ordinance in Vidaurri's arsenal. It is an inventory down to the rifle. He also offers details on the availability of copper and lead, including where and how it is mined, its quality and production for ammunition, and the standard prices for them. He continues by noting the abundance of saltpeter and explaining the process by which Mexicans manufacture and transport gunpowder. Rich with details that establish his mastery of resources in the region, the letter closes with Quintero "regretting that my information is so meagre on this subject and that I was not aware of the wish of the Government [for the information] while I was in Monterrey."[44] His report is obviously not meagre, but his more subtle point is his wanting to be better apprised by military leadership when it comes to their need for information about the border region. It's a rhetorical jab to remind the Confederacy that, on matters of the Texas-Mexico border, he is not simply their agent. He is their authority.

Quintero's strategic forms of self-fashioning should be understood in the context of their military power relations. Dispatches from the secretary of state are bound by formality, the conveyance of orders, and official responses to requests of approval, yet Quintero's forms of self-expression can be found in the subtle rhetorical moves his letters make. Through the span of his missives, for instance, the self-effacing stance of his early letters gives way to the self-affirming position he takes when it comes to maintaining his authority on matters of border conflicts. At one point, he offers to resign his post if Confederate leadership continues to ignore his concerns about Colonel John Ford's complicity with filibusters in the region. "The general government of Mexico as you are well aware," he wrote to Secretary Browne, "sympathizes with the Black Republicans. We have, however, succeeded in securing the friendship of the governors of the frontier States and now on the eve of incurring their enmity on account of the band of robbers who are permitted [by Ford] to abuse of the hospitality of Texas. . . . I earnestly request the Department to appoint a person to succeed me, who may have more influence than myself with the military at Brownsville and avoid the *serious difficulties I believe to be near at hand*."[45] Expressions of Quintero's agency in his dispatches can be found in such moments of discursive dissonance. He mobilizes the racial undertones of language, such as his use of the pejorative "Black Republicans" to refer to Republican Party members who supported abolition, and he masters rhetorical movements, like his feint to resign, to leverage his noncombatant authority over the War Department. He presents himself as so committed to the Confederacy that he would rather resign his post than be party to its self-inflicted border trouble. The rhetorical threat proved just how much influence the civilian agent held—the War Department reassigned Colonel Ford to desk duty.[46]

Three undated documents, likely produced at the start of his mission, mark how the Confederate *letrado* weaponized writing to protect the borderlands and preserve the potential for creating a greater Southern confederation of Mexico's northernmost states. The first are his notes on Mexico and the other two consist of his Spanish transcription of the Mexican Laws on Peonage in Nuevo León y Coahuila and his accompanying translation of them. Together, these dispatches begin to map the imaginative "third space" of a borderlands Confederacy. His notes on Mexico are not addressed to the secretary of state, but they're written to convey Quintero's assessment of the state of Mexico's political situation. His opening line presents the grim view that "Mexico as a federated Republic has virtually ceased to exist." Explaining that Mexico is composed of over twenty states and six territories, he emphasizes that the federal government's power "does not extend beyond a few of the central states for any effective purpose." Yucatán is "desolated" by "savages"; Guerrero is under the rule of a governor "whose power is supported by a horde of savage *pintos*"; a governor with "absolute power" heads Sinaloa; Sonora is "mostly Americanized" and divided by two parties; Governor Vidaurri "reigns supreme" in Nuevo Leon; Tamaulipas is under the "arbitrary sway" of a governor; states such as Chihuahua, Baja California, Oaxaca, and Chiapas are too far to be under the central rule of the government; and "Durango and Zacatecas are a constant prey to the Indian tribes of the North." More, "Durango is now being settled by Americans." Quintero presents Mexico in disarray to emphasize the central government's weak hold on the precarious states that seem—to the Confederate agent, at least—ripe for annexation or susceptible to secession, which might explain why his notes include commentary on Mexico's racial population. Citing a recent report, the *letrado* summarizes "the different races of the population as follows: One sixth part European, one half pure Indian and one third a mixture of the European Indian and African. The law of increase or decrease is not defined with any certainty, but the general impression is that the Indian race experiences a constant decrease."[47]

Synthesizing observation, rumor, news reports, and census data, the notes give rare, clear expression to Quintero's opinionated assessment of Mexico. Most of his reports tend to provide information rather than open opinion, and when he does offer his judgment, usually later in his service, it's steeped in his knowledge about the border and the political and economic dynamics of the region. His notes on Mexico are different. Rather than presenting Mexico as a fettered republic, as was standard in Cuban independence writing, Quintero characterizes it as a failed one because its federal government cannot serve the interests of its marginal states and territories, as indicative in his emphasis that the northern states are overrun by "savages." He describes Mexico, in other words, through rhetoric that Confederate leadership would understand, not just in terms of their prejudicial presumption of Mexican ineptitude but also through an anti-Indigenous language that highlights the disasters that befall a centralized republican government that does not tend to its marginal states. They are subject to racial ruin. From Quintero's Southern sympathetic perspective, the present state of Mexico's disarray offers a lesson that validates the secession of the South's slaveholding states. His "Notes on the Present Conditions of Mexico," then, is only nominally about Mexico. It also conveys to Confederate leadership the confluence of their cause with the conditions in the borderlands, which explains why of all the governors of the northern border states, Quintero presents Vidaurri as a Confederate in the making: "he has annexed the State of Coahuila to his own without the Federal power being able to prevent it."[48]

The *letrado*'s translation and transcription of the region's laws on peonage bolster the notes on Mexico. The documents are not specifically addressed, but their inclusion at the beginning of reel 8's chronologically ordered addenda suggests that, alongside the Mexico notes, Quintero produced and submitted the peonage laws for the Confederate record at the start of his appointment. Mexico's 1857 Constitution, which reaffirmed the prohibition of slavery and declared free "any slave who set foot" in Mexico's national territory, made the prospects of extending the slaveholding Confederacy questionable. However, the region's debt bondage system seemed to provide a labor structure akin to slavery that held Confederate interests in the early war years. Control of the borderlands would at the very least stem the movement of enslaved people into Mexico. Alternatively, even though Article 5 of the 1857 Constitution also prohibited bondage labor, the codes governing peonage in Mexico's northern states developed as indentured people increasingly escaped debt by crossing into Texas. Contra to the Mexican federal government's official position, regional peonage codes were linked to border-crossing regulations that controlled the trafficking of goods, limited the escape or harbor of outlaws or so-called bandits, and provided for the return of fugitive enslaved people. "Ultimately," Andres Reséndez concludes, "the persistence of coercive labor regimes both in Mexico and the United States, in spite of the rhetoric of free labor both federal governments espoused, raise profound questions about the limitations of state power and its limited ability to transform regional labor systems favored by local and regional elites."[49] Quintero's translated transcription of peonage codes for Nuevo León and Coahuila leveraged the governing dissonance in the centralized control of labor practices. He provided a literal and accurate translation of the 1851 laws, which superseded the 1828 and 1849 codes, and the stand-alone English translation of the 1851 codes he provides to Confederate leadership gives the impression that servitude remains in good legal standing in the borderlands.

However, his archive battles itself once again. His addendum also includes a handwritten transcription of the region's peonage codes in Spanish from 1828 through 1857, the latter of which includes two additional articles adopted from the 1857 Constitution. One article pronounces that the 1857 laws supersede the 1851 codes and another article reads in part, "Nadie puede ser obligado a prestar trabajos personales, sin la justa retribucion y sin su pleno consentimiento. La ley no puede autorizar ningún contracto que tenga por objecto la pérdida or el irrevocable sacrificio de la libertad del hombre, ya sea por causa de trabajo, de educación o de voto religioso." (No one can be forced to provide personal work, without full remuneration and without their full consent. The law cannot authorize any contract that has as its object the loss or irrevocable sacrifice of man's freedom, whether due to work, education, or religious vow.) The *letrado* translated the 1851 laws for the Confederate record but excluded the 1857 codes that superseded them. A bracket mark in the left margin of the archived document indicates that he deliberately expunged the 1857 articles in his translated transcription.[50] As with Chacón's and Tafolla's respective autobiographies, Spanish and English do battle in Quintero's archive, raising interpretive questions about authority, accuracy, and autobiographical intention between the English-language translation he writes for Confederate leadership and the Spanish-language transcription he provides for the record. The former is not simply a mistranslation of the latter; it's a strategic misrepresentation that gives promise in English to a potential slaveholding confederacy in the south Texas-northern Mexico borderlands that the Spanish-language codicil already foreclosed. His omission of the 1857 articles is just as meaningful as his addition of one sentence to his duplicate letter about Puebla. As Gregory Eiselein says of self-writing, "Autobiographies hide things they don't want you to see, and they reveal things they never intended to show you."[51] Quintero's small gesture of omission marks a creative act that, as with his unnaming of Texas on the map, holds open the possibility of realizing the CSA's short-lived plan to annex the region in a greater Southern Confederacy.

Even Quintero's statements in support of the Confederate cause are embattled. Though he often uses "our" to refer to the Confederate government, its military, or its goods and supplies, he states his support for the Confederacy three times. The first is his brief declaration to Secretary Browne mentioned previously, and the other two are a study in the competing rhetorical registers that pull at the *letrado*. Accompanied by a letter of appointment from then Confederate Secretary of State Robert Toombs, Quintero added his own letter of introduction to Governor Vidaurri that explained the Confederate agent's mission and captured the occasion to proclaim the Confederate cause. The agent takes such ornate care to explain the US South's secession that it's worth quoting at length:

> The political occurrences of the last few months in the United States of the North are too well known to your Excellency to need recapitulation here. It is only necessary to state as has been done by a higher official than the undersigned at the Federal capital of Mexico, that the primary object of the Confederate States in withdrawing from an oppressive and uncongenial alliance with their former co-States was to form a new Confederacy among homogeneous sovereign communities in which the elements of discord which divided the old one should not enter. This has been happily accomplished and my country presents to day the grand spectacle of a whole people united as one man to change their Government by peaceable and constitutional means in order to adapt it to the better protection of their rights and liberties. If the United States should persist in denying this right and compel the Confederate States to defend it by force it will not alter the principle of self government, but will only manifest the barbarism of its opponents.[52]

Toombs's orders gave no instruction to defend the Confederate cause. Just the opposite. He instructed Quintero to take a high-handed approach to the Mexican governor, assuring him of the Confederacy's good will, directing him to see to the security of the Mexican side of the Rio Grande, and threatening him with military action if he failed to do so.[53] Toombs's letter to Vidaurri that accompanied Quintero's undiplomatically repeated the Confederacy's grievances. But in neither Toombs's order nor his letter to Vidaurri did the secretary of state proclaim the Confederacy's secession as a just cause for independence. Instead, Quintero took the opportunity to downplay Toombs's blunder with an impassioned declaration of states' rights, political independence, and the formation of heroic, masculine national unity that carries echoes of the exile's lute, to recall the name of the Cuban revolutionary anthology that featured Quintero's verses. His description of the Confederate states as "my country" speaks to the way the Cuban understood the South's secession as the embodiment of national independence that he once imagined was on the island's horizon, with the strategic omission that such liberation was in the name of preserving slavery. The entire rhetorical situation of his letter, accompanied by Toombs's, drives Quintero's Confederate patriotism. He understood much better than the Confederacy's secretary of state that proclamations of self-governance would resonate with the Mexican border governor. He continues, "It is proper to state to your Excellency also that the Confederate Government disclaims all the ideas of invasion and conquest of other territories [a position Toombs certainly did not state in his orders], which was so conspicuous in the policy of the United States. On the contrary, they accord to their neighbors what they claim for themselves, the absolute sovereignty and control of their own dominions subject only to the laws of nations and the requirements of treaties."[54] Quintero's rhetorical gambit hit its mark, as it was at their first face-to-face diplomatic meeting that Vidaurri proposed annexing Nuevo Leon and Coahuila into the Confederacy.[55]

Quintero's third declaration for the Confederacy is no less rhetorically complicated in the context of his letter and the imbroglios of the borderlands. In an eleven-page detailed dispatch from Monterrey to Secretary Browne that Quintero started on March 22 and continued on March 24, 1862, he describes *la frontera* as a region besieged with internal conflicts that threaten the hold the Confederate agent managed to establish with Governor Vidaurri. His letter reports that, besides facing a British, French, and Spanish blockade at the mouth of the Rio Grande, a Texas parson turned Union spy attempted to establish a Lincoln consul in Monterrey with the aid of "runaway Germans and negroes from Texas." The issue points to the larger problem of Texas being used as a staging ground for incursions into northern Mexico that challenge Vidaurri's governance of the region. On this latter point, Quintero indicates that the biggest threat to the Confederacy comes from within, as he suggests that Colonel John "Rip" Ford, a man for whom he once vouched, is aiding filibuster incursions launched from Texas by General José María de Jesus Carvajal. The two are old filibuster friends, and in a frenzied attempt to establish his dream of a republic on the Rio Grande, Carvajal staged an assault on Reynosa, Tamaulipas, armed with munitions secured in Brownsville, the letter reports. The situation jeopardized the good relations Quintero worked to establish with Vidaurri, and the attacks on the Mexican governor's hold on the region risk the Confederacy's tenuous access to circum-Gulf ports. While Quintero notes that Vidaurri has opened Matamoros, Brownsville, Mier, and Reynosa for Confederate agents to import arms and supplies, Carvajal "has neither means nor ability to carry out any enterprise." Bound, perhaps, by friendship, Ford's soft support of Carvajal's incursions threaten nothing short of losing the region for the Confederacy: "I fear if Gen. Carvajal continues to be permitted *to organize troops in Texas to attack Gov. Vidaurri's [troops] we will soon lose the friendship of the latter.*" Sensing that his work and the fate of the Confederacy are on the brink of colossal collapse, he closes by proclaiming to his command,

> The disasters which have over taken the arms of the South have disheartened many of our friends here. It, however, animates and makes me stronger than I would have been if victory had crowned our efforts. Our people were accustomed to successes and this tended to render them lukewarm. They will now wake up and with one heart and soul defend their country against the common foe. Mishaps may be in store for us, but we are destined to become independent.[56]

Quintero's closing comments conflate the Confederacy's challenges with his own struggle to keep up a successful mission on the Rio Grande line when Confederate officers do not act in concert with the information provided by their agents. The telltale fissure comes with the *letrado*'s use of pronouns. His shift from "our" to "them" draws a hard distinction between his full commitment to the cause and Colonel Ford's half-hearted understanding of the careful diplomatic balance the Confederacy must maintain with the most powerful sitting Mexican governor of the region rather than a career filibuster with little political clout. The passage also gives expression to the revolutionary verve that characterized the Cuban's earlier poetics of liberation and his zeal for Lamar's poetic prowess. He even echoes Lamar's fire-eating poem by noting the hazard that disunion poses to "the arms of the South." "And let no feuds divide you; / On tyrants pour your hate," Lamar had written in his ode, a sentiment Quintero seems to have taken to heart. Alongside the words and phrases underlined throughout his letter for emphasis, his closing declaration is a rare impassioned personal proclamation in a formal diplomatic dispatch warning that the imminent threats to the Confederacy in south Texas are not the international blockade of the Rio Grande, the possibility of a French monarchy, the feeble mobilization of Juárez's military, a "miscreant" parson from Texas, or even Carvajal's filibustering fever. The threat to the Confederacy in the region is the disunion of Southern Confederates and the petty discord that stands in the way of the Confederacy's "destin[y] to become independent."[57]

The brief declaration is reminiscent of Quintero's poetics of liberation and indicative of his nuanced understanding of the relational power structures that govern the region. Better than Toombs or Ford, the Latinx *letrado* recognized Cuba's struggle, the US South's secession, and the condition of Mexico's northern states as on the same continuum for the dream of a greater circum-Gulf slavocracy. He rarely linked them directly in his dispatches, only noting on a few occasions that Cuba could serve as a hub for cotton and munitions, but unlike his Anglo Confederate counterparts, he held on to the idea of a confederation of Mexico's northern states and the US slaveholding states that seceded. He left figurative space for it in his archive and continued to pursue it outside Confederate records. When his relations with Vidaurri soured over the control of the cotton trade in Nuevo León, Quintero reached out to Pedro Santacilia, his fellow exiled Cuban *letrado* who married Juárez's daughter and advised the Mexican president. As he explained to Santacilia,

> Yo fui quien traje ese comercio al Sr. Vidaurri hace más de dos años y hoy podré llevarlo a Tamaulipas si se restablece la paz en Matamoros y el Gobierno del Sr. Juárez protege nuestros intereses. . . . En nombre de nuestra antigua amistad, en nombre de los grandes intereses y ventajas que resultarán a este país y en nombre, en fin, de la sinceridad y honor que usted sabe muy bien han distinguido siempre mi conducta, le reugo encarecidamente hable con el señor Presidente sobre los particulares que arriba he mencionado y me informe sobre decisión. Si usted cree necesario que vea en persona al Sr. Juárez lo haré inmediatamente.

> (I was the one who brought this business to Mr. Vidaurri more than two years ago, and now I will be able to take it to Tamaulipas if peace is restored in Matamoros and the Government of Mr. Juarez protects our interests. . . . In the name of our old friendship, in the name of the big interests and advantages that will result in this country, and finally, in the name of the honesty and honor that you know have always distinguished my conduct, I sincerely ask you to speak with the President on the particulars mentioned above and inform me of his decision. If you think it necessary for me to see Mr. Juarez in person, I will do so immediately.)[58]

Quintero's letter to Santacilia makes palpable the political and personal circuits of connection between Cuba, Mexico, the United States, and the Confederacy. The two revolutionary poets were exiled together in the United States, where they met Juárez and Vidaurri during their respective flights across the border, and several years after civil wars have pulled them apart, the idea of a greater Southern Confederacy momentarily reconnected them through a Spanish-language missive that does not appear in the CSA's archive. It remains with Juárez's papers, an exiled dispatch with a proposal that the beleaguered Mexican president did not accept. However, the personalized note and unsanctioned outreach to broker with Mexico's liberal leader via his Cuban compatriot shore up the degree to which Quintero leveraged his "ties of *la patria*, suffering, friendship, and literary kinship" to realize the dream of national independence that started in Cuba and fell with the Confederacy.[59]

Coda: Lamar's *Laúd*

After the Civil War, the Confederate *letrado* returned to New Orleans following a brief trip to Cuba. The Ten Years' War seemed to have curbed the exile's return, and despite his early hopes for the island's independence, he kept his distance from another civil war that countenanced the abolition of slavery as a *casus belli*. Besides, the composition of Cuba's revolutionary freedom fighters changed from Quintero's early days. "From a slave society formed by a fear of slave and black rebellion," Ada Ferrer writes, "there emerged a movement that came to attack slavery and colonialism, to mobilize free and enslaved black and mulatto men, and to enable the rise of nonwhite leaders."[60] This wasn't

Quintero's movement. Postwar New Orleans, where the racial legacies of slave culture die hard, was more to his liking. He settled with his family, resumed his work as a lawyer and a newspaperman, and took up a post as the federal government's consul to Costa Rica. He returned somewhat to his literati life, Kirsten Silva Gruesz has shown, by heading up a local literary circle and keeping an active journalism career.[61] In terms of his poetry, however, his lute was quieter, and one postwar ode might explain why. His Lost Cause "Memorias del Alma" seems to close the door on his poetics of liberation. The poem opens with the speaker addressing Rebeca (which recalls the name of Lamar's deceased daughter, Rebecca) in a wooded grove before the war pulled them apart:

> I flew to fill a position among the ranks
> of a heroic legion, and my existence
> I consecrated on the altar that a cultured people
> erected to their holy independence.
>
> At tremendous cannon roar
> and at seeing the lit bombs rise into
> the blue atmosphere, how much I remembered
> you then! But fate wanted brutal force, not heroism,
> to decide the fight, since justice and patriotism
> do not always manage to win.

Moving from sylvan to elegiac, the speaker pays homage to Confederate officers, such as General Hugh McLeod and Colonel John F. Marshall, before closing with a paean to Mirabeau Buonaparte Lamar, who died a year and a half before the outbreak of the Civil War:

> Lamar, incomparable on the platform,
> inspired poet, a lightning bolt in battle;
> To you, my good friend,
> who shared your home and bread with me,
> I consecrate a memory to you! Your name
> that the victor does not acclaim,
> with my lute, in the Spanish language,
> I will carry through the fields of fame.[62]

"Memorias del Alma" brings Quintero back to the antebellum moment when *Verse Memorials* and *El laúd* intersected on the *letrado*'s Latinx continuum, echoing each other in a poetics of liberation that inspired the Cuban revolutionary to embrace the Confederate cause via Lamar's poetic influence. The poet hardly carried Lamar's name through "the fields of fame," however. The piece appears to be a shard of one of Quintero's last postbellum poetic efforts. He chose to write it in Spanish, which limited its readership; its original print venue remains obscure; and only "el más interesante pasaje" (the most interesting passage) remains extant in print.[63] Nonetheless, one of the last tunes from the exile's poetic lute sounds a Latinx note for the Southern statesman who inspired the Cuban's literary secession.

The poem marks a pivotal moment in Latinx literary history. It is a rare Reconstruction-era piece in Spanish by a US Latino who weaponized writing in English on the CSA's Latinx front. On the one hand, Quintero returns to his characteristic "masculine sentimentalism," as the ode is reminiscent of his antebellum verses dedicated to Cuban heroes; on the other, the postwar verse takes on the hues of the Lost Cause poetics that distinguish so much Southern literature after Appomattox. Its three movements map the connections that intersect Quintero's Civil War writings. The ode's opening movement, with reference to Lamar's deceased daughter, Rebecca, marks the imagined pastoral days of the antebellum age that the Civil War disrupts in the antistrophe middle stanzas: "We left, alas, perhaps to never see each other / on earth, when the bloody war raised its head / and roared around a horrid storm." Finally, the poem's epode, in its homage and elegy, closes with a self-referential nod to the era of Cuban revolutionary poetics that inscribed Quintero's name in the "republic" of Cuban letters. Exile no more, Quintero's lute sings for Lamar—the pro-filibustering expansionist poet-politician whom Ambrosio José Gonzales, another Cuban Confederate, once approached to solicit aid for López's incursion on the island.[64] Quintero's poem pulls Lamar's legacy into Latinx literary history. The gesture raises the question about who and what resides in our so-called Hispanic literary heritage. Or better put, what does Latinx literary history inherit from the white sheep in the family?

For instance, while Quintero seems to have turned away from poetry after the war, he published a manual on the *code duello* in 1873. *The Code of Honor*, which Quintero revised for another edition released in 1883, is a long overlooked Latinx Reconstruction text. Put out in pamphlet form, the text lists the rules and guidelines for engaging in duels of honor, and while the 1873 edition has a relatively brief introduction, the 1883 edition opens with a revised introduction that puts dueling in the context of Southern Reconstruction through language that's reminiscent of Quintero's review of Lamar's poetry:

> So long as the foul flood of radical aggression does not overwhelm true civilization in the United States—so long as radical license does not render all too deeply degraded to be sensible of their own degradation—so long as radical levelling does not reduce all to the semi-savage state of the social hog—so long as the gentleman is not eliminated from existence—until the advent of the millennium, the Code of Honor will be used.[65]

Published in the same decade that saw María Amparo Ruiz de Burton's 1872 *Who Would Have Thought It?* and her 1885 *The Squatter and the Don*, *The Code* positions the Cuban Confederate *letrado* as a founding Latinx literary figure, as Silva Gruesz rightly argues.[66] Much like Ruiz de Burton's first novel, Quintero's text is also steeped in ideas of Southern honor that he revives literally. His editions are reprints of former South Carolina Governor John Lyde Wilson's *The Code of Honor*, which was first published in 1838 and saw reprints in 1845 and 1858. For his editions, Quintero added his own introductions, provided several footnotes, expunged the appendix matter in Wilson's original, and changed the subtitle for the 1883 edition. Otherwise, minor emendations notwithstanding, the text is a verbatim copy of Wilson's *Code*, without attribution. Granted, Quintero does not hold an author byline on his editions, but his *Code of Honor* is a reconstruction of Wilson's text, tying the Latinx *letrado*'s literary heritage back to South Carolina's fire-eating lineage.[67] A nullificationist and early advocate for states' rights, Wilson is also arguably the foundational figure of South Carolina's early nineteenth-century dueling culture, from which the term "fire-eater" first emerged before it was used to refer to staunch secessionists. Wilson's edition, which Campbell argues presents the author's ambivalence about dueling, opens with an unambiguous stance in relation to political and personal sovereignty: "If an oppressed nation has a right to appeal to arms in defence of its liberty and happiness of its people," Wilson writes of his code, "there can be no argument used in support of such appeal, which will not apply with equal force to individuals."[68]

Wilson's 1838 comments signal the way the South Carolinian called on the sentiments of US independence as coded rationale for the state and individual rights to uphold a sense of honor through arms. The kernel of such thought, of course, would grow into Southern secession over slavery, the Civil War, and the feelings of presumed white disenfranchisement that characterize the racial violence of Radical Reconstruction in the United States. This is the genealogy we inherit with Quintero's *Code of Honor* editions. He pulls Wilson and the US South's long-lasting rhetorics of and rationales for racial violence into the "Latino continuum" because they are familiar (familial) structures of feeling in the Cuban's slaveholding consciousness. "To be 'Cuban' not as a subset of, but rather than, 'Latino' is to be, quite often, associated with whiteness, and thereby disassociated from blackness," Lamas explains.[69] The troubling legacy of the white Cuban's dream for a greater independent confederation of a Southern slaveholding nation is evident in his archive and can be traced through the poetics of liberation that connect the United States, Cuba, and the Confederacy to the history of slavery and its anti-Black legacies that give us an altogether different iteration of the *x* in "Latinx." It recalls the saltire of the Confederate battle flag and its trappings of white power, privilege, and passing at the expense of Black, Indigenous, and Latinx communities, then and now.

4

When Cubans Go South

White Nationalism and the Cuban Confederate Cause

If José Agustín Quintero presents what we have characterized as a borderlands Confederate willing to cut a tenuous pan-Latinx front with Mexican *caudillos*, his older Cuban counterpart, Ambrosio José Gonzales, gives us a similar confederation of *cubanidad* during the mid- through late nineteenth century. He is most known as Narciso López's adjutant general and translator during the Cuban filibustering movements, though he wasn't at the general's side during the second, fateful August 1851 incursion on the island that left the famous filibuster garroted. For South Carolinians, Gonzales is also remembered for his impassioned duty in the Confederate ranks, serving alongside his Creole *cuate*, General P. G. T. Beauregard, as a colonel and chief of artillery in charge of protecting South Carolina's coast.[1] Whether it be for Cuba or the Confederacy, Gonzales had a flare for touting his military record: he claims to have been the first Cuban to have "shed blood" for the island's independence during the May 1850 filibuster skirmish; he squabbled with Jefferson Davis over military appointments and defensive strategies; and he seems to have penned, anonymously, several newspaper pieces praising his own valorous service to the CSA. He was a "soldier under two flags but one cause; that of community independence," Jefferson Davis reportedly said of the Cuban Confederate, suggesting with the euphemism of "community independence" the presumed white rights that Gonzales advocated for before, during, and after the US Civil War.[2]

As Ella Lonn explains, "The cause of southern self-government made an overwhelming appeal to this Cuban patriot. The official records show that he was perhaps the earliest volunteer, having made the tender of his services on November 30, 1860, to the state of South Carolina, and among the last in service—three weeks after Appomattox."[3] Rather than a foreign freedom fighter joining the Confederate ranks, however,

Gonzales threw in with the South Carolina secessionists as an adopted Southerner: "It is reported by telegraph," he wrote to South Carolina Governor William Gist, "that it is the intention of the Federal Government to coerce South Carolina into submission. In such a contingency I beg respectfully to proffer my humble services to the state of my adoption. I have served as adjutant genl & chief of the staff to the lamented patriot, Genl. Narciso Lopez."[4] The language of "coercion" and "submission," and by implication, resistance and independence, were familiar positions to Gonzales, who was in part responsible for circulating similar rhetoric in the late 1840s and early 1850s in the name of the Cuban cause. Along with other elite Cuban exiles, such as Miguel Tolón, Cirilo Villaverde, and Gaspar Betancourt Cisneros, and other members of the Cuban Junta, as they called themselves in the United States, Gonzales advocated for the island's independence and annexation in the press, parlor rooms, and private letters. However, unlike his Creole confederates, many of whom remained in New York after López's death and continued their fight for the island, Gonzales went in a different direction: he married into a slaveholding South Carolina family and, by 1860, upheld secession and the Confederacy in the same language and spirit he once circulated for the cause of Cuban independence.

My argument here is that Gonzales was certainly a Cuban and a Confederate, torn between two flags, as the saying went, but he bridged both of those positions by becoming a Southerner, of the US South's plantation master class. It's this transition that marks the disconcerting process by which a Cuban revolutionary adopted the racialist rhetoric of the South, primarily to make a plea for the liberation of the island (with its slave system intact), but also as a way of learning how to become a Southern white nationalist. While Creole elites may have accepted the preservation of slavery as key to the island's annexation, Gonzales goes south with his sentiments about Cuban nationalism, liberation, and racial identity. His is a story that underscores a nineteenth-century US Latinidad defined by a process of adoption and assimilation into the South's slave society and its race-based nationalism rather than rooted in a collective filiation and shared struggle with a Hispanophone community. At stake here is unmasking the racial violence that undergirds the adoption of dominant culture, for Gonzales's life and writings underscore how the process of becoming a Southern Latinx subject in the

United States was predicated on the protection of Black enslavement and the entrenchments of its race-based social codes. Unlike notable Creoles, such as Tolón, Villaverde, or José Martí, who maintained a radical vision for Cuban independence from New York that, to differing degrees, imagined independence for Creoles and the enslaved alike, Gonzales adopted his understanding of Cuban independence into the culture of secession that surrounded him, advancing a Southern Latinx literary culture that was anti-Black, pro-slavery, and as much a lost cause in Cuba as it was in the Confederacy.[5]

Gonzales belongs to that class of Southern settler-planters whose entire economic and cultural world system, as Matthew Pratt Guterl explains, stemmed from the day-to-day operations of slavery and enslaved labor across the circum-Gulf South. The "master class of the Americas," as Guterl calls them, imagined their white power across national boundaries because slavery moved transnationally. "They understood African slavery as a universal system of labor for the Americas and searched for best practices in other slave societies. . . . Despite their particular regional preferences . . . they believed that the fate of slavery in the South was closely intertwined with the fate of slavery elsewhere in the Americas, that the line separating master from slave could, if the circumstances were right, cut across the foreign policies and international debates of various republics and colonies." The polyglot Gonzales, Guterl points out, was a "fluent, native speaker of the only other language that mattered to the Deep South: the language of slaveholding."[6] Like his Hispano counterpart, Miguel Otero, who also married into a South Carolina family of enslavers, Gonzales had an investment in whiteness that offset the markers of racial otherness that his name or nationality betrayed, and after his 1856 marriage to Harriet ("Hattie") Elliott, the youngest daughter of William Elliott (the South Carolina politician, planter, enslaver, and minor nonfiction writer), the Cuban became enmeshed in the extensive slave labor system and plantation profits of the well-connected lowlands family.[7]

Yet he also belonged to a first-wave cohort of Cubans who agitated for the island's independence during and after the Narciso López movement. These exiled Creoles, many of whom owned, operated, or published in New York's Spanish-language press, kept the question of Cuba alive after the López movement expired, and the longer they remained in New York, the more the movement's shaky stance on slavery became apparent, culminating with the 1854 appearance of *El Mulato*, "the most radical of the transnational newspapers published by Cubans in the 1850s," which advanced in unambiguous terms complete abolition on the island.[8] The fate of slavery was always a blight to Cubans calling for the island's independence. Many of these same Creoles were either enslavers or hailed from an elite class that slavery buttressed. As we saw with Quintero, they no doubt saw the contradiction of rallying arms for an independent Cuba while also countenancing the economic or social necessity of slavery. For some exiled filibusters, annexation promised the best protection of slavery, "but the vast majority of planters," especially in western Cuba, "were unwilling to free their slaves or to support an insurgency likely to encourage their mobilization."[9] Initially, Creole exiles tended to elide the question, sometimes using the familiar rhetoric of "slavery" as an ambiguous term that could refer to political or human bondage. However, by the mid-1850s, US politics and the abolition movement swayed some exiled Creoles toward a more radical position, with *El Mulato*'s editors and contributors embracing universal freedom as part of the island's anti-colonial independence, much to the chagrin of Cuban elites who wanted to skirt the issue and contra to trends on the island that saw it as "one of the principal consumers of African slaves specifically in the context of the rise and growing hegemony of antislavery."[10]

Gonzales did not remain in New York, though, nor did he own, operate, or edit a Spanish-language paper. His is not the story of the literary *filibusteros*, whose essays, poems, plays, and novels fashioned Cuban nationalism in exile in the pages of the Spanish-language press for transnational Hispanophone communities.[11] Instead, Gonzales waged a war for Cuba in the English-language papers, radiating from Georgia and the lowlands of South Carolina, where the Elliotts' Oak Lawn plantation served as his cultural ground zero during the mid-1850s. The difference between South Carolina as a slave society and New York as a society that benefited from slavery is pivotal for understanding the development of Gonzales's ideological alignment. In slave societies such as Cuba and South Carolina, Edward B. Rugemer explains, "slavery shaped everything from the aspirations of the poor to the political calculations of the rich," whereas in emergent, mercantile industrializing centers, such as New York, "slavery played a subordinate role" in competition with diverse labor resources, economies, and social structures.[12] It is for the latter reason that the mid-nineteenth-century Cuban cause in New York became increasingly abolitionist and more diverse in its literary and print cultures, but it is for the former reason that Gonzales's Cuban nationalism gave way to the Confederate cause and its brand of Southern independence that sought to protect slavery and white power.

Gonzales's War for Slavery

An 1849 letter to Caleb Cushing, the former Massachusetts congressman and filibustering *aficionado*, marks the opening moment of Gonzales's transition into a US-based white nationalism that will take hold in the South during and after the Civil War. "I have always been American *de jure*: so far as what a man carries in his heart can counter that right. But now, I am glad to say, that since Monday last, I am also *de facto*. . . . I have come to the determination of fixing my residence in this country now my own, until the day in which my native island shall also be a *land of the free*. I am deeply interested in becoming thoroughly acquainted with your, I should say, our, institutions and to practice the English language in connection with diplomatic business to all possible extent."[13] Nearly three decades later, Gonzales wrote another letter to solicit a diplomatic post of some sort—this time to then President Ulysses S. Grant. "Although my sympathies have always been with the Cubans," he writes to Grant, "I have taken no part in Cuban Movements since the time of Lopez expecting to act in the future as a citizen of the United States. When you were in Charleston, after the War, on a tour of inspections, I was one of a deputation of merchants and planters who called on you to request the removal of colored troops."[14] Between the two letters is the story about Gonzales's transformation into a US citizen-subject of Cuban birth whose fight for the protection of Southern white power is the embodiment of his Americanized Latinidad. In 1849 he set out to become "thoroughly acquainted with your, I should say, our, institutions," as he said to Cushing. His decision to become a US citizen is strategic, as he understands it as the best way to secure a paid political appointment in the US government, and his writing to Cushing is calculated. The Democrat politician did not hold a government post at the time, but Gonzales recognized their shared filibustering sympathies as a common cause. By 1876, his letter to Grant affirms that the Cuban has indeed mastered the institutionalized racism that props up white power as a perceived protected privilege of US citizenship, especially in the postwar South. He pleads to the former Union general to heed the region's white racial resentment and remove Black troops from Charleston.

How did Gonzales come to such a position, and more, how did that process lead the once eager Cuban filibuster away from the mission of Cuba's independence? After all, as he boasts to Grant, he did not participate in any more movements for Cuba after López, but what does his being a US citizen have to do with his later decision to forgo fighting for Cuban independence during the Ten Years' War? The answer, I think, lies in Gonzales's acculturation into the US South and his incorporation into its slave society. In the early years, he ambiguously advanced positions to preserve the practice of slavery and to protect the white racial power he enjoyed as an elite Creole, but his arguments for both took different forms the longer he stayed in the United States and adapted to South Carolinian culture: his adoption of the South's pre–Civil War politics transformed his push for Cuban independence into an advocacy for Southern nationalism that twinned the island's longtime struggle for liberation with South Carolina's growing secession movement, even though the question of Cuba's annexation was hotly contested among South Carolinians.[15]

Gonzales came to such a position slowly, for his initial writings about the island's independence took great pains to navigate the relationship between the López expeditions and slavery. He maintained the line that the liberation of Cuba through filibustering was an anti-colonial movement to allow the island to determine its fate: secure independence; join the United States by becoming part of its circum-Gulf Southern states; and, in either case, decide through self-governance the future of slavery on the island. In US Southern parlance, he was proffering a states' rights argument for Cuba. Comprised of Gonzales, Cirilo Villaverde, José Sánchez Iznaga and J. M. Macías, the Cuban Junta's first public announcement in the US press, for instance, walked the rhetorical line around slavery with familiar language in the United States about enslavement to tyranny. The *junta* announced that it will "serve as a centre for correspondence, with a view to concert to the thousands of noble spirits who, *in all sections of this Union*, sigh to behold the slavery and sufferings of Cuba, and long to contribute any aid, honorably and legitimately in their power, to her relief."[16] The proclamation conveys a keen understanding that in 1849 the issue of slavery divided the United States just as much as it vexed the island, so in an effort to appeal to "all sections of the Union," presumably Southern and Northern, the *junta*'s statement references "slavery and sufferings of Cuba" without clarifying whether slavery means chattel slavery or the symbolic political enslavement of white citizen-subjects. Seeking widespread support for the filibustering movement, the call means to be cagey. It invites Southerners to believe that they would be gaining Cuba as a slave region and leads Northerners to fancy that they would be liberating oppressed Cubans from the tyranny of the Spanish yoke and toward a "republican nationalism" that "embraced universal white-male suffrage, popular sovereignty, laissez-fair individualism (for whites), slavery, and territorial expansion."[17]

In a direct appeal to Mirabeau Buonaparte Lamar to solicit aid for the movement, Gonzales fed the pro-slavery expansionist politician-poet a healthy dose of the *junta*'s mastery of English-language duplicity by calling on Lamar to help in "the redemption of the hundreds of thousands of Cubans who labor under Spanish tyranny and the selfishness of a few of their own people."[18] With a significant population of enslaved Black people living on the island, free Creoles hardly did much "labor" in the sense of work, but Gonzales is using the word in the sense of having to endure, to suffer even, under the rule of the Spanish colonial government. The conflation of these two conditions—to work and to endure—is indicative of the great lengths Gonzales leveraged the English language to draw on a double structure of feeling in Anglo America: the prevailing nationalist sentiments of freedom and independence as the natural condition of white people and the equally prevailing panic that white people would be forced to live under conditions reserved for enslaved Black people. The Cuban's pitch for support even positioned Lamar as a potential liberator who could grant "redemption" (a term in the United States' slave culture that referred to the practice of purchasing the emancipation of an enslaved person) to the scores of Cubans ostensibly held in political bondage. The telling aspect of Gonzales's rhetoric is not that he's familiar with the discourses of white slavery, which was common rhetoric at the time, but that his rhetoric draws on the language of enslavement but does not include the enslaved in his vision of a free Cuba. Gonzales likely did not see the enslaved Blacks on the island as "Cubans," and he certainly did not think that they warranted the same independence as their free Creole counterparts.

For instance, the *junta* made clear in a private letter to General John A. Quitman, whom they were recruiting to head the filibustering expedition after failing to secure William J. Worth, Robert E. Lee, and Jefferson Davis, that Cuban independence meant annexation into the Union as a Southern slaveholding region that liberated whites from Spanish rule but kept Black people in bondage.[19] "The freedom of Cuba and her annexation to the United States with the least possible effusion of blood," the *junta* wrote to Quitman in 1850 from New York, "have been resolved upon by several patriots and property-holders of Cuba now residing here. . . . Having one common interest with the Southern States, we ask their protection and aid." The *junta* further requested that if Quitman were to lead the mission, he would agree to take care to avoid poor, disorganized planning or any other strategic mishaps that might, in the end, "be more favorable to emancipation of the blacks than to the freedom of the whites."[20] Knowing that Quitman and his Southern circle were already circulating secessionist rhetoric, the *junta* sought to recruit the Mississippi governor's pro-slavery stance, as well as his reputable military experience, as double solutions to Cuba's independence: a well-led military expedition on the island that ousted Spanish rule but kept slavery intact, guaranteeing "freedom" for whites without extending "emancipation" to Blacks. Five years later, José Agustín Quintero even published a Spanish-language biography of Quitman, presumably to introduce him to Cuban and Hispanophone readers "por cuya independencia i libertad politica, nuestro heroe ha sentido siempre hondas simpatias" (for whose independence and political freedom, our hero has always felt deep sympathies).[21] "Now," John McCardell concludes about this 1850 moment, "the character and purpose of filibustering changed: it became a tool for creating a southern nationality and precipitating secession."[22]

By 1854, sectionalism and the problem of slavery became the dividing line in the Cuba debate, with *El Mulato* launching the opening salvo against the Creole caginess about the issue. The paper, Lazo explains, "unmasked how the racial ideology of filibustering and annexation rested on an ambivalence between a claim to Cuba based on Creole (and thus unstated white) right to land and a simultaneous refusal to discuss race and the influence of Africa and slaves on the island's society."[23] Gonzales promptly lambasted *El Mulato* in a *Washington Daily Union* editorial that discredited the "hybrid" organ as representative of the Cuban cause: "The 'Mulato,'" Gonzales proclaims, "is no Cuban paper" but an "abolitionist sheet of very small dimensions and much smaller influence." He continues in a telling description of the Cuban newspaper scene,

> The "Verdad," established in New York as far back as 1847, and supported for gratuitous circulation by Cuban patriotism, was the first organ of the Cubans in the United States. It still exists, and no accusation has been brought against it for misrepresenting Cuban interests in regard to slavery. The "Cubano," the "Correo de Ambos Mundos," and the "Filibustero," in New York; the "Beacon" and the "Independiente," in New Orleans, have been co-laborers of La Verdad in the work of Cuban regeneration, and have abstained from meddling with the question of domestic slavery, which, Cuba being free, will, as naturally as in South Carolina, take good care of itself. The separation of Cuba from Spain has been the goal of the aspirations of all true patriots.

At first glance, Gonzales's position applauds the Creole avoidance of the slavery question, but in the process, he introduces an analogy between Cuba and South Carolina that culturally translates for his Anglophone readers the fight for Cuba in the Spanish-language press. In fact, Gonzales's impetus for penning the piece is not to chastise *El Mulato*'s abolitionist stance per se, but to correct a *Charleston Evening News* report that *El Mulato* revealed the true "scheme" of Cuban annexation: "*universal* liberty with abolitionism." Such a statement, Gonzales assures the Southern Democrat-leaning readership of the *Union*, is far "from being founded on fact." Instead, he insists that the Cuban cause is akin to South Carolina's supposed sovereignty.[24]

What is also telling about his *Union* editorial is his familiarity with the Spanish-language press as well as his distance from it. Obviously, Gonzales kept abreast of the main Spanish organs out of New York and

New Orleans; he's an avid reader of English-language periodicals too, such as the *Charleston Evening News* and the *Charleston Messenger*. Yet, keeping true to his plan to "practice the English language," as he wrote to Cushing in 1849, Gonzales seems to have primarily written to and for the Anglophone press, with nary an extant publication in any of the *filibustero* sheets, some of which were founded, printed, or edited by his early *junta* compatriots. His dexterity with English might be one reason for his choice of venues, though Spanish was his native language. His sense of audience might be another reason: from the start, Gonzales's mission was to elicit support for the López expeditions from Anglo-Americans. Whatever the case, his decision to write to and for the Anglophone press points to a significant moment in nineteenth-century Latinx literary and cultural history. It signals a shift in the direction, readership, and reception of writings by and about Latinx subjects from a Hispanophone minority community to an English-speaking majority readership. There are very few Latinx writers during the 1850s deliberately, directly, and consistently engaging Anglo-American readers in English about the hot-button issues pressuring Latinxs across the United States. Perhaps only Miguel Otero, the New Mexican politician and fellow Latino-in-law to a South Carolina family of enslavers, engaged the English-language public so directly in his writings before the war, but throughout the nineteenth century, Gonzales was the most prolific Latinx published writer in English about Cuba, the Confederacy, and Cuban independence before, during, and after the Civil War. Even after López's death, he continued to make the case for Cuba to Anglophone readers, putting him well before María Amparo Ruiz de Burton or Loreta Janeta Velazquez as our first Southern Latinx writer whose investment in the South estranged him from his respective Latinx community.

In an 1853 letter to Caleb Cushing, for instance, Gonzales distanced himself from the *junta*'s activities in New York, claiming "that to such movements I have been & am an absolute stranger."[25] A year later, he announced in the *New York Times* his departure from the *filibusteros* entirely: "I prefer, for the present, the action of the Government to that of individuals. Should my confidence in the former ever be shaken, I shall go with the foremost for that 'ultima ratio *civis*,' in favor of oppressed humanities: the right to expatriation, and of meeting the tyrant hand to hand upon the soil he desecrates."[26] In private, he further explained to

Laurent Sigur, former filibuster and editor of the *New Orleans Delta*, that he has "kept aloof" from the *junta* because of "the antislavery notions of its members & my utter dislike of the personal character of others."[27] So, after the New York *junta* reconstituted itself in 1852, leaving Gonzales out of a leadership position, he seems to have decided to become the self-appointed spokesperson for Cuban affairs in the pages of the *New York Herald*, the *New York Times*, and the *Washington Daily Union*, among other organs, penning articles, letters, and announcements to make the case for Cuba to the American reading public. His is a different imagined community, then: not the robust literary, cultural, and political production of Cuban exiles who imagined, fashioned, and debated the fate of the island, but the heated arena of Anglophone papers, where Cuba hung in the balance of US politics, sectionalism, expansionism, and abolitionism. Not surprisingly, the South's growing secessionist and nationalist movement influenced Gonzales and his writings, leading his war for the Cuban cause to become an argument for slavery and white power that appealed to the Southern sentiments of his Anglophone readers. His letter to the *Times*, for instance, announced his break from the New York *junta* as a secession: the "right to expatriation," as Gonzales puts it, is what South Carolinians were calling their movement to break from the Union in the 1850s.

Gonzales found a kin figure in his father-in-law, William Elliott, a South Carolina politician who maintained a Unionist stance to his political peril until he embraced the Confederacy after secession.[28] The two men were Masons, and a year after Gonzales's 1856 marriage to Elliott's youngest daughter, Elliott published in installments his account of traveling through Cuba at a time when travel narratives to the island were a popular genre for Northerners and Southerners to advance arguments for or against annexation, slavery, and Cuba's racial compatibility with the United States. "A Trip to Cuba" is a literary probing of the island's potential as an annexed slave state. Elliott takes a coy position on the filibustering movement proper, supporting it in spirit but balking at it in practice, but he makes apparent the attraction Cuba held for the US South's slaveholding class and its related racial codes. En route to Key West, for instance, he reflects on the war then being waged against the Seminole, the so-called Third Seminole War: "While the brave, indomitable Indian dies in battle, or pines away in imprisonment, the African, in the self-same connection, thrives best, and reaches his highest elevation, in the conditions of a slave!"[29] Further, he outright concludes that it is Cuba's slave system that makes it such a prosperous island in relation to the rest of the Caribbean and, by extension, makes it the best option for annexation: "The peculiar source of the prosperity of Cuba then, is, her possession of slave labor! She owns six hundred thousand slaves!," and whoever controls Cuba's slave system, the South Carolina planter salivates, inherits the wealth to be gained from African labor.[30] If his isn't an open statement for annexation, it is one that sees the protection of slavery on the island as paramount to the protection of the peculiar institution in the United States.

Gonzales echoed Elliott's position, articulating it across a handful of published newspaper pieces that called on the Monroe Doctrine to protect slavery on the island. The Spanish government's effort to increase African and Chinese laborers, the Cuban argued, amounted to a form of racial colonization that threatened white interests across the Americas. In an 1854 editorial admonishing the Pierce administration for its inaction against the so-called Africanization of Cuba by way of Spain's plan for Black labor apprenticeship, Gonzales proclaims, "Mr. Monroe was called upon to meet a certain case—the schemes of Europe through white colonization. The present executive [Pierce] may find himself constrained to oppose the much more evil ones through black apprenticeship. In that, the European system was rejected; in this, the African should be, with all of its barbarism and concomitant results." Gonzales's missive trucked in familiar formulations of white fright, often noting that Blacks outnumbered whites on the island, that slavery tended to keep Blacks in check, and that the large-scale program of the importation of Blacks and Chinese as indentured labor was tantamount to Spain weaponizing the island's racial tensions. "Shall Spain be allowed to trade in slavery . . . and deluge her West India islands with ferocious Africans, while England . . . hangs over us—Cubans and Americans—like Damocles' sword, the dread of their sudden liberation; which means the ruin to our commerce, destruction to our interests, and the obliteration of our race in Cuba and Porto Rico?"[31] He was, in part, describing the Spanish regime's deliberate program of keeping the Creole revolution in check by increasing the importation of Black people, loosening the social codes separating the races, and threatening universal emancipation. By

1854, his characterization of the crisis had an uncanny ring to his Anglophone readership, with Gonzales presuming in his writings a common white cause in the protections of "our race" in the circum-Gulf South.

As his possessive plural pronoun further suggests, Gonzales found in Southern white nationalism arguments for Cuban independence that mimicked anti-colonial struggle, on the one hand, and provided an answer to the problem of Cuba's slave question, on the other. A series of pieces on Cuba that he published in the *Detroit Free Press* in 1858 and 1859 give expression to the "shifting grounds" of his Southern nationalism and also highlight the degree to which the Cuban's writings can and should be recovered as part of a Southern Latinx literary heritage.[32] While his 1853 *Manifesto on Cuba* is widely understood as the Cuban's position on the island's independence, the more obscure installment pieces in the *Free Press* point to the transformation of Gonzales's thinking about Cuba, slavery, race, and his place in the South in the five years that separate the *Manifesto*, published in New Orleans, and the *Free Press* articles, published in Detroit. The difference between the two outlets is significant. The *Manifesto* appeared in pamphlet form by way of New Orleans's *Daily Delta* press. Considering its location, print venue, and appearance a few years after the López expeditions, the *Manifesto*'s argument for Cuban independence makes sense in the way that it aligns American revolutionary rhetoric with Cuban grievances over taxation without representation, lack of a free press, and the restriction of personal liberties: "The Cuban is, moreover, deprived of all liberty of conscience, of speech, and of the press," Gonzales proclaims in the *Manifesto*. Further, to a Southern audience that would understand the nuance of his point, he continues about the slave trade, "Through this horrid traffic, declared piracy by existing treaties, and secretly connived at by the cabinet of Madrid, it is estimated that over half a million of human beings have been imported into Cuba since 1846. . . . While slaves and Asiatics are thus introduced, white colonization is discountenanced, that the threat of a colored population may be held to the Cubans, while 24,000 bayonets are pointed at their breasts."[33] With the same rhetorical dexterity as the *junta* communiqué, Gonzales's *Manifesto* advances a brand of white Creole republican nationalism that uses American revolutionary rhetoric and anti-slavery language to drum up white fright of being outnumbered by Black people. His characterization of the slave trade as "horrid traffic," for instance, invokes an objection to the trade that appeals to white racial hysteria: it is "horrid" because, if left unchecked, the trafficking of enslaved will bring too many Blacks to the region. It is a stance against the slave trade, in other words, because of the threat it ostensibly poses to white people.

In 1858 Gonzales selected an unlikely organ for his second extended writings about Cuba at the request of James Orr, the staunch secessionist and pro-slavery Democratic Speaker of the House who proffered the need to reopen the African slave trade.[34] The *Detroit Free Press* was at the time a hotbed of the Democratic cause for Northern readers. Before Wilbur Fisk Storey became the editor of the *Chicago Times* during the Civil War, he ran the *Free Press* from 1853 to 1861, and his commitment to reactionary Democratic politics led him to edit a vitriolic newspaper that focused its attention on whipping up racism against Black people and, in conjunction, puffing states' rights over the federal government when it came to deciding the issue of slavery. Two core beliefs structured Storey's editorship, Justin E. Walsh explains: "First, racism," and second, "the unquestioned supremacy of the state governments vis-à-vis the central government." Put bluntly, "Underlying all of Storey's other convictions was the certitude that the Anglo-Saxon race was ordained by the Almighty to spread the blessings of American liberty to all in the Western Hemisphere except Negroes. . . . At best, in his view, the Negro was a subhuman species who should preferably return to Africa, but under no circumstances was it possible for him to co-inhabit the continent with white men in freedom."[35] Racial fear about free Blacks, abolitionists, and Black enfranchisement litter the paper's editorials and news coverage, alongside running commentary about Congress, South Carolina's emerging secessionist sentiments, and advertisements for sugar, molasses, coffee, syrup, cigars, and sundry spices, all for sale on arrival by way of New Orleans. So it is not exactly the place of publication that makes Gonzales's writing Southern. It is the sentiments of his writings that go south: the *Free Press* proved to be the perfect venue for Gonzales to write about Cuba and its independence in the language of Southern white nationalism emerging from his adopted state.[36]

Gonzales penned his Cuba series from the Elliott family's Oak Lawn, South Carolina, plantation, between October 1858 and January 1859. The introductory article ran in the November 25, 1858, issue, with the editorial announcement that the installments would be a series of informational pieces about Cuba "by one of the best Cuban minds," with the intent to inform toward annexation.[37] The series is similar to a variety of pieces about Cuba in circulation at the time (some of which Gonzales quotes and references) and should be considered within the Anglophone genres about the island: speeches, addresses, public pleadings, travel accounts, novels, histories, and extended op-ed columns all weighed the merits or risks of annexing the island for American readers. The opening salvo makes clear that Gonzales is entering the same debate: "Such is, in fact, [Cuba's] importance to the Union, that her relation to it may almost be viewed as of a domestic character." His is an expansionist position about Cuba, seeing it as practically a part of the Union and thus unnecessarily apart from it in the same way that John O'Sullivan imagined the future annexation of California and the rest of Mexico's far northern frontier as a foregone conclusion of a destiny made manifest.[38] He goes so far as to explain the proper relevance of Manifest Destiny in relation to the Cuba question: "'Manifest Destiny,' so often quoted, so seldom understood, simply the obvious relation in *our* political sphere between cause and effect, or in other words, the visible process of *our* characteristic national political gravitation, is written in this great conquest of *our* people and institutions, for, unlike any other power in ancient or modern times, through peace *we* conquer."[39]

Behind the somewhat convoluted explanation of O'Sullivan's mantra, Gonzales's statement betrays the competing interests of his Southern cause by way of a pronoun slippage that recalls his 1849 letter to Cushing and his invocation of "our race" in the May 3, 1854, *Washington Daily Union* editorial.[40] In the first and second instances above, "our" references an American citizenry, the very same "Anglo-Saxon" advance guard O'Sullivan imagines en route to California, of which Gonzales fancies himself a part in adoption and spirit. "Our political sphere" and "our characteristic national political gravitation" refer to the United States and its people, and Gonzales sees himself as a citizen-subject of both. However, in the third instance—"the great conquest of our people and institutions"—his use of "our" refers to Cubans and Cuba, seeing Manifest Destiny as a *fait accompli* on the island. It's a subtle rhetorical gesture that splits the plural possessive pronoun, making it refer in two directions at once, with a Hegelian annexationist synthesis in the end:

"through peace *we* conquer." The slippage in referent is significant for the way it traces Gonzales's shifting nationalism and his process of incorporating his *cubanidad* into the ideologies of Americanization that leaves his self-referentiality as confused as his explanation of Manifest Destiny:

> Born in Cuba, but educated in the United States, of which I have been more than fifteen years a resident; an American by alliance, engaged for the last ten years in the cause of Cuban annexation, formerly as a Cuban, in the field, and for several years in the character of an American citizen, I trust that I may claim to speak for both my native and adopted lands words of a union which it is my pride humbly to impersonate, believing, as I do, that upon that union depends nearly all that is dearest to the American and the Cuban heart.[41]

Unlike most of the other fissured, fractured, or embattled Latinxs on the Civil War front, Gonzales envisions himself as a unified subject with bi-national filiations. His is a strikingly modern claim to be both a Cuban and an American, a "Cuban-American" who is not split or divided between the two positions but at "union" with them at "heart." His declaration is reason enough to agree with Antonio Rafael de la Cova that at first, like his father-in-law, Gonzales was a steadfast Unionist, whose political stance mirrors his personal understanding of his identity.[42] But the glue that holds the hyphen between Cuban and American is Gonzales's unflagging belief in white racial superiority. Put another way, we see how Cuba's anti-colonial independence movement, as it was articulated by elite exiles like Gonzales, was ideological cover for the island's master class to promulgate political independence from Spain but preserve the island's slave structure and economy, independently or in confederation with the United States, where whites were a socially and politically protected ruling class in the North and the South. "The growing increase of the free colored population of Cuba," Gonzales says of Cuba after comparing the island to Virginia, "is, to my mind, the very reason why she should pass as speedily as possible into safer hands than those of her present rulers."[43]

Writing to make the situation of Cuba legible to Southern readers, he further explains, "The population of Cuba is, like that of our southern states, composed of but two races—the pure, dominant, energetic white race, and the African. . . . The majority of the former are Cubans which means *white natives*." The equivocation here is important, for while the phrase "our southern states" indicates that Gonzales imagines himself speaking to Southerners as a fellow white citizen-subject, his explanation of Cubans as "white natives" indicates the degree to which he must still insist on the argument of Creole racial identity as the same as Southern whiteness. He goes on: "The word Creole is equally misapplied; it is used sometimes in this country to designate a mixed race of blacks and whites; but a creole means a Cuban born, as contradistinguished from the Spaniard or foreigner; if the word mulatto or negro is appended to it, or if used when speaking of blacks, it means a Cuban born mulatto or negro, to distinguish him from the imported African or mulatto."[44] Elite Latinxs throughout the nineteenth century labored to broker their "off-whiteness" into the Anglo-American political system, often going to great lengths to insist or imagine Latinx white purity as either an antidote to disenfranchisement or an answer to the United States' blanket racism against racial others.[45] Gonzales here is no different from, say, Miguel Otero, María Amparo Ruiz de Burton, or José Agustín Quintero, all of whom fancied white Latinidad along similar south-by-southwest axes. However, Gonzales doesn't labor to make the case that white Latinidad is adjacent to Anglo-American whiteness. Instead, his writings incorporate Creole whiteness into the South's brand of white nationalism that militantly upholds slavery and the race-based politics of slave culture society.

As with all nationalisms, Southern nationalism, especially on the eve of secession, wasn't monolithic. Southerners held vexed Unionist sentiments during these heady years, with outright calls for secession—like the nullification movement years earlier—seen as a radical fringe position. The more tempered tended to balance their sense of nationalism between personal feelings for the sovereignty of their home state and political filiation for the United States, if not as a nation than as a political institution of federal representative governance.[46] As it gained momentum, Southern nationalism accrued different, sometimes competing structures of feeling. Some proclaimed Southerners to be the true bearers of the spirit of 1776; others argued for a distinct Southern culture in language and literature; and still others looked toward revolutions in Europe as models for nation building. Despite its different forms, though,

Southern nationalism had one common cause: "Already dependent upon racial arguments to defend the logic of their social system and their daily lives," Drew Gilpin Faust explains, "southerners eagerly embraced the notion of a racially determined nationalism."[47] A better way to put this might be that, regardless of the thread of nationalism emerging from the South, its mission was always the preservation of white power and the protection of the enslavement of Black people. Moreover, in South Carolina, "overt appeals for the protection and extension of slavery rather than notions of southern liberty and honor inspired the secession movement."[48]

That Gonzales is writing from the Elliott family plantation is in this regard significant, for while his Creole counterparts waffled on the problem of slavery, Gonzales used the English-language press to advance an argument for Cuba's independence through the language of Southern nationalism and its entwined *sine qua non*: slavery and white power. "No intelligent American need be told," Gonzales continues in his article on labor in Cuba, "that slave labor is, if not more so, as necessary in Cuba for the cultivation of her staples as it is in South Carolina for that of rice and cotton. . . . This labor is in jeopardy from a continuation of political and economic disturbing agencies, and must carry in its fall the labor of the South, and thus directly and indirectly endanger the happiness, the peace, and the prosperity of the other sections of the Union."[49] In language and sentiment, Gonzales molded and modeled his arguments for Cuban independence along the same lines that Southern nationalists were calling for the South's independence from the Union, giving rise to a Southern Latinx literary production that looked away from the Spanish-language press. Instead, with the *Free Press* Cuba pieces, he launched a mission for Cuba to Southern nationalists who, at the time, were so invested in preserving slavery and its racial structures that the island seemed more of a liability than a solution to the South's peculiar institution.

On the congressional floor, South Carolina representative W. W. Boyce argued against the annexation of Cuba, and Gonzales's *Free Press* pieces read like point-by-point rebuttals to the statesman. Boyce maintains, among other things, that free states would benefit most from Cuba because slavery on the island would cripple the South's economy through the importation of tariff-free plantation products that would continue to bolster Northern markets and manufacturing. He also notes with considerable anxiety Cuba's free Black population, pointing out that "our free negroes are American free negroes, dwarfed by being in contrast with the greatest white race on the globe," while "the free negros of Cuba are Spanish free negroes, elevated relatively by going in contrast with an inferior white race." Finally, in what speaks to the direct opposite of Gonzales's arguments, Boyce maintains, "There is only one race of people in modern times who have shown the capability of self government, that is the Anglo-Saxon race. . . . The Spanish Creole race of Cuba are the worst kind of materials with which to build up republican institutions," because, Boyce explains, "for the last thirty years in particular, they have lived under martial law. They have had no political privileges, and are utterly ignorant of the machinery of free institutions."[50] South Carolina planter, enslaver, and former nullificationist Lewis M. Ayer Jr. reiterated Boyce's position in a July 4, 1855, speech delivered at Whippy Swamp. Notable for its fiery stance against the federal government on the patriotic occasion, Ayer proclaimed that Cuban annexation would inhibit Southern independence by embroiling the South in a foreign war, when resources could be better spent establishing a Southern Confederacy: "It would cost us more men and more money . . . to take and hold Cuba twelve months," he announces, "than it would to establish the undisputed and undisturbed existence of our Southern Confederacy forever."[51]

Gonzales's arguments for Cuba rebut the points by his South Carolina counterparts, which explains why his *Free Press* pieces broker in the language of slavery and white power. His engagement with the Anglophone press has put him on the front lines of a crusade that labors to argue for Cuba's relevance to the South in the wake of South Carolinians' rejection of the island's pull. Gonzales's penultimate piece speaks to pundits opposed to Cuba's annexation, including James H. Hammond, who in October 29, 1858, gave a speech at Barnwell Court House in South Carolina that addressed the question of Cuba in the aftermath of the Kansas-Nebraska Act: "We might expand slavery by acquiring Cuba," Hammond postulates, "where African slavery is already established. . . . But if we had Cuba, we could not make more than two or three slave States there; while . . . she would, besides crushing out our whole sugar culture by her competition, afford in a few years a market for all the slavery in Missouri, Kentucky, and Maryland."[52] To "dissipate the fears of Senator Hammond," Gonzales rejoins two months later, citing a Spanish colonial fiscal report proclaiming "That from *natural reproduction, the slave trade once abolished, the necessary slave labor can be obtained in Cuba*."[53] His is a strange stance. He corroborates Hammond's fear that Cuba's slave population will jeopardize the South's slave economy because of the availability of slaves on the island. However, it is not the argument per se that is significant as much as it is the conversation that Gonzales is joining in the first place. Citing and translating Spanish colonial documents, the *New York Tribune*, the *Edinburgh Review*, the *Kingston Journal* (out of Jamaica), Hammond himself, and even his own father-in-law's travel narrative in *Russell's Magazine*, Gonzales makes the case to his Anglophone Democrat readers that, contrary to growing sentiment otherwise, Cuba provides a significant slave society that can help to protect and sustain the South's slave system in the face of abolition or disunion—that, in effect, annexation is the solution to protecting the slave society of Cuba and the US South.

Gonzales shared with Southerners one key sentiment that fell out of public favor with many Cuban exiles: slavery. "I believe that God created negroes for no other purpose," Hammond proclaimed, than "to be the slaves of the white race; and I wish to see them in that capacity on every spot on the surface of the globe where their labor is necessary or beneficial."[54] On this point, the Cuban agreed, noting in his final piece that, among the other annexationist arguments for Cuba, the most pressing is that the island presents a natural bulwark against the rising tide of Black emancipation and abolition: "In *our* hands she would form a wall against the negro system of Jamaica and St. Domingo: possessed of Cuba, practical abolitionism would turn her guns against *us*, and any maritime power would be enabled to use her to *our* injury."[55] With a return to his most telling pronoun, Gonzales goes Deep South in his last *Free Press* piece, speaking to Cuba's cause as a white Southerner would to protect the South's slave society from the fear of Black emancipation and the imagined onslaught of abolitionist attack. He likely always held pro-slavery sentiments, but while other exiles inched toward abolition on the island, Gonzales trenched further into the pro-slavery stance to the point that his arguments for Cuban independence became Southern nationalist in word and spirit. His position was not just rhetorical. When

South Carolina seceded, Gonzales threw in with Southern nationalism *de facto*, as he once put it, by volunteering to serve in the CSA. "Gonzales now supplanted the fight for Cuban freedom," de la Cova says, "with the independence struggle of his adopted state."[56] As the *Free Press* installments make clear, the "one cause" between his two flags, to recall Jefferson Davis's purported praise of Gonzales, is his war for the preservation of slavery as the last stand for the protection of presumed white freedom and independence across Cuba and the Confederacy.

Defending the Self

When Gonzales decided to join the secessionists, he was choosing to fight for slavery through a logic that understood Cuba and the Confederacy as extended home fronts of white nationalism presumed to be under siege by Spain's weaponized threat of emancipation on the island and the Union's militant abolitionism from the North. The urgency with which he tendered his services speaks to his commitment to the cause, and the type of service he offered reflects the Cuban's strategic martial spirit. A skilled marksman, he proposed that the Maynard Rifle Company hire him to be their paid arms dealer to the Confederate army; he offered his service as chief of artillery; and he proposed and oversaw the fortification of the South Carolina coastline. If he saw battle action, he did not write about it but instead worked most effectively as a defensive strategist with a keen vision for mobilizing forces and arms across terrain he knew well. It is difficult not to sense that his experience with planning an island invasion of Cuba informed his proposal to Jefferson Davis to fortify Edisto Island, with its "5,000 negroes and one hundred or so odd voters," off the South Carolina coast, as "an omnipresent fort along the whole extent of our seaboard."[57] With some modification, Davis took up Gonzales's proposal, but he did not take up his requests for promotion: the two carried on a brief but bitter war of words when Davis passed up Gonzales's repeated petitions for a generalship in favor of friends and former West Point classmates of the Confederacy's president, as Gonzales accused.

We might even say that Gonzales's frustration with Davis resulted from his hitting the Creole glass ceiling—the same one that his friend and childhood classmate, General P. G. T. Beauregard, hit with the CSA president after the Battle of Corinth. After over a decade in the United States as a naturalized citizen who married into an elite family of enslavers and worked assiduously to argue for white rights and the protection of slavery through a brand of nationalism that envisioned the annexation of Cuba as part of the Southern cause, Gonzales reached the limits of his assimilation into the Confederacy even as he served to protect the Confederate front. When he finally did receive promotion to lieutenant colonel and chief of artillery, he took his praise to the press in a piece anonymously published in the *Charleston Daily Courier* that bears a striking resemblance to his hand and contains details specific to the fight with Davis he had waged a year prior:

> No citizen, native or adopted, has labored more zealously, efficiently, and disinterestedly for South Carolina since the opening of the war, than General A. J. GONZALES, as he is known to his friends. He bears the title of General, not from a militia pastime, but from active and honorable service under another flag, but for the cause of Independence and Self-Government, now involved in the contest of the South against the North. Although of military studies, habits, and experience, General GONZALES was not in the line of promotion, not being a West Pointer, and has accordingly served thus far without adequate commission or reward, beyond the consciousness of duty, and the flattering testimonials of all under whose commands he has acted.[58]

Referencing the private war of words Gonzales exchanged with Davis in which he accused the Confederate president of nepotism, the anonymous piece narrates the process by which Gonzales became recognized as a South Carolinian. The article is a testament to the culturally familiar American story of his transformation from a Cuban national to a US citizen who, through hard work, perseverance, and loyalty, accomplished military and social promotion in the war for "Independence and Self-Government," despite his lack of West Point credentials. This could be the story of Benjamin Franklin, Frederick Douglass, or any number of Latinx subjects who survive ethnic Americanization, save for the detail that independence and self-government under the Confederate banner constitutes an active investment in white power and privilege that Gonzales fought to protect. De la Cova notes that

Gonzales's "self-aggrandizement usually appeared in his correspondence when he suffered great stress," as he did in his campaign against Davis, but I venture that such "self-aggrandizement" is evident as well in the *Courier*'s anonymous pieces, marking them as Gonzales's embattled autobiographical entries.[59]

Besides official letters, orders, and other forms of military records, Gonzales's presence in print during the Civil War years takes the form of third-person snippets in the *Charleston Daily Courier* that suggest that the Cuban Confederate heeded Hattie's advice: "Tis a miserable thing to be a great man in this country," she tells her husband. "I want you to have your promotion advanced in the papers. No one will know of it if you do not have it noticed."[60] Whether by his hand or a friendly editor's, the *Courier* promoted and defended Gonzales with as much gusto and strategy as the Cuban protected the South. The press touted his successes, aired his grievances, and preserved his commitment to the Confederacy in print, often with his name shouted in capital letters: GONZALES. The pieces in the *Courier*, which was a Confederate organ, refer to Gonzales under his rank as general in López's filibustering army rather than his designation as lieutenant colonel in the Confederate army, and the entries often praise his military duties when Gonzales felt he was not getting his due from the Confederate leadership. "No citizen has done more without office for South Carolina and the South, since the commencement of the present war, than A. J. Gonzales," the *Courier* again announced. "He spent two months in Richmond, directing and urging the foundry operations, which gave us some valuable supplies of ordnance. That some of these pieces of ordnance were lost at Port Royal was not the fault of any engineering or plan of Gen. Gonzales. . . . Through all this course of service he has gone without regular commission or position, although every list of appointments has contained names of men less qualified."[61] The *Charleston Mercury* followed suit with its own notice that echoes Gonzales's tendency for hyperbolic self-praise: "Among the many who, since this contest began, have constantly and ungrudgingly bestowed all their energies for the advancement of the Cause, without ever having receiving adequate acknowledgement of their services, is Gen. A. J. Gonzales."[62]

True to his initial mission of using the press to muster support for the López expeditions, Gonzales seems to have leveraged Charleston's two

Confederate papers to preserve and protect his reputation, actions, and record of service. When General Beauregard rebuffed Gonzales's complaints that his roles as chief of artillery and ordnance had him doing double duty that warranted a promotion, an extended piece that reads like a résumé of Gonzales's Confederate service appeared in the April 26, 1863, *Courier*. "The manner in which the duties of this post—or of the two posts combined, the Artillery and Ordnance being generally separated—deserves special regard and commemoration. The Chief of Artillery and Ordnance is Col. A. J. Gonzales. . . . Fertile in resources and prolific in suggestions, he is ever eagerly ready and willing to receive, apply and acknowledge the suggestions of others." Given his voracious appetite for reading and writing to a variety of newspapers, Gonzales understood the fortifications of print, for even if his bids for promotion were often rebuffed, his general orders often reversed, or his proposed defensive works and fortifications credited to higher-ranking officers, he ensured that his standing and reputation as an unwavering Confederate remained intact among the readers who mattered to him most: the real and imagined community of South Carolina's white readership. His use of the press also strategically entwined him with General P. G. T. Beauregard, who often denied Gonzales's requests but held the rank the Cuban Confederate coveted: "Apart from his military skill and inclinations," the *Courier* piece concludes, "the most prominent trait in his mind is a devoted love for his Chief and General, to whom in his person he bears a resemblance, which is often noticed, and which with the same uniform might confound any but the most discriminative eyes."[63]

As a CSA colonel and chief of artillery, Gonzales armed, supplied, fortified, and worked to protect the South Carolina and Georgia low country "in defence of this State where my family reside," he explained to Jefferson Davis.[64] Yet, while his extant military letters are scant on details of direct military action, his anonymous print pieces stage a different civil war. Sometimes, the language of the pieces closely matched his official dispatches; other times, their timing corresponded with his military movements. On October 31, 1861, for instance, one month after Gonzales requested promotion from Davis, the *Charleston Daily Courier* posted a short notice that "Gen. A. J. Gonzales has arrived on a brief visit. He is engaged with characteristic zeal and energy in public defences, in which field he has done and is doing noble service." A week later, the *Courier* further crowed, "Gen. A. J. Gonzales is ready and prepared to do duty as a full private in one of the regiments now engaged in the defence of our coast. He has labored ably, perseveringly and zealously, as far as he has been permitted to do, for the public defence, and without adequate position or recognition."[65] The British spelling of "defence" in Gonzales's private letter to Davis and in the *Courier* announcements is perhaps an indication that they're by the same hand, and even if they're not, their confluence invites a double entendre that connects Gonzales's military maneuvers to his rhetorical salvos of self-vindication. His "engagement in public defences" could refer as much to his anonymous print pieces as it does to his proposed plans for the South Carolina coast. He pursued the latter in defense of the South and penned the former in self-defense. He was wily in this way, waging a form of discursive warfare that outflanked his Confederate leadership, for even though he never garnered a generalship in the CSA, the Cuban colonel referred to himself as "General" in newsprint in recognition of the title he carried in Narciso López's insurgent army of freebooters. The title stuck with him in public and private writings well after the US Civil War ended. He promoted himself.

Raising the Dead

Gonzales's postwar life probably produced more trauma than his days fortifying the South Carolina lowlands and squabbling with Jeff Davis. After the war, he took Hattie and their growing family to Cuba, much to the dismay of the Elliott family. Even General Beauregard offered a word of caution to his Creole counterpart. "I hope you do better in Cuba," he wrote after receiving a note from Gonzales about his postwar struggle to become financially stable, "although matters there appear 'Trés en broilléss.' You may, ere long, find yourself in the midst of another revolution. Your past experiences will give you, at once, an important position there, should you desire to take a part in the coming struggle."[66] He had no desire to do so. Spanish authorities watched him closely, and the island's growing revolutionary movement was more inclined to emancipate the enslaved than it was during Gonzales's early days. He would in later letters state that he avoided participating in the Ten Years' War because he was acting and living as "an American citizen," and as de la Cova shows,

Gonzales seemed earnestly intent on trying to resettle in Cuba, although why he would return there with his young family during the island's growing civil turmoil is unclear. Perhaps he fancied himself as part of the exiled Confederate class that migrated to Cuba, Mexico, and greater Latin America out of a sense of defeat, a resentment of the Union, a rejection of the idea of living among free Black people, or a fantasy for a new Confederacy further south. Either way, the "former revolutionary and Confederate chief of artillery," de la Cova explains, affirmed to Cuban officials "that he was there 'to make a support of his family' and not to succor the new independence movement."[67]

The trip to Cuba proved fatal. Shortly after giving birth to her daughter Ana Rose, Hattie contracted yellow fever and died on the island in September 1869. Her death did long-lasting, irreparable damage to Gonzales's relationship with the Elliotts and with his own children, who, after spending a short time in Cuba, returned to South Carolina to be raised by the Elliott family while Gonzales struggled to find the economic means and social clout he enjoyed in the 1850s. Hattie's death and its familial aftermath left Gonzales alienated from his children and most of the Elliott clan.[68] Her death also sparked the Cuban's turn to spiritualism later in life, culminating with the publication of *Heaven Revealed*, his 1889 collection of spirit writings ostensibly from Hattie, who by then had been twenty years deceased. The necro narrative should be understood in its personal and cultural context. It registers Gonzales's deep mourning, his loneliness and isolation from his family, and in older age, his longing for his wife. While readers of the time—and now—might have grave skepticism about spirit writings, the book registers Gonzales's profound sadness. It should also be put in relation to the history of spirit writings of the day and the debates that spiritualism raised at the time. There is no doubt that Gonzales believed in the spirit messages he was receiving—at one point, he mentions to his eldest son, Ambrose, that he speaks to Hattie and her father (William Elliott), and he includes a sample spirit message from them to him in a letter as proof.[69] However, in the late 1880s the skepticism over spiritualism was at a fever pitch. Convened at the bequest of an ardent spiritualist, for instance, the Seybert Commission investigated rapping, spirit writings, ghost hands, and other phenomena related to communication with the dead, under the academic auspices of the University of Pennsylvania. Noting that the "belief in so-called Spiritualism is certainly not decreasing," the committee members attended different spiritualist sessions, including those by the famed medium Pierre L. O. A. Keeler, whose materialization séances the commission specifically labeled "highly deceptive" in its 1887 report.[70]

Two years later, Gonzales responded in kind by publishing *Heaven Revealed*, which is a long-dead Latinx-authored text worth resurrecting because of the autobiographical insight it provides about the Cuban Confederate during the post-Reconstruction era. As Molly McGarry shows, spirit writings saw a resurgence in the aftermath of the war: "The language of reconstruction infused Spiritualist writing," explains McGarry, "as well as the larger political culture, before Reconstruction itself." Contra to most spiritualists, however, who were also reformists, free thinkers, and abolitionists, Gonzales seemed more convinced that its "magical metaphysics," as McGarry calls it, could conjure Hattie and the world they shared before and immediately after the Civil War.[71] Gonzales was a true believer in the spirit world, and the prolific writer was equally captivated by the process of spirit writings and their technologies of expression. After explaining the process of the slate-writing sessions, for instance, he affirms, "The hand-writing is his wife's whether on the slates, or in pencil on paper, and is identically the same from the first message, at the end of December, 1887, to those at the end of April 1889. It is very much the same as hers in mortal life, only smaller, to crowd as many words as possible into a small space." With few exceptions, the slate messages Gonzales reprints lack specific personal details. Only the final message, published by Occult Telegraphy in New York's *Celestial City*, a spiritualist newspaper, directly addresses Gonzales as "Gonzie," his family nickname, and is signed by "Harriet R.E.G."[72]

Conjured by Pierre Keeler, the same medium the Seybert Commission dismissed, the messages in *Heaven Revealed* take on an intimate tone that shores up McGarry's point that writings from the dead raise queer spirits.[73] The medium ostensibly communicates to Gonzie as Hattie, addressing him in slate writings as "Darling Lover," signing off as "Thy loving bride," and exclaiming disembodied forms of love that, as the sessions progress, become increasingly erotic. "How good, how generous, how noble the impulses of thy soul for so frequently to provide a way for me to come with my impassioned devotion. . . . To feel that a loved one is lost in death is not so bad as to know that the dear one is separated from you by subjection, yet longing, longing, longing, constantly longing, to be together." It's difficult not to read these spirit messages cynically as ruses for Keeler to keep Gonzales returning for sessions, and even though he realizes that scammers could take advantage of more gullible clients with means, poor Gonzie seems smitten by the séances. On one occasion, he attempts to grasp the "materialized" hand behind the curtain from which the slate writings appear, and on another, he tries to kiss the materialized specter summoned through Keeler. Finally, after a steamy session, he receives the following slate: "How wonderful it did seem to me last night to be wrapt in your loving embrace. Oh, my own dear one, you have no idea how I longed to be in your arms like that. . . . It did seem so like the old, old time of our honeymoon, didn't it? You were so kind to come and receive me as you did." In a footnote, Gonzales adds that Hattie was sixteen when they married, making her twenty years his junior.[74]

As a post-Reconstruction narrative, *Heaven Revealed* shows Gonzales to be lonely and unsettled personally in the late 1880s, but the spirit writings are also part of the Cuban's late attempts at self-writing. For as much as he worked to publish praise and self-aggrandizement in the press, Gonzales tended to avoid extended self-writing. His anonymous newspaper pieces are, at best, veiled autobiographies. Otherwise, he kept his life to the basics: he fought for Cuban independence, threw in with the Confederacy, and was an American citizen, though Cuban by birth—these are the details he often reiterated when summarizing himself in letters of introduction or application. What we get with *Heaven Revealed* is Gonzales's unabashed and unwavering belief in the pseudoscience of metaphysics, in the technologies of spirit conjuring, and in the power of writing to raise the dead. While much of the text purports to be copies of the slate writings he received, he frames them with an introduction that corroborates or authenticates the disembodied dispatches, and his footnotes provide intimate scenes of mourning, desire, and perhaps even desperation. He recounts holding a spirit wedding in private with his corpse-bride Hattie, for instance; he notes clasping her "materialized" hand through a curtain; and we learn that Hattie writes to him "in his room through his own powers of mediumship."[75]

This last note sheds a different light on Gonzales's late writings about Cuba, published in two extensive installments in the *New Orleans Times-Democrat* a few years before *Heaven Revealed*. In its March 30, 1884, issue, the paper announced its invitation to "Gen. Ambrosio José Gonzalez" to share his recollections about the first and second Cuban filibustering expeditions some thirty years in the past. Gonzales is happy to oblige and frames his first installment with the structuring thesis that "Had success attended the effort of American statesmanship, and Cuban patriotism, the Union would have been strengthened and our civil war would have been averted." Of all his writings, the first installment is his only sustained narrative that details his military action. He recounts the incursion on the island, the landing of the filibusters, and their initial volleys with Spanish forces: "The moment we were seen by the garrison they opened fire upon us, and I received in the left thigh two musket balls, Gen. Lopez being unhurt. I may be pardoned for saying it was the first wound a Cuban ever received in battle for his country's cause." His is a firsthand account that underscores his central role in politicking in the United States for support, plotting with key leaders, and serving at López's side in the thick of action. While his narrative primarily offers a historical account of the first filibustering movement, Gonzales slips into a literary mode to emphasize the tension and proximity of battle. Describing the tense standoff between the filibusters' retreating *Creole* and the Spanish *Pizarro* in close chase, he writes, "On came the Pizarro like a huge shark, on the Creole minnow and passed but a few yards astern of us. As I looked around through the cabin window, I could distinctly see the faces of the admiral and his officers standing on the upper deck to have recognized them had I known them."[76] The simile and metaphor (shark and minnow) are uncharacteristic of Gonzales's writings, but the scene also stages a haunting memory for him as he recalls with clarity faces of the unknown. The brief recollection is a spectral past, a ghost ship of the uncanny from his early days, as if in the moment of his writing about the escape, Gonzales conjures the recognizable faces of the unfamiliar crew of Spanish colonial power.

A week later, the *Times-Democrat* published his second installment, "The Cuban Crusade," which takes a dramatic shift from his first piece. Here, Gonzales must account for López's second incursion on the island indirectly because he did not participate in it. He explains that he was convalescing from fever at Sulfur Springs, West Virginia, at López's instruction, when the general hastily led a second incursion on the island, following fake news reporting that support for the filibusters was high. "He failed to carry out the plan agreed with me," Gonzales explains, "and did not even write or communicate with me, then in West Virginia, considering the condition of the island so favorable, as all the papers stated, that he would miss the opportunity of marching in triumph into Havana." Because Gonzales was not part of the second expedition, his account of it relies on 1850s press coverage, demonstrating that he preserved an archive of Cuban news pieces and exhumed the nearly thirty-five-year-old articles and editorials to animate his account of the second expedition. Even though he provides specific dates and places of publication, he quotes freely from different sources without making clear distinction in print between the quoted material and his own words. Moreover, in remembering the fateful expedition that saw the capture and execution of López and his band of filibusters, Gonzales resurrects the voices of the American dead by including their last letters: "were taken prisoners by the Habenero, were brought to Havana last night, and condemned to die this morning. We shall be shot in an hour," one note reads. "My Dear Friends—" another opens, "I leave you forever, and I go to the other world. I am a prisoner in Havana, and in an hour I shall have ceased to exist." Like the spirit writings that comprise *Heaven Revealed*, the letters from filibusters long deceased conjure them from the past. They are messages from the dead that, along with the 1850s news pieces Gonzales reprints, revive the Cuban issue for a new era: "Cuba still lies at the entrance of the Gulf of Mexico; it is still the clasp that holds the southern part of North America; it still lies in the path of our coastal trade; but it is of more vital importance than it was then," Gonzales closes, noting that the annexation of the island would protect US interests, security, and control of the modern development of Gulf Stream shipways and canals.[77]

Gonzales's last installment on Cuba's annexation ends on a telling note of his transformation. He signs it as Ambrosio Jose Gonzales, "of South Carolina, formerly of Cuba." His signature is a departure from his earlier ways of describing himself as "adopted" into the South, but it also speaks to the ways the naturalized US citizen saw himself late in life as a South Carolinian—of the region by way of Cuba. Capturing in miniature his long-standing effort to become *de jure* and *de facto* an American, as he once proclaimed to Cushing in 1849, the self-designation is also a reminder that Gonzales's united loyalties were in the service of what he understood to be the region's twin commitments: the preservation and protection of white power and privilege in the circum-Gulf South. With another Cuban independence movement on the rise in the 1890s, Gonzales found himself an unlikely figure of a few commemorative pieces in *Patria*, the main Spanish-language organ of new insurgent sentiments that rejected annexation and embraced emancipation as part and parcel of the liberation of the island.[78] If his response to the Ten Years' War is any indication, Gonzales would have kept his distance from this last bid for independence too, but *Patria* presented him as a living memory of Cuba's long-standing fight for independence. After Gonzales's 1893 death, the paper ran an extended memorial that brought the general back from the dead for a new generation of revolutionaries, including José Martí, who mobilized their movement from the hub of Spanish-language print from which Gonzales went south so many years earlier—New York.

5

From Union Officers to Cuban Rebels

The Story of the Brothers Cavada and Their American Civil Wars

Latinx Confederates highlight the ways filibustering, independence, rebellion, and revolution connected Cuba, the US South, and northern Mexico in shared civil wars before and after the War Between the States. To be sure, there were Union sympathizers in the region, especially as Juárez gained political and military traction against the French, but the circum-Gulf space not surprisingly leaned toward maintaining slavery and its related regional labor practice of debt peonage. Ambrosio José Gonzales's movement south underscores the cultural confluence of circum-Gulf slave societies and their familiar racial structures. José Agustín Quintero's plasticity also embodies such connectivity, as he ventured from Cuba to New England, from Boston to New York, from New York to New Orleans, and then from the Crescent City to south Texas and Monterrey, Mexico, before returning to New Orleans after the Civil War. Their migrations from Cuba to the United States and its Southern states map the mobility of their whiteness and the transformation of their Latinidad from Cuban-identified revolutionaries to Confederates in their sympathy with the Southern cause during and after the US Civil War. Their filiation to slave culture ran so deep that it displaced their initial advocacy for Cuban independence. Both did not revive their Cuban revolutionary sentiments during the island's Ten Years' War because it countenanced Black emancipation as integral to Cuban independence—a position that in theory distinguished Cuba's 1868–1878 civil war from the López incursions twenty years prior.

The lives and writings of two Cuban-born Union brothers, however, tell a somewhat different story of coming into Cuban revolutionary consciousness. Federico and Adolfo Cavada were family products of Cuba's long-standing rifts, but their coming of age in the United States and their service in the Union embody the way the Civil War initiated their social, gendered, and ethno-national process of becoming revolutionary US Latinxs in Cuba. The brothers Cavada—there were three of them, actually—were born in Cienfuegos, Las Villas Province, Cuba, to Isidoro Fernández Cavada y Díaz de la Campa of Santander, Spain, and Philadelphia-born Emily Howard Gatier. "Ironically," Michael A. Dreese explains, "the three sons of Isidoro and Emily Cavada would be key figures in the independence movement that sought to overthrow the yoke of colonial power under which both branches of the family had prospered."[1] Fernández Cavada, a loyal *peninsular*, served as the Spanish crown's tax collector in Cienfuegos, where he met and married Emily Howard, the youngest daughter of French émigré Louis Howard, a wealthy landowner who fled the Saint-Domingue revolt and settled in Cienfuegos, where he traded in sugar and cattle. After Fernández Cavada's 1838 death (he was thirty-six at the time), Emily Howard taught school briefly before she returned with her sons to Philadelphia in 1841 and married Samuel Dutton, a banker and ship chandler who became stepfather to Emilio, Federico, and Adolfo. Not much is known about their early years. The eldest, Emilio, became a New York and Philadelphia sugar merchant and served as a medic during Cuba's 1895 war for independence, while Federico started his US education in a boarding school in Wilmington, Delaware, and finished it by graduating from Philadelphia's Central High School in 1846. Afterwards, he served as an engineer for the transcontinental railroad along the Isthmus of Panama, where he contracted malaria and returned to the city of brotherly love a little worse for wear. In July 1861, he and his younger brother, Adolfo, joined Company C of the Twenty-Third Regiment of Volunteers of Pennsylvania, recruited in Philadelphia, and later, they enlisted with the Zouaves Company under Captain Collis in the 114th Pennsylvania Regiment.[2] As Federico's recruiting officer, O. W. Davis, later recalled, "On the twentieth day of July, 1861, a delicate looking young man entered the business office . . . and asked for a position in the Twenty-third Pennsylvania Volunteers."[3] He proclaimed that he had no knowledge of "military matters"—"None whatever"—but was willing to pay for the cost of raising his own company; he also affirmed that he did not have a job; was out of work because of his health; and when asked whether he "could endure the exposure of a soldier's life," he responded, "I do not know, but have made up my mind to try it."[4]

The brothers Cavada comprise a class apart from the large groups of émigrés in New York, New Orleans, Key West, and Philadelphia who agitated for Cuba during the 1850s and 1860s. This émigré class, as Gerald E. Poyo has shown, was responsible for fostering a sense of Cuban nationalism that encompassed the United States and the island through print culture, political pressure, and labor politics. Separatists, annexationists, cultural and political nationalists, abolitionists, and radical anarchists all converged on the United States during the island's heady mid-nineteenth century, and through organs such as *El Filibustero*, *La Verdad*, which was backed by *Democratic Review* editor and expansionist pundit John O'Sullivan, *La Voz de América*, *El Pueblo*, and *El Mulato*, Creole leaders such as Cristóbal Madan, José Luís Alfonso, Gaspar Betancourt Cisneros, and Cirilo Villaverde, to name a few, debated Cuban independence, separatism, or annexation from political exile.[5] They organized influential *juntas*, such as the Club de la Habana and the Sociedad Republicana de Cuba y Puerto Rico, and seem to have applied as much pressure on US politics and culture as they did on Cuban military and political change on the island. While Cuban émigré ideologies were anything but homogeneous, the elite Creoles in US urban centers shared a common ground: "the reform movement's liberal vision and strong sense of Cuban national identity."[6] They were Cubans in the United States politicking for the future of their homeland.

But the Cavada brothers were different on this score. First, they were not émigrés in the sense that there is no indication their mother moved them from the island out of separatist politics. Her domestic arrangement changed, and since Federico and Adolfo were relatively young, they followed their mother; oldest brother Emilio joined too, as his stepfather trained him in the business world. Second, the brothers grew up in the United States. They attended school in Delaware and Philadelphia, mastered English, secured US citizenship, and saw the US military as a venue for social mobility. In a telltale sign of Latinx transformations, Federico also went by Frederic, Fredrick, or Fred, and in Union records and his published writings in English, he put his names under erasure by using "F. F. Cavada."[7] Third, they came to their Cuban revolutionary politics when they returned to Cuba as official US consuls. Much of their writing in the United States makes nary a mention of Cuban independence, but just as reformist leaders were leaving Cuba for the United

States en masse in January 1869, the brothers Cavada were resigning their official posts to throw in with the rebels in Trinidad and Cienfuegos. They provide an instructive paradigm for understanding how nineteenth-century *latinidades* emerged unevenly on the transnational scene during the long Civil War years. As young boys, the Cavadas move from Cuba to the United States, experience there the process of American socialization, and then, after serving in the Union with mixed records, they return to their native Cuba, where they become rebels, despite having been raised for much of their lives away from the island in relative privilege as members of Philadelphia's wealthy merchant class. Theirs is a return to the "ever-faithful isle," where they (re)discover their Latinidad in the thick of Cuba's own civil war.

A Tale of Two Brothers

In themselves, the brothers are a study in contrast. While older Federico suffered an embattled Union career, younger brother Adolfo rose rapidly through the ranks, and while his older brother took ill often and injured easily, Adolfo was almost an army overachiever whose field diary charts his penchant for military details and his rise in rank. Penned in English, the journal spans nearly two full years, from August 1861, when he enlisted as a Philadelphia volunteer, to New Year's Eve, December 31, 1863, when he closes his diary "ready to begin another year" and wondering what 1864 will bring.[8] In between, the entries chart his transformation from a greenhorn to an experienced combatant as he weathers skirmishes and pickets at Warwick River and the subsequent battles of Fredericksburg, Chancellorsville, and Gettysburg, the latter of which is figured as the culmination of his military experiences and personal development.

At Yorktown, Adolfo sits on picket along the banks of the Warwick and alternates between fear, adventure, awe, and humor during the monthlong campaign. On April 8, 1862, he writes, "Brisk musketry firing ahead—Began to feel a little green—The skirmishing very lively," but only four days later, the green captain gets daring: "On picket still at Warwick River: Occasionally I go in search of adventure—crawling on hands and knees opposite to the rebel batteries; by Captain Hilderbrand, Fred, and myself was considered fine fun."[9] That same evening, shells, musket fire, and a thunderstorm all rouse Adolfo from sleep as "rapid volleys were fired—artillery began to push further, shells whizzed and burst—the lightening flashed, the thunder crashed, and the rain plashed. Altogether about the grandest piece of music in nature's repertoire."[10] The light action he sees is enough to inspire some literary pretension in his journal too. In the previous entry, for instance, "lightening flashed, the thunder crashed, and the rain *plashed*" in the heat of the skirmish—not "splashed" in the diary but "plashed," an accidental or deliberate rhymed onomatopoeia that captures the sound and action of water as it puddles around him amidst rebel fire and a fierce thunderstorm. Finally, come May, he gives a more lighthearted entry, one that points to either the folly of warfare or its absurdity: "May 1862—Bang! Whiz, whiz! Look out for your heads! Men rushing ahead eager for the fray; men rushing back eager to get out of it."[11]

By June 2, 1862, Adolfo has grown accustomed to picket duty—"Getting shelled every day but don't mind that now," he says, but six months later at the first Battle of Fredericksburg, he encounters real action on the front, and his journal entry betrays his excitement, trepidation, and relief at surviving one of the most lopsided Confederate victories of the war: "Fix bayonets—Charge! . . . Hurrah! The Rebel artillery and musketry all concentrated on us. Terrible fire—our men fall by hundreds . . . The air is full of flying bullets, . . . men falling in groups. List of wounded: Lt. Humpherys—slightly wounded; Genl Humpherys—two horses killed. Capt. Cavada—allright."[12] His May 7, 1863, entry, one day after Union forces suffer more heavy losses at the Battle of Chancellorsville, is more grim: "In camp—Reflections—Another ground movement, another terrible, bloody battle fought by the Army of the Potomac resulting in *so* many killed, *so* many wounded, *so* many prisoners."[13]

It is of course monumental for US Latinx literary and cultural history that Adolfo Cavada, a Cuban-born US citizen, was a participant at the early battles of the US Civil War and kept a diary about it, putting to rest Walt Whitman's misconception that the war would remain unwritten.[14] With Cavada's diary, we have both the written war and the interiority of an "actual" soldier, to recall Whitman's pronouncement, and here is where the journal takes significance for understanding Cavada's identity formation. His interiority—his excitement, anxiety, fear, and joy—is aligned with the Union cause. The diary maps the battlefronts of his Americanization. It is not coincidental that the diary opens with Cavada at Yorktown, which is more memorable as the last battle of the American Revolution than one of the first skirmishes of the US Civil War. Meanwhile, the excitement and gloom he feels at Fredericksburg and Chancellorsville, respectively, mirror the ebb and flow of the federal army's momentum, as it weathered Confederate General Robert E. Lee's lopsided victory at Fredericksburg only to face a worse fate at Chancellorsville. In short, Cavada figures himself in his military diary as a synecdoche for the Union at the start of the war and, by extension, he fashions himself as a quintessential United States citizen who begins as a greenhorn picket at the site of the American Revolution's siege of Yorktown and comes of age at the Civil War's most significant engagement: the Battle of Gettysburg.

Just as the Union victory at Gettysburg marked a turning point in the war, it also signals a change in Cavada's diary. His July 2, 1863, entry seems self-consciously aware of the impending battle's importance, and as if to respond in kind, he takes more care to narrate it poetically: "[The rain fell—deleted]. No sound broke the stillness of the air except the pattering rain drops in the grass. . . . It was a grand sight—one to make one['s] blood warm and tingle through its channels—all sense of danger—the past abolished in that great present—that surrounds us." It is at Gettysburg that Adolfo comes of age as a soldier and US citizen-subject. He proclaims a day after the battle, "July 4, 1863—The Fourth of July! A day made doubly dear by the victory of liberty over slavery on the fields of Gettysburg. . . . A short distance from here I could see the hill where I encamped with the 23rd Regiment during the 1st and 2nd of November 1862. Things have changed in my favor since then."[15] That Gettysburg takes place around the Fourth of July is perhaps a historical coincidence but symbolic nonetheless as Adolfo narrates his transformation through a national imaginary that begins with the American Revolution and culminates with a celebration of US independence. It is also the first and only time that Adolfo mentions slavery as a *casus belli*, as if his transformation as a US Latinx is tied to his awareness about slavery and independence, a point that will return with a difference after the Civil War.

If Gettysburg is the culmination of Adolfo's Union career, however, it marks his older brother's misfortune on the field. July 3, 1863: "No positive information had been received of Fred's fate.—Some thought he had escaped, others had seen him wounded and [taken] prisoner, others still had seen him struck down by a cannon ball—amid so many contradictory statements I still hoped for the best."[16] Adolfo's concern is not new. Throughout his diary, he is called to attend to Federico, who is often ill, absent, or broke. He recounts taking leave to go retrieve his AWOL big brother; other times he mentions letters received from his mother, reminding him to watch after his brother; and always, when they share the field, his diary entries express concern for Federico. Throughout most of the time Adolfo is coming of military age, his brother's health wanes. On December 16, 1862, Adolfo hears that his brother had been wounded and goes to visit him at camp; a month later, Federico comes to stay with Adolfo at camp, and he's "very sick"; a day later, Adolfo secures leave papers for his brother and sends him home to recuperate, under the escort of Lieutenant Colonel O. H. P. Carey of the Seventy-Seventh Pennsylvania Infantry. Four months later, on April 4, 1863, Adolfo must go find his brother and bring him back to camp.

Federico at first proved to be a precious war participant. In May 1863, he was found guilty of and cashiered for three related charges of "behav[ing] himself in a cowardly manner in the presence of the enemy" at the Battle of Fredericksburg by absenting himself from the battlefield, taking shelter at the rear of the battlefield, and deserting his men under fire for shelter in the rear.[17] It was at Fredericksburg that Cavada was injured and convalescing perhaps in the same hospital Whitman wandered in search of his brother George.[18] While recovering, he passed the time by reading *Harper's* magazine, where he came across A. R. Waud's illustration *Gallant Charge of Humphreys' Division at the Battle of Fredericksburg* in the January 10, 1863, issue's coverage of the battle. The black-and-white two-page spread must have struck a chord with Federico because he painted a replica of it, with a few significant changes that, like his younger brother's diary, give expression to his interiority in response to his first Civil War battle encounter. Waud's sketch is standard for his and other Civil War illustrations in *Harper's*: it depicts the battle scene, captures the grand scale of it, and presents in the foreground a body count that borders on realism were it not for the black-and-white medium. It's by no means a sanitized depiction of the battle, but its title heading announcing the division's "gallant charge" puts the soldiers' strewn bodies in the foreground in stark contrast to a greater cause, though despite Humphreys's heroics on the field, the Confederate army won the day at great cost to both sides.

Cavada paints a different picture. The oil painting's colors bring out with dramatic contrast the battlefield's confusion as the scene meditates on the horrors of war. Shells explode on human bodies; ghostly figures emerge from pits in the background; and Cavada's use of light is even more menacing as apocalyptic smoke and destruction provide the color counterbalance to the foreground's darkness. All is chaos and destruction surrounding and obscuring Humphreys's "gallant charge." Moreover, the painting's two major alterations to Waud's illustration forward the piece's stark realism and highlight Cavada's split self-representation in the scene. First, Cavada centers a prostrate corpse in the foreground and, contra to Waud's illustration, obscures the face of the man; second, Cavada adds into the foreground the figure of a soldier, turned away from the battle, looking up either in pain or supplication, and holding his wounded head, the white head bandage standing in subtle but obvious relief to the other headgear on the field. Cavada has painted himself into the illustration, both as the wounded soldier who is at the rear of the action (for which he was charged with cowardice), but also, I maintain, as the (now) faceless prone corpse facing (without a face) the viewer. It's a painting that Don Diego Velázquez himself would appreciate for the way the painter triangulates the foreground with a self-representation looking away from the scene and a faceless self-reflection staring back, if you will, at the painter and the viewer.[19] In miniature, it's a representation of Cavada's post-traumatic experience on the battlefield, and it's also emblematic of his embattled process of becoming Latinx on the Civil War front. He is left fissured in his own painting.

That Federico would turn to self-expression to convalesce is not surprising. Of the Cavada brothers, he was the artist. On December 15, 1847, a year after his graduation from Philadelphia's Central High, the precocious Cavada started his journal with a juvenile ditty that shows that he was thinking about his writings for posterity. His self-labeled preface begins,

> This book contains perhaps little wit
> Of sound sense or good deal less;

Figure 5.1. Federico Cavada's rendition of the Battle of Fredericksburg captures his internal struggles. Frederick Cavada, *The Battle of Fredericksburg on 13th December 1862*, c. 1863, Philadelphia History Museum at the Atwater Kent. Courtesy of the Historical Society of Pennsylvania Collections, Bridgeman Images.

Figure 5.2. Cavada based his painting on an illustrated two-page spread that appeared in the January 10, 1863, issue of *Harper's Weekly*. A. R. Waud, *Gallant Charge of Humphreys' Division at the Battle of Fredericksburg*, Morgan Collection of Civil War Drawings, Prints and Photographs Division, Library of Congress, LC-DIG-ppmsca-22749.

But would its pages their composer bless
If they contained of true poetry a bit.
Unfit to be read, but by his own eyes,
In reading them you may ill-use your time
For bad the metre, and worse the rhyme,
You'd little know what they imply.
Still, a glimmering hope remains,
You may grasp [?] the author's thought
And add the truths he's left unsought
To those his humble verse contains.[20]

The nearly 275-page journal spans a year and includes love poems to a variety of young women but especially one "Mary Ellen"; he has an attempt at an epic poem, a long ballad, several pieces in Spanish, and moody poems titled "Anger" and "Aspirations Blasted!" His diary also lists the books that the young Cavada read over the year. By his account, he devoured the histories of Rome, England, Scotland, Greece, China, and the United States, to list a few; he also covered Prescott's histories of Peru, Brazil, Mexico, and the reign of Ferdinand and Isabella; and he notes that he read in both English and Spanish histories of the West Indies, Granada, and the Crusades. In poetry, he read Byron, Scott, Milton, Shakespeare, and Burns, alongside Rousseau, Paine, a history of the French Revolution, and Burton's *Anatomy of Melancholy*, to name only a few. Young Federico fancied himself an author, as his journal includes a table of contents that not only indicates the page numbers for his poems and entries, but also notes which are "not worth reading."[21] Though he was at the time receiving training as a civil (topographical) engineer, the then five foot five, 110-pound precocious Cuban kid preferred the arts. His journal can be understood as a study of how a young, displaced Cuban becomes a US subject citizen—through books, language, and literacy. That he takes up his education more evenly than the Jimeno brothers of California further highlights the significant degree to which Federico mastered the cultural literacies he needed to pass.

Still, on the battlefield, he did not fare any better at Gettysburg than he did at Fredericksburg. He was in the melee long enough to get captured, and once again, charges of cowardice were leveled against him. In his July 12, 1863, report, Captain Edward R. Bowen of the 114th

Pennsylvania Infantry notes that he "saw Lieutenant-Colonel Cavada, who was then commanding the regiment, stopping by a log house in an orchard on our right. I inquired if he was wounded; he replied that he was not, but utterly exhausted. I begged him to make an effort to come on, as the enemy was only a few yards from him and advancing rapidly. He replied that he could not, and I left him there, and not having heard from him since, I have no doubt he was taken prisoner there."[22] He was, and his commanding officer, Colonel Collis, who himself was accused of cowardice a few months later, filed formal charges against Cavada and waged a nasty public campaign, accusing him of cowardice at the Battles of Chancellorsville and Gettysburg. As Collis explained in a letter to Assistant Secretary of State Seward, "At Chancellorsville, on the 3d May, 1863, when the first shot was fired at my regiment, Colonel Cavada disappeared, and when, after two hours' incessant fighting, with but ninety men and four officers left, . . . we marched to the rear, we found Colonel Cavada sitting in the woods more than two miles distant from the line of battle"; he claimed he was "suddenly attacked with a very severe headache."[23] Cavada's capture at Gettysburg, Collis argued, was indicative of the cowardice he displayed at Fredericksburg and Chancellorsville. The fact that Lieutenant Colonel Cavada was captured alongside General C. K. Graham was probably the only reason Collis's and Bowen's reports gained little military traction.

Meanwhile, to pass his time as a prisoner of war, Cavada drew sketches and wrote anecdotes and stories about prison life on contraband scraps of paper. One sketch details the restless boredom he tried to stave off by reading the *Richmond Enquirer*. The single-page sketch captures a series of postures and positions the prisoner takes to get comfortable with the South's leading Confederate rag, with a brief description under each image that narrates the humorous and symbolic war against an "ennui" so great that the prisoner wrestles with reading the Richmond paper to pass the time. The sequential "imagetext," to recall W. J. T. Mitchell's term, captures an especially difficult position for a prisoner like Cavada, who read widely and avidly but is stuck with only a Confederate newspaper to peruse.[24] He's torn between reading and discarding it, having to stomach the Southern press and having nothing else to do but serve time. While his sketch's solution makes light of the situation, the images themselves resemble body studies that reinforce the idea that he painted

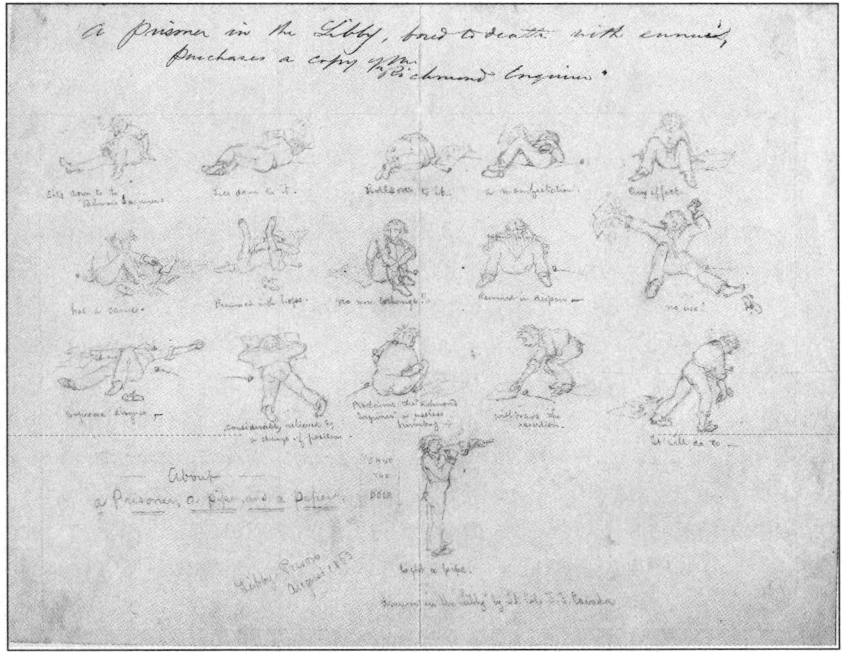

Figure 5.3. Cavada passed his time as a prisoner of war reading and drawing. F. F. Cavada, *A Prisoner in Libby Bored to Death*, 1863, Edward Carey Gardiner Collection (#227), Historical Society of Pennsylvania.

himself into his copy of Waud's *Harper's* illustration. Many of the individual postures recall the scores of prostrated bodies that populate Civil War battle scenes in print media, like *Harper's*, and the details of a few sketches mirror from different angles the corpses and shell-shocked bodies he painted into his Battle of Fredericksburg. If the battle painting is a scene of his trauma, the Libby sketch, with its traces of battle scene contortions, narrates a process of survival, recovery, and rejection of Southern print culture through humor. The Richmond paper is only good for lighting the prisoner's pipe.

A few months after his 1864 release, Cavada transformed his study of prison boredom into the first (to date) Latinx prisoner of war narrative. King and Baird, the same company that printed Collis's incendiary pamphlet against Cavada, published *Libby Life: Experiences of a Prisoner of War*, which was republished in 1865 by J. B. Lippincott (the Philadelphia publishing house that would release Ruiz de Burton's *Who Would*

Have Thought It? in 1872). As the *Daily National Intelligencer* announced in June 18, 1864, "The narrative abounds with scenes and incidents, the correctness of which is vouched for by his fellow prisoners, and will interest every reader."[25] Dedicated to the Union League of Philadelphia, a prominent organization of upper-crust, Republican Party businessmen who supported Lincoln's war effort to which the brothers Cavada and their stepfather belonged, Cavada recounts daily life as a prisoner—the boredom, hunger, and small celebrations the Union captives enjoy—with "freedom" as an underlying theme. "My chief aim in these humble pages," Federico explains, "has been to perpetuate for my companions in captivity, a compliance with their request, a truthful record of our prison experiences,—a record which, while it cannot fail to bring back upon our hearts some of the gloomy shadows which once darkened them in the prison-house, may also renew upon our lips the irrepressible smiles which were wont to wreathe them at times, in spite of hunger, suffering and despair."[26] His sentiment gives truth to the power of language, especially during wartime, to be subversive and transformative. "In prison camps and torture blocks," James Dawes postulates, "the achievement of communication and recognition through an undetected note or an answered whisper is the first step in rebuilding the world."[27]

Nearly all Civil War prison camps were notorious, and Libby Prison was no exception. Part of Richmond, Virginia's prison complex, which included Castle Thunder and the nearby Belle Isle Prison, Libby was a warehouse turned jail for Union officers between 1861 and 1864, when it was then used for Confederate military criminals. By all accounts, sanitary conditions due to overcrowding were deadly, so much so that in February 1864, Libby Prison was the site of a sensational and sensationalized escape attempt by way of a fifty-seven-foot tunnel. "By February 9, 1864," William Best Hesseltine explains, "the tunnel was opened and a hundred and nine prisoners made their escape during the night. Forty-eight of the hundred and nine officers . . . were captured before they reached the Union lines." Of the ones who did make it, Hesseltine continues, several offered exaggerated official reports, newspaper accounts, and personal narratives about their escape.[28] Cavada was not one of the escapees, but he recounts the event in his narrative after it occurred, and in his preface, he situates his book contra the overblown accounts. He states that his "sketches . . . were drawn, not with the object of presenting a sensational picture of the military prisons of the Confederacy, but simply to while away the idle hours of a tedious and protracted captivity."[29] Though he understates his intentions, his prefatory comments shed light on his sense of aesthetics, as he presents his narrative as an extension of his "imagetext" studies of a prisoner fighting boredom. The narrative unfolds through vignettes, and even though the book is illustrated (not by his hand), Cavada's visual artistry leverages the symbolic power of the imagetext as "a principle of thought, feeling, and meaning as fundamental to human beings as distinctions of gender and sexuality," Mitchell explains, and in Cavada's case, the contours of racial difference as well.[30]

He recounts laundry day, for instance, or "whitewashing" day, as he calls it, as a "torture and terror" "invented by the fiendish ingenuity of some monster in human shape" as the prisoners are hosed down from above by the prison guards, while "a dozen negroes from below" scrub out the prison quarters with filthy water.[31] Unlike Adolfo, who finds the triumph of "liberty over slavery" on the Gettysburg battlefield, Federico discovers the opposite as he becomes a POW and describes his conditions as akin to suffering the tortures of enslavement, but when we recall that Libby is in the heart of the Confederacy, then his longing for freedom in the face of captivity must be read in the context of Black enslavement and the North's sensationalized accounts of white slavery. It is a brief but telling scene as Cavada and his Union compatriots literally and symbolically find themselves stuck between enslaved Black people below and white overseers above, with no escape from either of them. The vignette draws on the defining characteristic of their imprisonment—a lack of freedom—as a condition that puts the white Union soldiers on the same level as the enslaved Black people who clean up after them.

He narrates a similar, if not more bizarre sketch of the "Grand Ball" of New Year's Day, 1864, in the prison's kitchen. With a small band, accompanied by a man "well blacked up" as a "negro woman" and another dressed as "a comical representation of [her] colored beau," the prisoners engage in a "heathenish" dance that leave the "Sioux and Camanches . . . utterly outdone."[32] On a lower floor, two men engage in a chess game that rivals Thoreau's symbolic "ant war" in *Walden*:

> On the floor below, two sane men are near the termination of a highly interesting game of chess; . . . Black's hand is outstretched, tremulous

> with ill-controlled excitement: White turns pale, for those nervous outstretched fingers clutch a portentous black rook, and in another instant the white king will be mated. . . . When lo! From the ceiling overhead, where it was hung, down comes a huge ham, and drops like a bomb-shell into the very midst of the contending hosts! The pieces are scattered right and left; the board, and the rickety table on which it stood, are overset; and the black and the white general both spring to their feet with a cry of horror. . . . The *war-dance* was still going on overhead, and a gigantic Indian warrior having leaped into the air, and come down directly above the suspended ham, had jarred it from the nail on which it hung, and had thus ruined the most brilliant game of chess ever played in the prison.[33]

The New Year's celebration gives way to a carnival scene of racial disruption and destruction, with the US Civil War figured as a chess game, not between Northern and Southern whites, but between Blacks and whites in a metaphysical struggle for dominance over a binary racial system already vexed by the presence of Native America. Cavada's simple sketches, then, represent in miniature allegories of race war that situate his imprisonment as enslavement to the United States' prevailing racial order, making his final acquisition of freedom even more ironic because he is "bought out" during a prisoner exchange in 1864 and becomes "once more substantially and positively—FREE!"[34]

After his release, Federico briefly reenlisted in the Union army under his friend General David Birney, but near the war's end, Secretary of State Seward named him US consul to Trinidad de Cuba. He promptly tendered his resignation from the Union army to take up his new post and return to his native island in 1866. It was a homecoming for him and also an awakening, as his dispatches to the US State Department urge it to aid Cuba's independence movement.[35] The freshly appointed consul and former Union officer was becoming rebellious, and three years later, after the outbreak of Cuba's Ten Years' War on October 10, 1868, Federico resigned his post and joined Cuba's insurgency, alongside Adolfo, who also returned to the island after the Civil War as the American vice consul in Cienfuegos. As the *New York Herald* reported on February 12, 1869, "It is reported that the leaders of the [Cuban] revolution in the sugar districts of Cienfuegos, Villa Clara and Trinidad are Adolfo Cavada and his brother, Frederick Cavada. The former was recently

American Vice Consul at Cienfuegos. He was a Colonel of a Philadelphia regiment of zouaves during the civil war in America. The latter was until last week the American consul at Trinidad de Cuba, and has just resigned."[36] Big brother Emilio joined the cause by using his New York and Philadelphia sugar businesses to supply funds, munitions, and other contraband to his brothers, while Adolfo commanded a small force of rebels in the province of Las Villas. However, it was middle brother Federico—the precious painter, POW, and would-be "coward"—who emerged as the commander in chief of Cuba's rebel army. He left one civil war to lead another.

Ever Faithful to the Island

Spanning 1868 to 1878, Cuba's Ten Years' War was yet another rupture of the anti-imperialist movements that had been bubbling on the island since at least the 1830s. Often linked to anti-slavery interests, sometimes fueled by arguments for annexation to the United States, and nearly always fostered by Creole desire for economic independence from Spain, Cuba's anti-imperialism took many forms throughout the nineteenth century, culminating with its final bid for independence in 1895—the war José Martí made famous. But Cuba's Guerra Grande, as it's also called on the island, is a significant event because Cuba's historic struggles over race, slavery, independence, and self-governance took on a different tone in the aftermath of the Southern secession and the subsequent US Civil War. As Ada Ferrer explains, the 1868 revolution began when Carlos Manuel de Céspedes, a wealthy sugar planter, lawyer, and poet, emancipated the people he held in slavery and then "invited them to help 'conquer liberty and independence' for Cuba."[37] They did, along with thousands of others, and thus waged an anti-colonial insurgency and independence movement three years after the end of the US Civil War that constituted rebellion against Spain and its ruling *peninsular* class on the island.

Cuba's relation to the United States and its secessionist states, then, is not anomalous but analogous insofar as the reverberations of the US Civil War rippled across the Gulf of Mexico to shape the contours and conflicts of the island's Ten Years' War. If some Creoles saw a common cause in the so-called Confederacy, the Union's victory put pressure on the leadership of the Cuban independence movement to stake an unambiguous position on slavery on the island. Almost always besieged by the fear of slave rebellion and the memory of Saint-Domingue, most Cuban leaders wavered on the issue. Spain was not unaware of this fact either, as it very often threatened to abolish slavery as a way of keeping revolutionary and reformist politics in check.[38] As we saw in Ambrosio José Gonzales's writings, the so-called Africanization of the island in effect weaponized Cuba's lingering racial tensions through a double front that threatened to increase the importation of Black laborers to keep the island's white ruling class in fear of a race war in the name of complete independence. Meanwhile, Creole independence leaders were just as vexed about the issue, for many of them had a direct investment in the island's slave economy, especially after the Haitian Revolution left the sugar market open to Cuba. They espoused independence from Spain but also realized that slaves and free people of color could use the exact same revolutionary sentiment against the Creole class. Revolutionary leaders "were men conversant in the principles of Enlightenment and convinced, in theory and—to a certain extent—in practice, of the justice of abolition. They shared the conviction that they could not declare freedom for themselves while enslaving their neighbors; and they criticized past Cuban patriots for having advocated the continuation of racial slavery on the island. At the same time, the men of 1868 were also members of a traditional land- and slave-owning class, accustomed to the economic, political, and social advantages that came with slave ownership in a slave society."[39]

Not so for the American-raised Federico Cavada. He became known as General Candela, or the Fire King, for the scorched-earth, guerrilla tactics he practiced against the island's economic staple, the sugarcane fields. The *Cincinnati Daily Enquirer* reported in a piece titled "War to the Knife and the Knife to the Hilt," "The insurgent General Cavada has issued the following order to the forces under his command: 'It is probable that the owners of plantations will begin to grind sugar cane at an early date and the General expects his subordinates to burn the cane fields as soon as the cane is dry.'"[40] A burn policy and other forms of property destruction were neither politic nor popular during the Ten Years' War. Rebel President Carlos Manuel de Céspedes worked to muster support from fellow landowners and enslavers by assuring them that the rebellion would respect property, including food, farms, land, and, of course, people. The insurgent leadership was forced to balance two competing impulses of their rebellion—namely, to protect the interests of the landed Creole class and keep at bay the idea that the rebellion opened the opportunity for immediate emancipation of enslaved Blacks.[41] This was especially true of mid-island locales such as Cienfuegos and Trinidad, which were in between eastern Cuba, the hotbed of the insurrection, and the more prosperous western Cuba, which became the Spanish stronghold. "Insurgent leaders were hopeful of obtaining material and financial support from their wealthy counterparts, and hence were reluctant to enact measures capable of antagonizing sugar planters in the west. Any prospect of obtaining the support of western planters required respect for their estates and their slaves. In 1869," Pérez concludes, "Carlos Manuel de Céspedes proclaimed the death penalty for any attack against sugar estates and slave property."[42]

Threats to people and property were not only bad politics in Cuba, but they also made the Cuban rebellion unpopular in the United States at a time when rebel leaders were soliciting US recognition of belligerency and intervention on behalf of the insurgency. An October 29, 1869, *New York Tribune* article, for instance, reported,

> We have singular news from Cuba that the negroes near Cienfuegos have driven off a body of insurgents, which, we imagine, answers in some way to the general order of the patriot Cavada for burning the cane-crop. These things, however, are not the worst of our friends of Spanish descent as seen through the transparent ingenuity of those from whose stock and kind they are supposed to have descended. . . . The Cubans may make them worse still if they quarrel overmuch among themselves; and if there is any danger of this for want of a strong executive arm in the Junta, by all means, let the arm be found and put in its right place.[43]

Bad politics and worse press do no good for mustering support for the rebellion on the island or in the United States, but Federico managed to practice both as General Candela, as if he was waging rebellion against the United States and Cuba's elite Creole class.

Yet he did not entirely put down the pen for the knife, as the aforementioned *Cincinnati Daily Inquirer* headlined. Instead, in 1870, somewhere between organizing a rebel army and leading it, he wrote a travel narrative for *Harper's New Monthly Magazine* praising the national wonders of Cuba's Bellamar Cave and, more strangely, inviting US visitors to see the cave for themselves. "Easy of access from Havana by railway," Cavada would have tourists believe, "and commodiously and safely prepared for the reception of visitors, [the Bellamar Cave] fully repays one from a day's absence from the busy scenes of the capital."[44] The article makes no mention that the capital, as well as the Cuban countryside, is "busy" with a civil war, led in part by Cavada himself, and for this reason, it might be better understood less as a travel puff piece and more as a complex autobiographical allegory of hemispheric history, trans-American rebellion, and masculinity found in the Cuban cause. As the write-up continues, it recounts Cavada's descent into the cave. At first, it continues feeding the tourist's gaze, noting the cave's natural wonders, its passageways, its columns, and the unique formations of its stalactites and stalagmites, but the further Cavada descends, the more gothic the experience becomes, most notably when he crosses a formation known as the "Gothic Temple." Soon, formations begin to take shape, and he encounters the "Mantle of Columbus," a solid column formation that has crystallized into a mass "as white as snow."[45] Beyond it is the "Devil's Gorge," a symbolic point of no return as he descends deeper into the cave, only to discover at the end of his journey a passageway named the "Avenue of Hatuey," which leads him to "a tall, keen stalagmite called the 'Lance of Hatuey.'"[46] In the deepest part of Cuba's Bellamar Cave, Federico "discovers," so to speak, the most celebrated figure of Indigenous rebellion in Cuba.

A Taíno chief from Hispaniola, Hatuey became Cuba's national hero for raising a guerrilla war of rebellion against the Spanish in 1511, until his capture and execution on February 2, 1512. He became a protean symbol of Cuban nationalism throughout the nineteenth century as a way of recalling the horrors of the Spanish black legend, reimagining Cuban Creoles as Indigenous insurgents, and spinning a romantic, heroic history to the island's legacy of insurgency. Pedro Santacilia's 1859 *Lecciones orales sobre la historia de Cuba*, which was published in New Orleans, emphasizes Hatuey's rejection of Catholic conversion, and Juan Cristóbal Nápoles Fajardo's poem "Hatuey and Guarina," also published around 1856, imagines Hatuey putting his patriotism before his love for Guarina.[47] Francisco Sellén, a revolutionary Cuban poet exiled to the United States in 1868, penned and published in New York *Hatuey*, a drama in verse that represents the Indigenous insurgent as a martyr for independence, patriotism, and the treachery of betrayal within his rebellion.[48] Cavada's *Harper's* article might be seen in the same vein, but with a difference in the sense that it narrates Cavada's coming to revolutionary *cubanidad* consciousness. His is a symbolic journey beneath Cuba and, by extension, within his own interiority as he takes the path for US visitors to the cave, throws off Columbus's mantle, so to speak, and in the end finds Hatuey's lance for warfare. In much the same way that Adolfo's diary charts his coming of age as a Union officer and US subject, "The Cave of Bellamar" narrates Federico's transformation from US citizen to Cuban rebel ready to take up Hatuey's war of guerrilla tactics—a far cry from the traumatized self-representation in his copy of the *Harper's* illustration of the Battle of Fredericksburg, though ironically, "The Cave of Bellamar" includes illustrations signed by "ARW," presumably A. R. Waud, the illustrator Cavada copied years earlier.

Cavada's newfound commitment to Cuba's independence as well as the discovery of his own martial masculinity under the rebel cause can also be seen in his insurgent manual to guerrilla warfare that he penned and published as a field guide for officers. The pamphlet gives military definitions of terms such as *hilera* and *fila* (line and ranks), *frente* and *flanco* (front and flank), and *vanguardia* and *retaguardia* (vanguard and rear guard)—the usual military terms, with the glaring omission of "retreat" and "surrender," that indicate Cavada was attempting to introduce military protocol to his insurgent troops. His field guide for officers emphasizes this point, as he recommends that officers follow a clear chain of command, establish military tribunals, and probably the most telling of his experiences in the Union army, that officers keep written copies of their orders to collect as a record of their rebellion. All this while advocating the use of guerrilla warfare whenever possible.[49]

It is not difficult to comprehend how both pieces can come from the same pen at the same time if we understand Cavada's life and imagination in the context of a trans-American formation. He is not torn between "Nuestra America and the America that is not ours," as Martí would later put it. Rather, both Americas are his in ways that produce two different bodies of writing: one in English, published in one of the leading upper-middle-class magazines of the time in the United States; the other in Spanish, written to make the insurgent war against Spain more efficient in terms of military policy and guerrilla tactics. One announces allegorically his coming to revolutionary consciousness in Cuba; the other employs strategies he learned in the Union to wage rebellion. His is a Latinx identity with a voice in both worlds (US and Latino), as Cavada is not so much torn by his doubleness as he is formed by it in the much same way that the outbreak and outcome of the US Civil War inflected the issues of race, anti-imperialism, slavery, and self-governance fueling Cuba's own war of rebellion.

In this regard, Federico embodies a profound historical relation between the US Civil War and Cuba's Ten Years' War—both are American civil wars that share a genealogy much like the Cavada brothers themselves, for if the US Civil War is the arena for Adolfo's coming of age, it is the Cuban war that turns the precious painter and poet into a general and later commander-in-chief whose scorched earth practices rivaled William T. Sherman's swath to Savannah. It also made him a trans-American hero, claimed by Cuban nationals as a prodigal son; by Philadelphians as a freedom-fighting brother; and by Unionists as a comrade in arms. It is thus not surprising that his capture by Spanish forces in late June 1871 garnered national headlines across the United States. A petition for his release even became a *cause célèbre* for high-ranking Union brass, including Generals Graham (his former Libby Prison compatriot), Sheridan, and Sherman, all of whom petitioned President Grant to seek Cavada's release. But to no avail. A week before his fortieth birthday, Federico was executed without trial on July 1, 1871 (almost eight years to the day that he was captured at Gettysburg). In his last letter to his wife, Carmela, dated June 30, he writes, "I am here as a prisoner of war due to circumstances that without a doubt are familiar to you."[50] They are of course uncanny to him too, a sickly, inexperienced lieutenant colonel of the Philadelphia Volunteers who passed his time in a rebel prison sketching anecdotes finds himself a prisoner of war again—this time as a rebel commander-in-chief who never quite realized the irony of quelling one rebellion in the states but leading another on the island. His last words were reportedly, "Adios mi Cuba, hasta siempre."[51] One story even says he tossed his cigar and hat in the air before the bullets flew. His obituary ran in the *New York Herald*, the *Cincinnati Daily Gazette*, the *Leavenworth Times*, the *Boston Daily Journal*, Philadelphia's *Public Ledger*, and the *Philadelphia Inquirer*, which closed its paean to him with the following: "He lived and wrought and died for the cause of Cuban independence. He was a brave soldier, a true patriot, and an estimable gentleman."[52]

Six months later, the *New Orleans Times-Picayune* made brief mention that Adolfo Cavada was also killed in action, leading the head of the Cuban revolutionary movement, Carlos Manuel de Céspedes, to write a condolence note to Emily Dutton, the mother of the brothers Cavada. "Cuba counts one more martyr to its cause, but it can never forget the great service of Adolfo," the rebel president wrote. "Our history will consecrate an imperishable monument to him and what Cuban heart but will feel for the mother that has sacrificed so much that was dear to her."[53] Céspedes was not wrong. Even though the Ten Years' War ended in 1878 without securing Cuban independence or the immediate abolition of slavery, the revolutionary spirit of the Cavada brothers in action and in writing laid the foundation for the anti-imperial movement of Martí's generation. At the risk of making too much of Federico's transformation from would-be coward to the Fire King, it is worth noting that his return to Cuba and subsequent insurgent leadership fulfilled a nostalgic fate he expressed in 1847 in his first published poem, "The Cuban's Adieu to His Native Land," which Cavada notes in his journal appeared in the *Philadelphia Evening Bulletin*:

> Adieu to thee! Queen of the sea,
> Adieu to the thoughts of the past,
> Though for e'er thy remembrance shall last,
> Wherever on earth I may be.
>
> Adieu to thee! Queen of the wave,
> Adieu! With many a regret,
> Thy sorrows I'll never forget,
> 'Till lost in the gloom of the grave.
>
> Adieu to thee! Isle I hold dear,
> 'Till thy people at Liberty's call,
> By causing Iberia to fall
> 'Neath the flag of the free shall appear.

Farewell to thy dearly loved shore!
Farewell to thy fading hills,
For encompassed by the world and its ills,
Perhaps we may meet no more.

At last adieu! And 'mid the future keep,
The bright ray of Columbia's star;
Alas! Thy mountains loom up afar,
As we cleave the foaming deep!

And now thou'rt gone, perhaps for ever,
But await with a patient heart,
Till Columbia by valour and heart
The chains of the tyrant shall sever![54]

At first glance, the poem reads like the scores of other Cuban exile verses penned in Spanish-language organs throughout urban centers like New York and New Orleans. It imagines the ever-faithful isle someday gaining its independence from Spain, perhaps with the United States' assistance, and combines the political rhetoric of revolution with the romantic, if not overly sentimental, view of the island. But there are two differences here. The first is that it is written by a fifteen-year-old boy rather than an adult poet, lawyer, property owner, enslaver, politician, or military man, as most of the Cuban exile writers were in the 1840s and 1850s. The second is that it is penned and published in English. Cavada's poem, like the brothers Cavada, marks a transitional generation of US Cubans in the nineteenth century—not quite at home but not quite in exile either. "Deterritorialized," to recall how Rodrigo Lazo characterizes the exile's status, meaning that the Cavada brothers and their writing move "in and out of one nation and then another."[55] But such motion is not seamless, for to traverse one nation to another means to betray them both, to rebel against their borders for a sense of transformational citizenship. We see such a movement in Cavada's poem, for in it is a glimpse at how the fire of rebellion fueled the precious poet to travel from Cuba to Philadelphia and back to the island, dreaming of independence the entire time.

Conclusion

Recovering Our Southern Latinx Literary Heritage: The Reconstruction of Latinidad

The Civil War years situated Latinxs living in the United States in contradictory spaces that pressured the transformation of US *latinidades*, especially for those whose class, connections, or cultural capital already had them on the fault lines fissuring within and across the United States, Mexico, and Cuba. I've made no pretense to position these lives and writings as representative of the greater Latinx population, which was no more homogeneous then than it is now, and these Civil War writers would likely not pass muster for scholars who define US Latinx identity "not based on the birthplace or nationality of the writers but rather on spatial or community identification."[1] My position is that the historical conditions of the war years deterritorialized these Latinxs in the United States, leaving them instead in geopolitical spaces that made "community identification" precarious at best and perilous at worst. They are pulled away from communities, exiled by or from them, disidentified and *desconocidos*, as James Santiago Tafolla puts it, strange or unrecognizable after crossing the personal, cultural, and national lines of US Latinidad. Besides, "As it is traditionally invoked, community offers us a romance in place of complex and contentious social relations," Saidiya Hartman notes. "This is not to minimize or neglect the networks of support and care that existed among the enslaved," Hartman says of the problem of "the romance of community" for studying the history of the enslaved, "but to keep in mind the limits and fractures of community precisely because of the routine of violence of slavery." Albeit in a different way, the civil wars over the nineteenth century's cultures of enslavement transformed the lives and writings of those Latinxs who were directly or indirectly complicit with slavery, indentured servitude, or other forms of anti-Black and anti-Indigenous politics and sentiments. These positions might seat them in communities anathema to us now (and perhaps some Latinxs then), but I agree with Hartman that "it is as crucial to engage the issue of community through the descension and difference that are also its constituents."[2]

From its inception, the Recovering the US Hispanic Literary Heritage project has wrestled with the problem of reclaiming writers and writings that espouse or uphold values of race, culture, and power that are difficult to square with contemporary expressions of Latinidad or current presumptions about Latinx communities, as anyone familiar with the scholarship on María Amparo Ruiz de Burton knows. Sketched broadly, Ruiz de Burton is often heralded as the first Mexican American female author to publish two novels in English: *Who Would Have Thought It?* (1872), a satirical romance, domestic, and captivity narrative framed by the civil wars in the United States and Mexico, and *The Squatter and the Don* (1885), a post-Reconstruction historical romance that ties the fate of its star-crossed Mexican-Anglo lovers to the future of California's development by way of the railroad industry and monopoly capitalism. The novels are remarkably racist and sympathetic to the Southern cause during the Civil War and its aftermath. After the Recovery's republication of both books in the early 1990s, scholars (myself included) launched impressive rhetorical, historical, and analytical gymnastics to stake three basic, interrelated positions about Ruiz de Burton and her novels: (1) acknowledge that her writings present Mexican American whiteness at the expense of Indigenous and Black peoples; (2) maintain that such constructions of whiteness, however disagreeable, are in response to the rampant racism Mexican Americans faced in the nineteenth century; and (3) argue that Ruiz de Burton advanced a Latin Americanist alternative to Anglo-American whiteness, one rooted in Mexican, Spanish, and European colonial caste systems rather than the United States' hypodescent racial logics. The sticking point is the degree to which the latter could be understood as a viable, valuable, vexed, radical, revolutionary, or resistant response to Anglo-American racism, racialization, and racial hatred or a questionable Mexican American repetition of them.[3]

Ruiz de Burton's ostensible standing as the "first" Mexican American female writer to publish her novels in English explains in part the burden she carries in Latinx literary history, but considering the storylines I've recovered, her work should be understood as a literary continuation of the racial and cultural legacies of similar nineteenth-century Latinx writings produced during the long Civil War years. There are several distinct firsts before the publication of our first Latinx Civil War novel: Quintero is the first (and likely only) Confederate *letrado* with an archive of English-language dispatches from the borderlands; Gonzales is the first Cuban American to publish a corpus of op-eds, essays, manifestos, propaganda, and articles about Cuba in English; Adolfo Cavada is the first to write a Latinx Civil War diary in English; and his brother Federico published the first Latinx Civil War POW narrative in English. Moreover, by studying the lives and writings of the Jimeno brothers, we witness up close the linguistic and psychological ramifications of learning English by reading Anglo-American print material, writing to Anglo-American readers (real or imagined), and, eventually, seeing the Latinx body through Anglophone eyes. In all these cases, English-language literacy marks a turning point that shaped and re-positioned Latinidad within the United States' white power structures. Whereas the predominately Spanish monolingual Chacón and Tafolla remained on the margins of white cultural power despite their respective efforts to fight for it in blue or gray, Union and Confederate Latinx subjects like Quintero, Gonzales, the Jimeno brothers, and the Cavadas secured and preserved their racial whiteness through English. Otero too maintained his political power by campaigning on his fluency in English, contra to his monolingual Spanish-speaking Hispano opponent.[4] Their writings mark a socially significant transition in the production of nineteenth-century print and expressive cultures that Ruiz de Burton inherits by publishing her novels in English.

While the Spanish-language press continued unabated during the nineteenth century across Florida, New York, Philadelphia, New Orleans, Texas, New Mexico, and California, Latinx Civil War writings ushered in a new body of work literate and literary in Anglophone traditions. Recall Federico Cavada's reading list, for instance, which included John Milton, Lord Byron, Sir Walter Scott, Thomas Paine, and Washington Irving, while Quintero tied his literary legacy to Lamar, Longfellow, and the South Carolina nullificationist John Lyde Wilson. For these Latinx Civil War writers, English reorients their Latinx identities—it gives them access to Anglophone audiences; it provides cultural literacy and capital among Anglo-Americans; and it facilitates their attempts at racial passing through the vocabularies of racial power in the United States. Ruiz de Burton's novels continue in the same Anglophone vein as the other Latinx "firsts" who resorted to English. She spoofs classical rhetoric in *Who Would Have Thought It?* and cites writers such as Charles Dickens and Thomas Carlyle throughout *The Squatter and the Don*. Her sharpest characters are avid readers of Anglophone newspapers or British and European historical novels, and probably, the most declarative statement that her otherwise sentimental Mexican American waif utters in *Who Would Have Thought It?* comes by way of her introduction: "'My name is María Dolores Medina, but I have been always called Lola or Lolita,' she answered *in the plainest English*."[5]

The statement is an embodiment of the transformations of Latinidad that I've mapped across the Civil War writers who came of age in the United States at the same time as the fictional Lola Medina. Their lives and writings provide the Latinx legacy that frames Lola's magical transformation from an orphaned girl whose skin is dyed dark to a young, white-skinned Mexican woman. With the transition from Spanish to English comes a change in name, standing, and status that, in Lola's case, leaves her infantilized in both languages. Education, geographical migrations, and marriage arrangements further mobilize the transformations for the Latinx generation, who, like Lola, didn't come out of the war years the same. Instead, their acquisition of English and its attendant cultural literacies invited the internalization of Anglophone norms that left mid-nineteenth-century Latinxs split, divided, or alienated from their sense of self-identity, community, and national belonging. Poor Lola fares no better than the Jimeno brothers if we follow her racialization to its bitter end: After she returns to Mexico via Cuba with her father, we're told she suffers "profound melancholy" because she misses her Yankee lover, Julian Norval. When he joins her after the war, "the roses and dimples which had fled when she went to Mexico returned with the Yankee lover. The coral lips parted in merry laughter again, showing the pearly teeth. And the lustrous black eyes . . . were once more brilliant with happiness or languid with love."[6] The character whose dark-skinned body started as the center of attention of the novel and its ridiculous New Englanders ends up a conglomeration of grotesque body parts: coral lips, pearly teeth, and black eyes. She's a dismembered casualty of the domestic, gendered, cultural, racial, sexual, linguistic, and transnational civil wars she weathered from the Southwestern borderlands to the Northeastern United States and back to Mexico by way of Cuba.

What we learn from Ruiz de Burton's predecessors is that the transition from Spanish to English is a civil war that had a profound impact on their Latinx racialization, representation, and self-identification via a language that viewed Latinxs as others. Reminiscent of Porfirio Jimeno's letter from Mexico to his stepfather, Ruiz de Burton's use of English risks representing her main Mexican American female character through an Anglophone male gaze, and Lola ends up the worst for it. The omniscient narrator frames her through and for Julian's eyes, leaving her to appear as a selection of sexualized body parts to the Yankee lover and the novel's wider Anglophone audience. There's hardly much difference between the racist objectification the narrative critiques and the grotesque abjection the novel reproduces at its end. Lola is left fractured and fissured in our first Latinx Civil War novel in English because, for mid-nineteenth-century Latinxs, English is a double-edged weapon of war. It was the *lingua franca* that facilitated the political and legal dispossession of most nineteenth-century Californio elites, but as Rosina Lozano shows, learning it could also alter familial ties and cultural connections, as evidenced by Mariano Vallejo's family's uneven movements between Spanish and English. "Tell Mama I do not write to her," explained one Vallejo daughter, "as I have become such a '*gringa*' that I cannot write her in Spanish as my heart would dictate."[7]

The point is not so much about the fact of language transition from Spanish to English, but the divisions such a move creates internally. María Vallejo's message to her mama, for instance, is torn between her written English and the emotional memory of her Spanish, and the rupture between them produces a conflicted sense of white Latinidad. She invokes the Spanish she says she cannot write to refer to herself as *gringa* because of her English. This epitomizes the Latinx civil war lives and writings I've recovered and analyzed. They mark an embattled transformation of mid-nineteenth-century US Latinidad that is reconstructed in the context of the US Civil War and its racial fault lines that stretch from the US Southwest to the Northeast Seaboard via the circum-Gulf South. Theirs is a "political formation" of Latinx identity, to recall Renee Hudson's explanation of the relevance of "Latinx" for nineteenth-century writers, but if they offer us a "history of Latinx resistance," as

Hudson adds, it takes place on different, intersecting battlefronts: the site of English-language learning, the muster roll, the ranks of the conscripted, the military diary, sketches on scraps of paper, personal letters, and archives within archives. These personal, cultural, and textual theaters point to how the Civil War years pressured Latinx writers into "hegemonic and conservative forms of revolution and latinidad" through language, racial identification, and the promise of white power and privilege in the face of dispossession, displacement, and deterritorialization.[8]

If her published writings and extant letters are any indication, Ruiz de Burton frankly didn't give a damn about the Union, despite being married to Union Brevet Brigadier General Henry S. Burton. She cared even less for the plight of the enslaved and the status of the Indigenous. Her eyes were on the so-called Napoleonic "Grand Design" for Latin nations, as Rosaura Sánchez and Beatrice Pita explain in their edition of Ruiz de Burton's letters.[9] In one of her 1869 letters to Vallejo, in which she reminds him yet again of his *atravesada* statement, she uses the phrase "la raza latina" three times—twice capitalized—to refer to the Eurocentric notion of the so-called Latin race being proffered by Napoleon III and his sycophants: "De las naciones latinas, ¿cuál es la única que progresa? La Francia" (Of the Latin nations, which is the only one that has progressed? France.)[10] Initially, she presented herself as a liberal supporter in the early 1860s, especially in her letters to Matías Romero, Mexico's republican liaison with the United States, but after Maximilian's 1867 execution, Ruiz de Burton seems to have changed allegiances: "Con Maximiliano murió nuestra nacionalidad, allí pereció la última esperanza de México, y ahora los Yankies sólo esperan la hora que mejor les convenga para enterrarla para siempre, y pisotear bien la tierra encima y barrer todo vestigo desagradable después." (With Maximilian our nationality died, there perished the last hope of Mexico, and now the Yankees are only waiting for the time that best suits them to bury it forever, and trample the dirt on top and sweep away all unpleasant traces afterwards.)[11] Scores of scholars have pinpointed the brief but wondrous appearance in *Who Would Have Thought It?* of Lola's Austrian-born blue-eyed father and her archduke-loving *abuelo* as embodiments of the Creole whiteness that Ruiz de Burton advances as an alternative to Anglo America. They may espouse similarly racist views about Indigeneity, the argument goes, but their whiteness presents a form of Latinx identity that counters Anglo America's prevailing racialization of Mexican Americans that the novel satirizes.[12]

Yet, in the context of the firsts that precede her, Ruiz de Burton's fabrications of whiteness also point back to our peculiar Southern Latinx literary heritage. She may be advancing an idea of Latin American Creole whiteness that's ostensibly different from Anglo America, but as with Ambrosio José Gonzales's English-language writings about Cuba, her decision to write in English situates her novels within the prevailing racialized norms of Anglophone print and its real and imagined audience in the United States. With *Who Would Have Thought It?*, she goes to war with the Yankees and in turn is sympathetic to the Confederate South and its preservation of slavery, as we see in her description of Isaac Sprig's time in a Confederate prison camp.[13] *The Squatter and the Don* too links the dispossession of Californios to the postwar plight of white Southerners—the eponymous Don's hopes for the future of California rest on reconstructing the two regions via a railroad that would connect them geographically and economically. Suffering from what an early Chicano critic derisively dubbed the "*hacienda* syndrome" of a mid-twentieth-century New Mexican text, Ruiz de Burton's novels inherit their Southern sympathies from her Latinx predecessors who also set out to protect and preserve the idea of white Latinidad through English and the United States' vocabulary of racial power.[14]

The Southern Latinx literary heritage that Quintero, Gonzales, Otero, and Ruiz de Burton produced is written to and for the United States' English-reading audiences (real and imagined). It connects Confederate nationalism to the cause of Cuban independence or links the plight of Mexican American dispossession to the fall of the South, drawing on Southern sympathy and its attendant cultural codes. This body of work is obviously not the norm—it's the writing of the elite, after all, and the Jimeno brothers and the Cavadas never express sympathy for the US South in English or Spanish. Further, the fact that Tafolla wrote his unpublished autobiography in Spanish might explain why the Confederate bugler doesn't trumpet the Southern cause, even though he is no less invested in protecting his white privilege. The volumes that Quintero, Gonzales, Otero, and Ruiz de Burton wrote, however, point to a Latinx literary history in English that's rooted in Confederate sympathy to the degree that it should challenge scholars of the Recovering the US

Hispanic Literary Heritage project to reassess the transformative moment in our literary production when Latinx writers began to engage an Anglophone audience during and immediately after the US Civil War. The "very notion of a Hispanic Confederate," Rodrigo Lazo mentions, "is a reminder that a scholarly enterprise is likely to turn up skeletons."[15] As it turns out, our literary history is a veritable battlefield littered with a corpus of Latinx Civil War writings that adopted and adapted the prevailing languages of race, power, citizenship, and independence that circulated in Southern circles and was often predicated on Black enslavement and anti-Indigeneity. Whatever forms of Latinx resistance they might express emerge from forces of reaction that put these writers at civil war with their standing in Latinx literary history.

For example, in a narrative characterized by ambivalence, ambiguity, fabrication, performativity, instability, lies, facts, fictions, and fabulations, the one constant in Loreta Janeta Velazquez's *The Woman in Battle* is its positive investment in whiteness. First published in Hartford, Connecticut, and Richmond, Virginia, in 1876, the book recounts the life and adventures of Cuban-born Loreta Velazquez, who fought for the Confederacy as Lieutenant Harry T. Buford before serving as a spy, drug runner, blockade buster, and double agent for the CSA in various guises. Ever since its publication, readers have expressed considerable skepticism, criticism, doubt, and incredulity about the veracity of Velazquez's exploits. The prevailing critical objections to the book and its author center on whether Velazquez participated in the battles mentioned in the narrative; the accuracy of the historical events and personages recounted in the narrative; or Velazquez's place among the documented cases of women who joined the war effort for both sides as nurses, spies, or combatants in petticoats or pantaloons. There are also those who suspect that Loreta Janeta Velazquez is not a Cuban-born person named Loreta Janeta Velazquez.[16] However, what makes *The Woman in Battle* a Latinx Civil War narrative is that it repeats the telltale signs of the lives and writings of earlier Latinx Civil War subjects who undergo similar personal, social, and symbolic transformations during the war years.

The narrative's unflagging and unambivalent fight for slavery and Southern white nationalism during and after the Civil War identify Velazquez as a "genuine Southerner" of the time, which has positioned the Cuban Confederate on the margins of US Latinx literary history.[17]

"While we acknowledge Velasquez's [*sic*] resolve," write one team of Recovery scholars, "we reject the cause of the slave-holding South she served."[18] Yet, by that standard, we would be bereft of most of our nineteenth-century Latinx literary inheritance, for what rings most true in Velazquez's seemingly impossible autobiography is the one fiction that it shares with other Latinx Civil War writings: the belief in white racial supremacy as a justification for Black enslavement. Ambrosio José Gonzales held the same belief, fighting to protect it "in the character of an American," as he put it in one of his *Free Press* pieces. Velazquez fought for it too as Lieutenant Harry T. Buford of the CSA, and even after the Civil War, Velazquez continued with a race war against Black people as "a Cuban" and "a true Southern sympathizer."[19] With Velazquez, we're faced with a literary heritage that can be understood not so much by birth origin as by the active investment in maintaining a brand of white power and privilege that imagines a connection between the transformation of Latinx identity and the rise and fall of the Confederate South and its postwar Reconstruction.

From the moment the young Cuban is sent to New Orleans for an education, Velazquez expresses a series of identity conflicts that put the Spanish language, Catholicism, and family and cultural traditions at war with the process of Americanization that leaves Velazquez "a good American in thought and manner," much like what Ambrosio José Gonzales aspired to in 1849.[20] Velazquez's story is about the civil war of becoming a Latinx subject, and the connection between Cuba and the Confederacy mirrors Velazquez's identity as Buford. "I rebelled," Velazquez says, linking the personal Latinx transformations to the rhetorics of the Cuban revolution and Southern secession.[21] They uphold the same cause and provide the backdrop for the other forms of identity battles that the narrative recounts. "The multiple metaphoric civil wars that appear within Velazquez's *The Woman in Battle*," writes Robin C. Sager, "speak to the ways that individuals contested the traditional constructions of race, ethnicity, class, gender, and sexuality during the US Civil War and Reconstruction periods."[22] With such indeterminacy, it is tempting to argue that Velazquez is our first "Latinx" in the sense of the term's gesture to signal sexual and gender neutrality by crossing out, *x*-ing, if you will, the regime of binary gender systems that "Latino/a" upholds. However, as we saw with Ruiz de Burton, the fate of "firsts" is a lost cause. Instead, suffice it to say that in the context of our Latinx Civil War writings, it would be more appropriate to understand Velazquez as trans^{x}.

I stake this position as a revision of my initial recovery and republication of *The Woman in Battle*, in which I understood Velazquez as Buford along similar wartime narratives that were popular at the time. I maintained that, while Velazquez as Buford followed the genre tropes of popular stories that included women in men's clothing, the performance indicated a greater crisis in gender that the war ignited and also marked a historical confluence between Cuba and the Confederacy through a "transvestism [that] goes transnational," as I worded it then, that demonstrated the degree to which the common investment in slavery traversed the circum-Gulf South.[23] The few scholars at the time who discussed the text in terms of its veracity, its relation to women's Civil War writings, or its clear demonstration of the performativity of gender framed my focus on gender expression and my understanding of it as a staging of gender as an enacted category on a historical scene. To my thinking, Velazquez becoming Buford was not just about following a husband to the front lines, living out a martial dream to go to battle, or trying to gain access to a masculine public sphere otherwise closed to Velazquez. It was also about the fall of domestic ideologies in the Confederate South, the desire to imagine Cuba as masculine, and the retrograde project of reconstituting ostensibly normative, heterosexual gender and sexual roles by making the butt of humor and critique potential scenes of same-sex desire between Velazquez as Buford and a variety of hapless Southern belles.

But the focus on Velazquez putting on a uniform to participate in the Civil War eclipsed the recognition of a more complicated civil war. Well before Velazquez joined the ranks as Lieutenant Harry T. Buford, their gender categories were already in formation. Early in the narrative, Velazquez states,

> I was especially haunted with the idea of being a man; and the more I thought upon the subject, the more I was disposed to murmur at Providence for having created me a woman. While residing with my aunt, it was frequently my habit, after all in the house had retired to bed at night, to dress myself in my cousin's clothes, and to promenade by the hour before the mirror, practicing the gait of a man, and admiring the figure I

made in masculine raiment. I wished that I could only change places with my brother Josea.[24]

The scene unfolds long before the Civil War breaks out; before Velazquez meets and elopes with the first of four hapless husbands; and before Velazquez decides to join the Confederacy. It occurs while Velazquez is living in New Orleans—somewhere between the ages of seven and nine—and takes place in private as opposed to the later, public performances of gender. With this passage, the focus on dress takes a different turn, as Velazquez clearly states, "I was especially haunted with the idea of being a man."

While *The Woman in Battle* frames Velazquez within what Talia Mae Bettcher characterizes as the "wrong body" narrative, the night scene in their cousin's clothes invokes the specter of an identity Velazquez cannot quite name but gives expression through the types of gender performances that would be pathologized a decade later in Richard von Krafft-Ebing's 1886 *Psychopathia Sexualis*.[25] The fact that Velazquez's nightly promenade occurs in front of a mirror over the course of the two years they are sent to live with an aunt underscores the scene as a transitional moment of identity formation on multiple fronts. It's not that Velazquez is confused, embattled, or "trapped" in the wrong body, to follow Bettcher; rather, the gender-sex norms of the day frame Velazquez's identity between a binary that Velazquez "frequently" traverses at night. Peter Boag says something similar in his understanding that "many nineteenth-century western Americans who cross-dressed did so to express their transgender identity."[26] However true this insight might be, it limits the understanding of trans* identities to the sum of its gender expression, whereas dress is only part of the scene's overall significance. First, the scene takes place during Velazquez's English-language education in New Orleans, so the intersectionality of language—the transition and translation, if you will, between Spanish and English—undergirds the entire narrative episode. Second, literacy frames the moment, with Velazquez finding particular inspiration not only in the romance of Joan of Arc but also in New World colonial legacies: "I wished that I was a man, such a man as Columbus or Captain Cook, and could discover new worlds."[27] Finally, Velazquez expresses the moment through a misogyny that will follow them throughout the narrative in the form of women as sexual competition, comic relief, or vapid complainers. "A woman labors under some disadvantages in an attempt to fight her own way in the world," Velazquez mansplains, "and at the same time, from the mere fact that she is a woman, she can often do things that a man cannot. I have no hesitation in saying that I wish I had been created a man instead of a woman. This is what is the matter with nearly all the women who go about complaining of the wrongs of our sex."[28]

To read Velazquez *cum* Buford as another sensationalist story of a woman dressed in male attire—as myself and others have done—is to misread the few times Velazquez emphatically declares, "I have no hesitation in saying that I wish I had been created a man instead of a woman." Such statements announce the historical situation of trans* identity for an early Latinx figure. As Jack Halberstam explains it, "The asterisk [in trans*] modifies the meaning of transitivity by refusing to situate transition in relation to a destination, a final form, a specific shape, or an established configuration of desire and identity."[29] Considering the questions and objections raised about the authenticity of *The Woman in Battle* and the author's so-called true identity, I propose "trans^{x}" instead as a more apt marker of the variables that constitute the transformations that Velazquez's narrative maps. "Trans^{x}" registers the Latinx transition between Old and New World customs; conversion from Catholicism to Methodism; and shift from Spanish to English as part of the educational process Velazquez undergoes in New Orleans. "Trans^{x}" also marks Velazquez's characteristic geographical mobility as actual and symbolic transition between places and spaces of Latinidad: it signals Velazquez's transnationalism across Cuba, the United States, and the Confederacy, and it's not by happenstance that the narrative closes with Velazquez again on the move along the US-Mexico border. Were it not for its obsession with white Latinidad, the text would embody what Francisco J. Galarte calls "brown trans figuration," insofar as *The Woman in Battle* and its author "*matter* (so they are important *and* are enmeshed in material relations) and *move* (circulate, navigate as in movement, and also move us in the affective sense)."[30] The *x* in "trans^{x}" marks the nature of the Velazquez narrative that has frustrated readers ever since its 1876 publication—its refusal to fit one shape as an identifiable, authentic "Hispanic" text. Instead, it sits comfortably between fiction and fact; travel, adventure, and domestic narrative; war memoir and espionage tale; sensationalist tale and historical account. Authored by Velazquez and ostensibly edited by C. J. Worthington, *The Woman in Battle* gives credence to Halberstam's point that the asterisk, and I would add, the *x* in "trans^{x}" too, "makes trans* people the authors of their own categorizations."[31]

The Velazquez narrative sits at the crossroads of nineteenth-century Latinidad. As with its Latinx predecessors, it chronicles in English the embattled process of becoming a Latinx subject in the United States. It also frames that transformation through a trans^{x} narrative that looks ahead, so to speak, to contemporary categories of gender and sexual identities that the *x* in "Latinx" signals. It is a nineteenth-century text with twentieth-century notions about the performativity of gender and sexuality and the transformation of Latinx identity in the twin theaters of Cuban and Confederate civil wars and reconstructions. "*The Woman in Battle* 'embodies and enacts' the international dimensions of the American Civil War," Coleman Hutchison explains, "and in so doing, continues the work of Confederate literary nationalism long after the fall of the Confederacy."[32] For this reason, the Velazquez narrative has been estranged from efforts to reclaim it as part of a Hispanic literary heritage not only because of the indeterminacy of its author but also because its unapologetic stance in support of slavery and the protection of white privilege makes apparent the implications of claiming whiteness as a viable identity for Latinx subjects in the United States. However, as María del Pilar Blanco reminds us, "In studying expressions of Latinidad as they manifest themselves in different points of the American hemisphere, it is crucial to entertain both the contact points and the digressions between past and present histories, and also to understand such enunciations of identity as open-ended, often contradictory narratives."[33] *The Woman in Battle* is one such "contact point" with earlier Latinx Civil War writings; it is also a "digression" from them that heralds turn-of-the-century Latinx narratives caught up in the nadir of Jim Crow and its policing of whiteness. For two Cuban heirs—Ambrosio José Gonzales's older sons, Ambrose ("Brosie") and Narciso (named after the famous filibuster)—their commitment to the Southern cause extended well into the twentieth century. Their work may be "contradictory" in its expression of Latinidad, as Blanco puts it, but their Southern Latinx literature is not so much "open-ended" when it comes to the

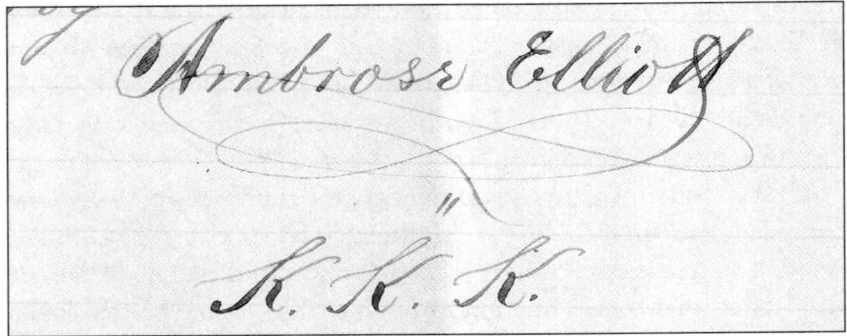

Figure c.1. Ambrose Elliott signs his name with a flourish of letters that announce his racial affiliation. Ambrose Gonzales to Emily Elliott, July 11, 1873 (from Buffalo Marsh), Elliott and Gonzáles Family Papers #1009, Southern Historical Collection, Wilson Library, University of North Carolina at Chapel Hill.

racial legacy it inherits from Ambrosio José Gonzales, Loreta Janeta Velazquez, and their ilk.

Ambrose was born in 1857, and Narciso was born a year later. After the Civil War, they both accompanied their father and mother to Cuba, where Ambrosio José took up a teaching job and, as we saw in chapter 4, kept his distance from the Ten Years' War. After Hattie Gonzales died of yellow fever in 1869, Ambrose returned with his father to the states while Narciso remained in Cuba for a little over a year before returning to South Carolina. For the duration of their teen and young adult lives, they were raised by the Elliotts, in part because their father was on the move for work, but also because the Elliotts blamed him for the death of their beloved Hattie. Either way, the Elliotts brought up the Gonzales children. At one time, they were so bitterly estranged from their father that they took up the Elliott last name. Under the eldest Elliott aunt, they learned the worst of Southern white racism during Reconstruction. In their letters to each other and to family members, they lament the presence of free Blacks in Charleston; rue with the rest of the Elliotts the loss of family land to former slaves; and as young adults, they mobilized with South Carolina's "red shirts," a white supremist group that terrorized Black voters.[34] Even after the third Enforcement Act of 1871 suppressed Klan activities and drove its members into further secrecy, Ambrose signed one of his extant letters as "Ambrose Elliott," with the abbreviation "K.K.K." beneath his signature.

The Gonzales brothers were also copious writers, with Narciso launching the politically pugnacious South Carolina paper *The State*, which he edited, while Ambrose worked as a contributing writer. Narciso found himself venturing to Cuba to fight for its independence during the 1898 Cuban-Spanish-American War and corresponded back to *The State* about the war front. At the same time, Ambrose published local color pieces about South Carolina's Gullah community in the vein of Joel Chandler Harris. At the turn of the twentieth century, Narciso's stinging political writings—some progressive and others invested in protecting elite Southern white power—landed him in a war of words with James H. Tillman, the lieutenant governor of South Carolina, who shot and killed the young Gonzales outside his newspaper office in Columbia, South Carolina. In the aftermath, Ambrose collected and published his brother's writings from the Cuban war front, titling the 1922 book *In Darkest Cuba*, and he continued writing his Gullah "folk pieces," publishing four volumes of his so-called "Black Border" series: *The Black Border* (1922); *The Captain: Stories of the Black Border* (1924); *With Aesop Along the Black Border* (1924); and *Laguerre: A Gascon of the Black Border* (1924)—all printed in Columbia, South Carolina, by way of *The State*'s press.

The books, their framing narratives, and Gonzales's expository work are on par with early twentieth-century racist caricatures of Black people living along the "black border" of the South Carolina coast—the former plantation belt of the Elliott clan, spanning from Beaufort to Edisto Island, that the elder Ambrosio Gonzales fought so hard to protect. In Gonzales's writings, there is no racial ambivalence, ambiguity, agency, double-voiced critique, or subtle reversals of power that characterize the tomes of African American folklore and its incorporation into fiction, à la Charles Chesnutt and his Uncle Julius. Instead, there is Joe Fields, who "was the most onery looking darkey on Pon Pon. Squat, knock-kneed, lopsided, slew-footed, black as a crow, pop-eyed, with a few truculent looking yellow teeth set 'slantindilarly' in a prognathous jaw."[35] And that's the first sentence of the first page of the first story of Gonzales's first three-hundred-page book in English. The work is in the same vein as the so-called Gullah craze of the 1920s–1930s, which trafficked in Southern fantasies of Black primitivism and the folklore of a better life under slavery. Such fictions garnered Julia Peterkin, Gonzales's

South Carolina contemporary, the 1929 Pulitzer Prize for her Gullah novel *Scarlet Sister Mary*. Peterkin "transformed her fantasies about the five hundred blacks who lived and worked on their two-thousand-acre plantation into fictional works that made her a historic literary figure."[36] Gonzales too likely picked up Gullah words and phrases from the enslaved people in South Carolina's Lowcountry region, including the formerly enslaved who continued with the Elliott family and from whom he would have taken their stories. But there was no Pulitzer for his mimicry of Gullah, which, "grotesque and interesting as it is," he says, "is only a vehicle for carrying to the reader the thought and life of an isolated group among the varied peoples that make up the complex population of this Republic."[37]

While there's something perverse about using a people's language to disseminate racial stereotypes about them, there's also a return here that's vexed by ethno-racial nostalgia: Ambrose returned to the language of the enslaved that surrounded him in his youth and resonated around him in postwar South Carolina. Narciso returned to Cuba to fight in its final bid for independence in the vein of his namesake and contra to his father's refusal to fight in a war that mobilized the island's people of color alongside white Creoles. Yet they are both still embedded in South Carolina's racial politics, policies, and policing, using their own English-language press to publish and disseminate their writings about, among other things, Cuba, the history of slavery, and the preservation of the Southern culture that their father fought to protect. They wrote to and for South Carolina's Anglophone readership, which might explain why they trafficked in racial caricatures, but like their father, neither looked completely away from Cuba even as they continued dreaming of the Confederacy. Instead, they inherited and perpetuated our peculiar Southern Latinx literary heritage, which may have emerged as early as the 1840s and peaked in the 1920s, but it took shape during the long Civil War years. These lives and writings require archival recovery, if only to recover from them and their anti-Black, pro-slavery legacy, which we should neither memorialize nor forget. They are our deplorables whose reconstruction of Latinidad emerged out of the ashes of the Latinx civil wars we continue to wage, weather, and survive.

ACKNOWLEDGMENTS

This book has been a battle of attrition for too many years to care. Two significant forms of institutional support turned the tide on the project. I was fortunate enough to be named a 2018–2019 Research Fellow at the University of Texas–Austin's Latino Research Institute, where I launched the book's research and writing in earnest, and I would still be clawing at the chapters were it not for the generosity, hospitality, and resources of the American Antiquarian Society, where I was named the 2023–2024 Mellon Distinguished Scholar in Residence. I owe the book's completion to my year in residency at the AAS, where I enjoyed the expertise, collegiality, and friendship of Scott Casper, Nan Wolverton, John Garcia, the outstanding library staff, and the cadre of fellows who joined me under the dome.

The camaraderie, company, and critical acumen of the AAS fellows kept up my spirits and improved my work during my residency. Alexander Chapa-Silva, Sam Plasencia, Andrew Porwancher, Adam Malka, Haven Hawley, Amy Gore, Eric Lamore, Ronald Angelo Johnson, and Gordon Fraser read drafts, shared a source or two, or listened to me talk through the project. I especially appreciated the company of Ben Davidson and Chip Badley, a Civil War historian and a nineteenth-century literary Americanist, respectively, who made happy hours a convivial combination of historical acumen and literary expertise.

I'm grateful to the librarians, archivists, researchers, and staff—too many to name individually—who helped me identify, access, or digitize the primary materials that comprise the book's bedrock. I always found a helping hand, a willing researcher, prompt replies, and enthusiastic aid from colleagues at the American Antiquarian Society, the Santa Bárbara Mission Archive Library, UC–Berkeley's Bancroft Library, the University of New Mexico's Center for Southwest Research and Special Collections, UT Austin's Benson Latin American Library and Dolph Briscoe Center for American History, the Haley Memorial Library and J. Evetts Haley

History Center, the Galveston and Texas History Center, the University of Miami's Cuban Heritage Collection, the University of South Carolina Library, the University of Georgia's Hargrett Rare Book and Manuscript Library, Georgetown University Archives, Special Collections at the University of Southern Mississippi library, University of North Carolina–Chapel Hill's Wilson Special Collections Library, the Boston Public Library, Harvard's Houghton Library, and the Historical Society of Pennsylvania. Support for this research was provided by the University of New Mexico College of Arts and Sciences, and a grant from the University of New Mexico's Center for Regional Studies facilitated the book's completion.

So many colleagues, scholars, and thinkers have shaped my writing, especially in relation to US Latinx literary history and cultural studies. Their work marks the contours of mine and cuts new routes for the future of studying our Latinx pasts. Over the years, I've benefitted from panel presentations, spirited discussions, and the innovative books, articles, and arguments by José F. Aranda Jr., Raúl Coronado, John Alba Cutler, Francisco J. Galarte, Laura E. Gómez, John M. González, Bernadine M. Hernández, Renee Hudson, Kelley Kreitz, Carmen E. Lamas, Rodrigo Lazo, Laura Lomas, Marissa K. López, Karen Roybal, Kirsten Silva Gruesz, Alberto Varon, and Maria Windell. My conversations with Sara E. Johnson, Koritha Mitchell, Carrie Tirado Bramen, and Elizabeth Young also sharpened my thinking on the intersections of race, writing, and history, while friends Margie Montañez, José Montañez, Bernadine Hernández, and Francisco Galarte more than once pulled me out of the trenches with dinner, beers, and laughs that threatened to blow our cover.

My appreciation goes out to the former students who weathered my Civil War interests during their doctoral days or kept in touch long after to see how the fight was going: Amy Gore, W. Oliver Baker, Lauren E. Perry-Rummel, Laurie Lowrance, Erin Murrah-Mandril, Leigh C. Johnson, and D. Noreen Rivera. A few colleagues have also been supportive over the years, including William Andrews, Minrose Gwin, Anita Obermeier, Chuck Paine, Gary Scharnhorst, Kathryn Wichelns, Marissa Greenberg, and Carmen Nocentelli. Eric Zinner and Furqan Sayeed have been exceptional to work with at New York University Press, and

I thank the anonymous reviewers whose detailed and substantial comments improved the book considerably.

I owe a special note of gratitude to Sara E. Johnson, Kirsten Silva Gruesz, and Rodrigo Lazo, the self-named Trans-American Writing Group. They pulled me through drafts of drafts of this book. Its completion is a testament to their willingness to spend the time, thought, care, and intellectual labor to see me through. They pushed on my ideas, pulled on my prose, opened new directions, headed off others, and gave me inspiration, especially during the pandemic, when I was tempted to go AWOL. I'm lucky to count such brilliant and dedicated scholars as my friends.

An army of sisters—Anita, Lupe, Elsa, Bertha, Lisa, and Becky—has always supported me; so too have my two brothers, David and Carlos. It's hard to go wrong with so many siblings on my side. I hope they find a minute to read this book. I've dedicated it to our parents, David and Felipa Alemán, who gave me their wit, wisdom, and humble wonder for the world, and I leave the book as a gift to Adelina, Alejandro, Miranda, Aviana, Leo, and Sebastian to remember stories of the past. To Melina, there isn't a word that will fail to write our future.

***

Portions of the book have been previously published. Part of my overall argument appeared in "Wars of Rebellion: US Hispanic Writers and Their American Civil Wars," *American Literary History* 25, no. 1 (Spring 2013): 54–68. A small section from chapter 2 appeared in "Narratives of Displacement in Places That Once Were Mexican," in *The Cambridge History of Latina/o Literature*, edited by John Morán González and Laura Lomas (Cambridge University Press, 2018). An earlier version of chapter 5 appeared in *The Latino Nineteenth Century*, edited by Rodrigo Lazo and Jesse Alemán (New York University Press, 2016).

APPENDIX

José Antonio Jimeno to William T. Sherman, November 9, 1850, William T. Sherman Papers

New York November 9th 1850

My dear friend Castañares
We did not write you because we did not know where y where, but Father Ryder wrote to Miss that you would like us to write to you, and told us your direction, and I am very glad to do so. I hope you will not be anscous that we are not in College, but you know that we were very ignorant besides our heads are not well yet, and Father Ryder thought we could have more care with Miss Meade than at the College, and our parents have written to her, to say that they wish her to keep us as long as she and Fr Ryder think it good for us to remain, as we require much training in many things, we could not get in College. We both thank you very much for all your kindness and care of us, also the kindness we received from your wife, when we were in Washington and we hope by good conduct and hard study to prove ourselves worthy of your friendship, and the interest you have taken in us. We received by Dr. Mory 2 pieces of gold as a present, and letters from our Mother who begs us to give her love to you and your wife, and she tells us that we have another little Brother but we do not know his name. Mr. Ord has gone to Monterey, Mrs. Sully the Mother of the gentleman who marriad Manuela came to see us the other day. She is a very good old Lady and invited us to her house in Phil[adelphia]. Mr Larkin called last week for the first time to see us but our aunt Robinson we have only seen once in sisc months. I saw her then at the Museum. I hear she is often in the City but she does not come to this house nor do we know where she lives or we could write to her but she told Mr. Larkin that our Grand Father is coming to New York and to pay a visit to Spain. and we will be very glad to

see him because we did not see him when we came from Monterey we all send our love to you and your wife and received the heart of your friend who never forgets you
José Antonio Jimeno

José Antonio Jimeno to William T. Sherman, February 15, 1851, William T. Sherman Papers

New York February 15, 1851

My dear friend Castañares
We received your letter in New York before Christmas and we thank you very much for it Castañares we received letters from home today with my Uncle Robinson but they do not tell me any thing about Mr. Ord and they dont say anything about the boys coming to New York. Castañares we received another letter from my Uncle Hartnell José H and from Carmen Loberanes, and Papa wrote us that the Colera went away and they are very well. Papá wrote me that Manuela comes see him nearly every day and do you know that Gillermito Hartnell married with the Sister of my Aunt Quintona the wife of my Uncle Pablo Noriega Castañares Don Enrique Melis came to see another gentleman from Monterey we are studying geography, grammar, tables, cyphering, spelling, definitions, dictation, and reading. we are very well escept my elbow is just alike my leg but it is almost well. Miss Meade is very well as ever and send her respects to you and your wife the boys send their regard to you and Mrs Sherman. Your gratefull friend and Hermano.
José Antonio Jimeno

José Agustín Quintero, "Memorias del Alma," in *Los poetas de "El laúd del desterrado": Quintero, Teurbe Tolón, Santacilia, Turla Castellón, Zenea*, by José Manuel Carbonell (Avisador Comercial, 1930), 27–28. In reprinting "Memorias del Alma," Carbonell provides only what he describes as "el más interesante pasaje de esa silva" (the most interesting

passage of this silva). The passages below are the ones he excerpted from a presumably longer poem.

MEMORIAS DEL ALMA

Susurraban las hojas,
en la arboleda el céfiro gemía,
y a nuestros pies el cristalino arroyo
suspirando corría.

Te vi entonces, Rebeca, palpitando
entre el cariño y la virtud luchando,
con tu semblante en lágrimas deshecho . . .
y a lo lejos el astro de la tarde
temblaba como el gozo dentro el pecho.

Dulces momentos esos
de emociones sinceras . . .
Si en el amor suelen mentir los besos
las lágrimas son siempre verdaderas.

Partimos, ¡ay!, tal vez para no vernos
en la tierra jamás, cuando sangrienta
la guerra su cabeza levantaba
y rugía en torno hórrida tormenta.

Volé a llenar un puesto entre las filas
de una heroica legión, y mi existencia
consagré en el altar que un pueblo culto
erigiera a su santa independencia.

Al estampido del cañón tremendo
y al ver surcar las bombas encendidas
la atmósfera azulada, cuánto entonces
me acordaba de ti! Mas quiso el hado
que la fuerza brutal, no el heroísmo,

decidiese la lucha, que no siempre
logran vencer justicia y patriotismo.

¡Nobel Mac Leod que la serena frente
erguías en el combate fragoroso,
como un león valiente,
como un Apolo hermoso!

Tú, Marshall esforzado,
que en mañana sombría
de tu corcel brioso los ijares
ante roja y tronante artillería
rasgabas entusiasta, acaudillando
tu valiente y fogosa infantería!

Lamar, incomparable en la tribuna,
inspirado poeta, en lid un rayo;
a ti, mi buen amigo,
que compartir supiste
tu hogar y pan conmigo,
yo os consagro un recuerdo! Vuestro nombre
que indiferente el vencedor no aclama,
con mi laúd, en española lengua,
llevaré por los campos de la fama.

NOTES

INTRODUCTION

1 Thompson, *Tejanos in Gray*, 71, 72, 33, 50, 53, 54, 58, 65. The twenty-four-year-old Manuel Yturri enlisted with the Alamo Rifles as a private. He then reenlisted as a first corporal in Company H of the Sixth Texas Infantry. He transferred to the Thirty-Third Texas Calvary under Colonel James Duff before joining Colonel Philip Nolan Luckett's Third Texas Infantry, where he moved in rank from second lieutenant to first lieutenant and then captain (xxiii).

2 Thompson, *Tejanos in Gray*, 8, 3, 5, 8–9, 11–12, 19, 22–24. Thompson notes that de la Garza enlisted with the Alamo Rifles under Captain Samuel W. McAllister on March 31, 1862: "The Alamo Rifles would eventually become Company K, 6th Texas Infantry" (xxiii).

3 See Thompson, *Tejanos in Gray*, xxv; and Gollar, "Jesuit Education." See also Schmidt, "Enslavement at St. Joseph College."

4 Glymph, *The Women's Fight*, 4.

5 Doyle, introduction to *American Civil Wars*, 3.

6 Hahn, *A Nation Without Borders*, 4. I introduced a similar understanding of Latinx civil wars in Alemán, "Wars of Rebellion."

7 Masich, *Civil War in the Southwest Borderlands*, 264.

8 Rothera, *Civil Wars and Reconstructions*, 10.

9 See Arenson and Graybill, *Civil War Wests*; Rothera, *Civil Wars and Reconstructions*; Armitage, "Civil Wars, from Beginning to End?"; Doyle, *American Civil Wars*; Hahn, *A Nation Without Borders*; and Taylor, *American Civil Wars*.

10 Arenson, introduction, 2. See also Nelson, *The Three-Cornered War*; and Scott, *Degrees of Freedom*.

11 Hahn, afterword, 339; Downs and Masur, introduction, 6.

12 See Lonn, *Foreigners in the Confederacy*; de la Cova, *Cuban Confederate Colonel*; Thompson, *A Civil War History*; *Vaqueros in Blue and Gray*; and *Tejanos in Gray*; and de la Teja, *Lone Star Unionism*. For lists of Hispanic participants in the Civil War, see O'Donnell-Rosales, *Hispanic Confederates*; and Rodríguez, *Hispanics in the US Civil War*.

13 See Owsley, *King Cotton Diplomacy*; Tyler, *Santiago Vidaurri*; and Daddysman, *The Matamoros Trade*.

14 "War Records," *St. Louis Post-Dispatch*, March 21, 1887.

15 White, "The Burden of History."

16 Put another way, I practice what Saidiya Hartman calls, in the context of writing the histories of the enslaved, "critical fabulation" insofar as my work "is a history written with and against the archive" that draws out speculative narratives of identity transformation. Hartman, "Venus in Two Acts," 11.
17 Taylor, *American Civil Wars*, 87, 187, 186.
18 A worm is a musket wipe. John [Juan] A. Quintero, Carded Records Showing Military Service of Soldiers who Fought in Confederate Organizations. For a note on the misidentification of José for Juan Quintero in *The War of the Rebellion* and the subsequent correction of the error in scholarship, see Tyler, *Santiago Vidaurri*, 36.
19 For a similar critique of Civil War historiography regarding Mexican Texans, see Valerio-Jiménez, "'Although We Are the Last Soldiers,'" 125.
20 Lazo, "Migrant Archives," 37; Lamas, *The Latino Continuum*, 12.
21 See Castañeda and Lomas, *Writing/Righting History*, for a history of the project.
22 Silva Gruesz, *Ambassadors of Culture*, xi. There are several exceptions in Latinx scholarship that bridge the gap between early writings and contemporary formations of Latinidad, including López, *Chicano Nations*; Bernadine Marie Hernández, *Border Bodies*; and Hudson, *Latinx Revolutionary Horizons*.
23 Anzaldúa, *Borderlands/La Frontera*, 3.
24 A more accurate translation of the line would be "when you said that you had 'el alma atravesada,'" because *tenía* lacks a clear pronoun referent (it could refer to "I" or "you" in the context of the letter), but considering that Ruiz de Burton indicates in two follow-up messages that she was the one Vallejo described as having *el alma atravesada*, I am choosing to translate the passage to mirror the subsequent representations of this scene.
25 Ruiz de Burton, *Conflicts of Interest*, 242, 262, 301.
26 Ruiz de Burton, *Conflicts of Interest*, x, 74.
27 "Tener el alma atravesada: Ser persona de malos sentimientos o intenciones" (to be a person with bad feelings or intentions). My translation. Rubio, *La anarquía del lenguaje*, 314. I thank Alexander Chaparro Silva for providing this citation. My understanding of the term has benefited from guidance provided by Chaparro Silva, Lillian Gorman, Kirsten Silva Gruesz, Rodrigo Lazo, Sara E. Johnson, and Mario Del Angel Guevara, though any misusage is by my own design.
28 Moyna and Martín, "'Un Alma Atravesada,'" 160, 168.
29 María Amparo Ruiz de Burton to Platón Vallejo, April 23, 1859, Vallejo Family Papers, MSS 76/70; emphasis in original. This letter foregrounds the risks of relying on Sánchez and Pita's collection of Ruiz de Burton's letters in *Conflicts of Interest*. Here, they do not italicize the words Ruiz de Burton underlines for emphasis ("own race," "some," and "judicious"), but they emphasize a phrase she doesn't underscore in her original letter ("a child's handful in their mighty grasp"). They address the letter to "Platón," though Ruiz de Burton greets him as "Plato," and she begins one sentence with the phrase "Shield it from the touch of the unsympathizing throng," but Sánchez and Pita render it "Shield it from the trash of unsympathizing things." Ruiz de Burton, *Conflicts of Interest*, 157.

30 Emparan, *The Vallejos of California*, 317.
31 Thompson, *Tejanos in Gray*, translator's note.
32 See Taylor, *American Civil Wars* for a study that demonstrates how Mexican nationals such as Romero, Juárez, and Ocampo engaged with US politics and politicians without being transformed by them in terms of their sense of *mexicanidad*.
33 Rivera, *The Emergence of Mexican America*, 19; Gómez, *Manifest Destinies*, 17; Alemán, "The Invention of Mexican America."
34 Lazo, introduction, 2.
35 González and Lomas, introduction, 2. See also Aparicio, "Latinidad/es"; and Caminero-Santangelo, *On Latinidad*.
36 Gerke and González Rodríguez, introduction, 9.
37 Thompson, *Tejano Tiger*, 77, 75.
38 Schmidt-Nowara, *Empire and Antislavery*, 17.
39 See Gómez, *Manifest Destinies* for a study of how Mexican Americans brokered their "off-whiteness" in the United States; and Guterl, *American Mediterranean* for an assessment of the overlapping interests of the circum-Gulf Southern master class.
40 Pino and Gallegos, "Address of the Legislative Assembly."
41 Pino and Gallegos, "Address of the Legislative Assembly."
42 Mora, *Border Dilemmas*, 91.
43 Stegmaier, "'A Law That Would Make Caligula Blush'?," 210.
44 Colonel John L. Gay Collection of Papers Pertaining to the Armijo Family, MSS-193-BC, box 1, folders 24, 25, 26, and 27.
45 Gómez, *Manifest Destinies*, 83–84.
46 I'm grateful to Santiago Guerra for first mentioning to me the "torna atrás" reference and to David Alemán Jr. for pointing out the connotations of "andar atrasado." Both comments have helped me make sense of the peculiar description.
47 Ruiz de Burton, *Conflicts of Interest*, xi. "Nearly every female Confederate diarist at some point expressed the desire to be a man," Faust asserts. *Mothers of Invention*, 231.
48 Young, *Disarming the Nation*, 17. See also Rable, *Civil Wars*; Faust, *Mothers of Invention*; Clinton and Sibler, *Divided Houses*; and Whites, *The Civil War as a Crisis in Gender*.

CHAPTER 1. WAR-TORN CALIFORNIOS

1 William T. Sherman to Francisco de la Guerra, Monterey, April 12, 1848, de la Guerra Collection, DLG 125 L4.
2 Pubols, *The Father of All*, 279.
3 Pubols, *The Father of All*, 276–80.
4 Rose Marie Beebe and Robert M. Senkewicz edited, translated, and published Angustias de la Guerra's *testimonio*, diary entries, and *recuerdos* in *Testimonios*.
5 Sherman, *Memoirs*, 81.
6 Sherman, *Memoirs*, 82.

7 Thomas, *Delmonico's*, 66.
8 The elder Jimeno brother signed most of his letters as José Antonio, which is the nomenclature I preserve throughout. I also retain the younger Jimeno's preference to refer to himself in his letters and in his service record as Porfirio.
9 Potter, *The Impending Crisis*, 16–17.
10 De la Guerra, "Angustias de la Guerra Ord Journal, 1846–1847," 275; de la Guerra, "Occurrences in California," 263.
11 Casas, *Married to a Daughter of the Land*, 52.
12 De la Guerra, "Recuerdos," 293.
13 *A Catalogue of the Officers and Students of Georgetown College, District of Columbia, for the Academic Year of 1850–1851* (John Murphy, 1851), 6.
14 William T. Sherman to Angustias de la Guerra, November 6, 1852, de la Guerra Collection, DLG 914 L01; Maguire to A. Robinson, May 31, 1856, de la Guerra Collection, DLG 618 L01.
15 Pubols, *The Father of All*, 234–35.
16 Brewster, "A Californiana in Two Worlds," 104.
17 See Robinson, *The Letters of Alfred Robinson*, 62.
18 Manuel Jimeno to José Antonio, July 1, 1852, de la Guerra Collection, DLG 560 L01.
19 Hague and Langum, *Thomas O. Larkin*, 202.
20 Hayes-Bautista, *El Cinco de Mayo*, 125.
21 Pubols, *The Father of All*, 273.
22 Francisco de la Guerra Jr. to Francisco de la Guerra Sr., April 5, 1853, de la Guerra Collection, DLG 0370 L02; emphasis in original.
23 Anita de la Guerra to Pablo de la Guerra, Boston, August 16, 1843, de la Guerra Collection, DLG 0837 L01; emphasis in original.
24 Robinson, *The Letters of Alfred Robinson*, 39.
25 Gómez, *Manifest Destinies*, 17.
26 Margaret Gordon Meade to William T. Sherman, November 9, 1850, Sherman Papers; Margaret Gordon Meade to William T. Sherman, February 18, 1851, Sherman Papers.
27 Porfirio Jimeno to William T. Sherman, November 9 [1850], Sherman Papers.
28 Porfirio Jimeno's November 9, 1850, letter addresses Sherman as "Castañares," and Sherman notes in his own hand at the bottom of the note that "I am known in California by that name." It is unclear why he went by the nickname, but it possibly describes Sherman's red hair as a dark, chestnut color.
29 José Antonio Jimeno to William T. Sherman, November 9, 1850, Sherman Papers.
30 Meade to Sherman, November 9, 1850. The Jimeno letters are enclosed with Meade's letter to Sherman, in which she writes, "I send you the boys' letters just as they have written them, but must remark that many of their mistakes proceed from carelessness."
31 James Ryder to William T. Sherman, November 18, 1850, Sherman Papers.
32 José Antonio Jimeno to Sherman, November 9, 1850.

33 José Antonio Jimeno to William T. Sherman, July 11, 1852, Sherman Papers.

34 José Antonio Jimeno to "Dear Sisters," February 17, 1853, de la Guerra Collection, DLG 545 L1.

35 José Antonio Jimeno to Pablo de la Guerra, February 20, 1854, de la Guerra Collection, DLG 544 L1.

36 José Antonio Jimeno to Sherman, July 11, 1852.

37 José Antonio Jimeno to William T. Sherman, February 15, 1851, Sherman Papers.

38 Meade to Sherman, February 18, 1851.

39 Meade to Sherman, February 18, 1851.

40 José Antonio Jimeno to Sherman, February 15, 1851.

41 Lazo, *Letters from Filadelfia*, 13, 14.

42 Meade to Sherman, February 18, 1851.

43 José Antonio Jimeno to Sherman, July 11, 1852.

44 Lazo, *Letters from Filadelfia*, 11.

45 See Clay, "Speech of Henry Clay," 9.

46 José Antonio Jimeno to Sherman, July 11, 1852.

47 Margaret Gordon Meade to William T. Sherman, July 17, 1852, Sherman Papers.

48 Bache, *The Life of General George Meade*, 557. Richard Meade Bache recalls of his uncle, General Meade, "He was, in a word, a dandy," outfitted in the latest fashions and with his long hair in ringlet curls.

49 Foster, "The Effeminate Man," 51.

50 José Antonio's name appears in the list of those who have unclaimed letters at the Boston post office as of June 19, 1854. See "List of Names," *Boston Herald*, June 21, 1854, 1.

51 See Chávez-García, *Negotiating Conquest*; and Casas, *Married to a Daughter of the Land*. Casas maintains that Californianas exerted agency by choosing to intermarry, and Chávez-García makes the similar case for the Californianas who pursued divorce.

52 See Robinson's March 3, 1854, letter to José de la Guerra, and his March 20, 1854, letter to Pablo de la Guerra in Robinson, *The Letters of Alfred Robinson*, 34, 35, 37.

53 Chávez-García, *Negotiating Conquest*, xvi.

54 Pitt, *The Decline of the Californios*, 195.

55 Hayes-Bautista, *El Cinco de Mayo*, 130.

56 Gray, *A Clamor for Equality*, 55.

57 Kanellos, "*El Clamor Público*," 10–11.

58 Benavides, "'Californios! Whom Do You Support?,'" 59.

59 Kanellos, "*El Clamor Público*," 14.

60 Prezelski, *Californio Lancers*, 26.

61 Prezelski, *Californio Lancers*, 81.

62 Prezelski, *Californio Lancers*, 73.

63 "Porfirio will kiss and pet you all day, but is averse to making any greater affection, being a *little* lazy in every way." Meade to Sherman, February 18, 1851; emphasis in original.

64 Porfirio Jimeno to Josefa Maria de la Guerra, February 18, 1861, de la Guerra Collection, DLG 551 L01.

65 Porfirio Jimeno to Josefa Maria de la Guerra, October 27, 1864, de la Guerra Collection, DLG 551 L05.

66 Porfirio Jimeno to Josefa Maria de la Guerra, November 29, 1864, de la Guerra Collection, DLG 551 L07.

67 Porfirio Jimeno to Josefa Maria de la Guerra, October 30, 1865, de la Guerra Collection, DLG 551 L14. Translation my own, but I'm guided by Prezelski's rendering of this passage (*Californio Lancers*, 120).

68 Prezelski, *Californio Lancers*, 120.

69 Porfirio Jimeno to Josefa Maria de la Guerra, September 24, 1864, de la Guerra Collection, DLG 551 L02; Porfirio Jimeno to Josefa Maria de la Guerra, October 2, 1864, de la Guerra Collection, DLG 551 L03; Porfirio Jimeno to Josefa Maria de la Guerra, October 9, 1864, de la Guerra Collection, DLG 551 L04; Porfirio Jimeno to [Concepcion and Josefa] de la Guerra, de la Guerra Collection, August 3, 1865, DLG 551 L13. "Cochina" is a harsh slang phrase that Porfirio uses to characterize his aunts as "dirty" or "filthy" women. "Pigs" might be one translation, but it does not carry the insult's moral and sexual undertones.

70 Varon, *Before Chicano*, 11.

71 Porfirio Jimeno to Rebecca R. (Ord) Peshine, December 22, 1864, de la Guerra Collection, DLG 522 L01.

72 Porfirio Jimeno to Pablo de la Guerra, August 3, 1865, de la Guerra Collection, DLG 554 L01; emphasis in original.

73 Whitman, *The Collected Writings*, 42. Lozano characterizes de la Guerra's English acquisition as a "conflicted" process toward "mastery of the language." *An American Language*, 75.

74 Prezelski, *Californio Lancers*, 146.

75 Porfirio Jimeno to James L. Ord, April 6, 1867, de la Guerra Collection, DLG 555 L01.

76 Jimeno to Ord, April 6, 1867.

77 Porfirio Jimeno, Compiled Service Records of Volunteer Union Soldiers Who Served in Organizations from the State of California. Porfirio's January–February 1865 company muster roll indicates one unnamed servant.

78 Porfirio Jimeno to Ord, April 6, 1867.

79 *El Nuevo Mundo*, April 2, 1866, 1, quoted in Hayes-Bautista, *El Cinco de Mayo*, 245.

80 William T. Sherman to Pablo de la Guerra, December 15, 1856, de la Guerra Collection, DLG 915 L02.

81 José Antonio Jimeno to James L. Ord, March 20, 1857, de la Guerra Collection, DLG 546 L1.

82 Kemble, *A History of California Newspapers*, 124. For more about the 1856 Vigilance Committee, see Taniguchi, *Dirty Deeds*. For a collection of primary writings from the warring sides, see Nunis, *The San Francisco Vigilance Committee*. For Sherman's open letter, see "General Orders—No. 1," *Daily True Californian*, July 19, 1856.

83 José Antonio Jimeno to Pablo de la Guerra, April 15, 1857, de la Guerra Collection, DLG 544 L2.
84 José Antonio Jimeno to Pablo de la Guerra, September 17, 1863, de la Guerra Collection, DLG 544 L5.
85 José Antonio Jimeno to Company C, October 25, 1864, de la Guerra Collection, DLG 547 L1.
86 Jimeno to Company C, October 25, 1864.
87 Meade to Sherman, July 17, 1852; emphasis in original.
88 Casas, *Married to a Daughter of the Land*, 182.

CHAPTER 2. SOUTHWESTERN MICROWARS

1 Mora, *Border Dilemmas*, 90.
2 Masich, *Civil War in the Southwest Borderlands*, 5. See also Nelson, *The Three-Cornered War*.
3 Thompson, *Vaqueros in Blue and Gray*, xii.
4 Valerio-Jiménez, "'Although We Are the Last Soldiers,'" 125.
5 Fletcher, *Territory of New Mexico*, 15.
6 Thompson's work is the most substantial in the history, recovery, and republication of Mexican American Civil War letters and documents. See his *Vaqueros in Blue and Gray* and *Tejanos in Gray*.
7 Rivera, *The Emergence of Mexican America*, 2.
8 Arenson, introduction, 3.
9 Masich, *Civil War in the Southwest Borderlands*, 276.
10 Montejano, *Anglos and Mexicans*, 81–82.
11 Brooks, *Captives and Cousins*, 306–7.
12 Stegmaier, "'A Law That Would Make Caligula Blush'?," 211–12. See Stegmaier for a complete transcription of the 1859 Slave Code.
13 "New Mexico," *New York Tribune*, December 31, 1860, 4.
14 "New Mexico: To the Editor of the *Constitution*," *Santa Fe Weekly Gazette*, February 16, 1861, 1.
15 Greeley, *The American Conflict*, 21.
16 "From Washington City," *Santa Fe Weekly Gazette*, December 8, 1860.
17 "From Washington City."
18 "From Washington City."
19 Gómez, *Manifest Destinies*, 115.
20 Gómez, *Manifest Destinies*, 83–84.
21 *New York Tribune*, December 31, 1860.
22 *Congressional Globe*, 36th Congress, 2nd session, January 21, 1861, 455.
23 *New York Tribune*, July 15, 1861.
24 *Santa Fe Weekly Gazette*, February 16, 1861.
25 Act Amendatory of the Law Relative to Contracts between Masters and Servants, 24–27.
26 *Santa Fe Weekly Gazette*, February 16, 1861.

27 Brooks, *Captives and Cousins*, 71.
28 Rael-Gálvez, "Identifying Captivity," 185.
29 Hermina C. Gonzalez to Mrs. Meketa, October 27, 1982, Charles and Jacqueline Meketa Papers; Genaro Padilla, *My History*, 153.
30 Meketa, introduction, 5–6.
31 "I feel like she is taking serious liberties with Chacon's intentions, and that her alterations do not improve on the original account. In my opinion she should get her own writing down to a minimum and let Chacon have the stage," an anonymous manuscript reviewer reported to the editor of University of New Mexico Press. See letter, anonymous reader report to UNM Press, Charles and Jacqueline Meketa Papers.
32 Genaro Padilla, *My History*, 158.
33 Chacón, *Legacy of Honor*, 132.
34 Chacón, "Memorias."
35 Chacón, *Legacy of Honor*, 242.
36 Meketa's translation of "resolví" as "decide" is accurate, but it's worth noting that Chacón did not use "decidir," a more exact word for "decide." He used the verb "resolver," which registers the state of resolving a crisis, solving a problem, or settling a conflict. Chacón, "Memorias," 75.
37 Chacón, *Legacy of Honor*, 118.
38 Rafael Chacón, Compiled Service Records of Volunteer Union Soldiers Who Served in Organizations from the Territory of New Mexico. Translation provided in Chacón's service record.
39 Chacón, *Legacy of Honor*, 127.
40 Chacón, *Legacy of Honor*, 130.
41 Chacón, *Legacy of Honor*, 131.
42 Chacón, *Legacy of Honor*, 131.
43 Chacón, *Legacy of Honor*, 132.
44 Genaro Padilla, *My History*, 178.
45 Chacón, "Memorias," 92.
46 Chacón, *Legacy of Honor*, 185–86.
47 Genaro Padilla, *My History*, 180.
48 Chacón, "Memorias," 124. My translations provided as counterexamples to Meketa's translated passage.
49 Gonzales, *Forced Sacrifice as Ethnic Protest*, 29–30.
50 Chacón, *Legacy of Honor*, 127.
51 Chacón, *Legacy of Honor*, 128.
52 Genaro Padilla, *My History*, 156.
53 Genaro Padilla, *My History*, 175.
54 For similar expressions of divided loyalties by Mexican American veterans, see Olguín, "Sangre Mexicana," 86–87.
55 Chacón, *Legacy of Honor*, 103.
56 Brooks, *Captives and Cousins*, 31.

57 Brooks, *Captives and Cousins*, 34.
58 Chacón, *Legacy of Honor*, 230.
59 Thompson, *Vaqueros in Blue and Gray*, 6.
60 Pino and Gallegos, "Address of the Legislative Assembly."
61 Chacón, *Legacy of Honor*, 102.
62 Chacón, *Legacy of Honor*, 251.
63 "Synopsis of Operations in the Department of New Mexico, May 16–December 28, 1863," in US War Department, *The War of the Rebellion*, series 1, vol. 26, part 1, 32.
64 Chacón, *Legacy of Honor*, 304.
65 Chacón, *Legacy of Honor*, 326; emphasis added.
66 Chacón, *Legacy of Honor*, 333.
67 Santiago Tafolla, "Nearing the End of the Trail."
68 Carmen Tafolla, introduction, xvi.
69 James Santiago Tafolla, *A Life Crossing Borders*, 4.
70 James Santiago Tafolla, *A Life Crossing Borders*, 5.
71 James Santiago Tafolla, *A Life Crossing Borders*, 6–7.
72 James Santiago Tafolla, *A Life Crossing Borders*, 15.
73 James Santiago Tafolla, *A Life Crossing Borders*, 17.
74 James Santiago Tafolla, *A Life Crossing Borders*, 23–24.
75 Foley, *White Scourge*, 23.
76 Juan Manuel Gallegos arrived in Washington, DC, as New Mexico's territorial delegate after beating Miguel Otero in an elected appointment that Otero successfully contested; José D. Sena was most likely en route to Alexandria, Virginia, to study law. He returned to New Mexico and served as a major in Colonel Miguel Pino's Second Regiment of New Mexico's volunteers in the Union army. He also served as captain of Company C of the reorganized First Cavalry, New Mexico, in which Chacón served as captain of Company E. See Twitchell, *The Leading Facts of New Mexico History*, 388; and Chacón, *Legacy of Honor*, 191.
77 James Santiago Tafolla, *A Life Crossing Borders*, 32.
78 James Santiago Tafolla, *A Life Crossing Borders*, 39.
79 James Santiago Tafolla, *A Life Crossing Borders*, 41; emphasis in original.
80 James Santiago Tafolla, *A Life Crossing Borders*, 41.
81 Foley, *White Scourge*, 25.
82 Brevet Lieutenant Colonel William Chapman to Lieutenant Colonel J. Francisco Chaves, November 27, 1861, Records of US Army Continental Commands; emphasis in original.
83 Thompson, *Vaqueros in Blue and Gray*, 6.
84 Thompson, *Vaqueros in Blue and Gray*, 56.
85 Thompson, *Vaqueros in Blue and Gray*, 98; James Santiago Tafolla, *A Life Crossing Borders*, 77.
86 James Santiago Tafolla, *A Life Crossing Borders*, 73.
87 James Santiago Tafolla, *A Life Crossing Borders*, 78–79.
88 James Santiago Tafolla, *A Life Crossing Borders*, 79; emphasis added.

89 James Santiago Tafolla, *A Life Crossing Borders*, 12.
90 James Santiago Tafolla, *A Life Crossing Borders*, 11.
91 James Santiago Tafolla, *A Life Crossing Borders*, 21.
92 James Santiago Tafolla, *A Life Crossing Borders*, 55.
93 James Santiago Tafolla, *A Life Crossing Borders*, 65–69.
94 James Santiago Tafolla, *A Life Crossing Borders*, 79.

CHAPTER 3. CONFEDERATE *LETRADO*

1 Quintero, "Review of *Verse Memorials*," 360–61; "Cuban Anniversary," *Daily Picayune*, September 2, 1854; Fuller, "American Literature," 124.
2 Marbán, *Confederate Patriot*, 16.
3 Silva Gruesz, *Ambassadors of Culture*, 152, 155. For biographies of Quintero, see Silva Gruesz, *Ambassadors of Culture*; Marbán, *Confederate Patriot*; Carbonell, *Los poetas de "El laúd del desterrado"*; and Brock, "José Agustín Quintero."
4 "Joseph A. Quintero," *Daily Picayune*, September 8, 1885.
5 Brock, "José Agustín Quintero," 85; *Daily Picayune*, September 8, 1885.
6 Pérez, *Cuba and the United States*, 31. For an analysis of Cuba's rise as a slavery stronghold in the midst of nineteenth-century anti-slavery movements, see Ferrer, "Cuban Slavery."
7 Lamas, *The Latino Continuum*, 7.
8 Echevarría, *Myth and Archive*, 68.
9 Silva Gruesz, *Ambassadors of Culture*, 16.
10 Lazo, *Letters from Filadelfia*, 10, 8.
11 For historiographic use of Quintero's letters, see Daddysman, *The Matamoros Trade*; Owsley, *King Cotton Diplomacy*; and Tyler, *Santiago Vidaurri*.
12 Hutchison, *Apples and Ashes*, 19.
13 See Shields, *Phillis Wheatley's Poetics of Liberation* for a different understanding of the poetics of liberation in relation to Black enslavement.
14 Ellis, *The Union at Risk*, 178.
15 Lamar, *Verse Memorials*, 173, 7, 174.
16 A transcription of Quintero's review can be found in Lamar, *The Papers of Mirabeau Buonaparte Lamar*, vol. 6, 360–61. The piece does not appear to have been printed in a US newspaper. It remains in manuscript form in the Lamar papers at the Texas State Archives.
17 Coronado, *A World Not to Come*, 353–54. For more on Quintero's 1850s newspaper work, see Silva Gruesz, *Ambassadors of Culture*, 145–60; Marbán, *Confederate Patriot*, 38–39; and Buenger, *Secession and the Union in Texas*, 88.
18 Quintero, "Review of *Verse Memorials*," 361, 359, 360, 361.
19 Quintero, "Lyric Poetry in Cuba." Brock dates the manuscript to 1850 based on Quintero's reference to Juan Clemente Zenea. Brock, "José Agustín Quintero," 16.
20 J. A. Quintero to Henry Wadsworth Longfellow, April 19, 1855, Letters to Henry Wadsworth Longfellow, bMS Am 1340.2 (4569). See also Silva Gruesz, *Ambas-*

sadors of Culture for an excerpt of this and Quintero's other letters to Longfellow (155–57). I've retained Silva Gruesz's translation.

21 Pérez, *Intimations of Modernity*, 9.

22 J. A. Quintero to Henry Wadsworth Longfellow, July 26, 1855, Letters to Henry Wadsworth Longfellow; Quintero, "Review of *Verse Memorials*," 356.

23 J. E. Hernández, "El laúd del desterrado," 3. While Quintero does not recognize the poets he commemorates in his early essay as capable of bringing literary liberation, he sang a different tune in the profile pieces of Cuban revolutionary poets he memorialized in the Spanish-language press. See Quintero, "Patriotas Cubanos," *El Bejareño*, April 19, 1856; and "Ramon Pinto," *El Ranchero*, July 19, 1856.

24 Quintero, "Review of *Verse Memorials*," 357.

25 Marbán, *Confederate Patriot*, 41. Marbán also draws attention to Quintero's use of "our" as indicative of his adoption of the Southern cause.

26 The Library of Congress's Confederate States of America collection provides the digitized microfilm rolls of the holdings that were previously referenced as the Pickett Papers. Reel 8 holds volume 8 and reel 32 includes volume 32, both of which contain Quintero's archive.

27 Judah P. Benjamin to José Agustín Quintero, September 30, 1863, Confederate States of America, *Confederate States of America Records*, microfilm reel 33.

28 Tyler, *Santiago Vidaurri*, 61.

29 Daddysman, *The Matamoros Trade*, 45–46. See also Owsley, *King Cotton Diplomacy*; and Thompson, *Tejano Tiger*.

30 Yolanda Padilla, "*La Crónica*, the Mexican Revolution, and Transnational Critique," 110.

31 Coronado, *A World Not to Come*, 15.

32 Saldívar, *The Borderlands of Culture*, 27. See also Américo Paredes, *With His Pistol in His Hand* and *A Texas-Mexican Cancionero*.

33 Kiser, *Illusions of Empire*, 3.

34 It is an "archive against itself," to recall Lazo's phrase in "Confederates in the Hispanic Attic," 52.

35 José Agustín Quintero to Judah P. Benjamin, June 1, 1863, Confederate States of America, *Confederate States of America Records*, microfilm reel 8; emphasis in original.

36 Quintero to Benjamin, June 1, 1863, Confederate States of America, *Confederate States of America Records*, microfilm reel 32; emphasis added.

37 Confederate States of America, *Confederate States of America Records*, microfilm reel 8.

38 Browne's letter to Quintero summarizes Davis's rationale for declining Vidaurri's offer. See William Browne to José Agustín Quintero, September 3, 1861, in Richardson, *A Compilation of the Messages and Papers of the Confederacy*, 77–80.

39 José Agustín Quintero to Judah P. Benjamin, November 9, 1863, Confederate States of America, *Confederate States of America Records*, microfilm reel 32. The

deciphering of Quintero's encrypted message is provided in the transcription of his letter.

40 Varon, "Archival Excess," 67, 69.

41 José Agustín Quintero to William Browne, June 1, 1861, Confederate States of America, Confederate States of America Records, microfilm reel 32.

42 John Pickett to Jefferson Davis, February 22, 1862, Confederate States of America, *Confederate States of America Records*, microfilm reel 5; emphasis in original. Referenced also in Kiser, *Illusions of Empire*, 193–94, n. 25.

43 Quintero to Browne, June 1, 1861.

44 José Agustín Quintero to William Browne, August 22, 1861, Confederate States of America, *Confederate States of America Records*, microfilm reel 32.

45 José Agustín Quintero to William Browne, March 28, 1862, Confederate States of America, *Confederate States of America Records*, microfilm reel 32; emphasis in original.

46 See Daddysman, *The Matamoros Trade*, 83; and Tyler, *Santiago Vidaurri*, 70–75.

47 José Agustín Quintero, "Notes on the Present Condition of Mexico," Confederate States of America, *Confederate States of America Records*, microfilm reel 8; emphasis in original.

48 Quintero, "Notes on the Present Condition of Mexico."

49 Reséndez, "North American Peonage," 613. For a translation of Mexico's 1857 Constitution, see Branch, *The Mexican Constitution of 1917*, 2, 3. For works that discuss slavery and peonage in the lower Rio Grande Valley, see Montejano, *Anglos and Mexicans*; Mora-Torres, *The Making of the Mexican Border*; Nichols, "The Line of Liberty"; Gurza-Lavalle, "Against Slave Power?"; and Baumgartner, "The Line of Positive Safety."

50 Mexican Laws on Peonage, Confederate States of America, *Confederate States of America Records*, microfilm reel 8.

51 Eiselein, "American Self-Fashioning," 233.

52 José Agustín Quintero to Santiago Vidaurri, June 19, 1861, Confederate States of America, *Confederate States of America Records*, microfilm reel 8.

53 Robert Toombs to José Agustín Quintero, May 22, 1861, and Robert Toombs to Santiago Vidaurri, May 22, 1861, US Naval Records Office, *Official Records of the Union and Confederate Navies*, series 3, vol. 3, 217–18.

54 Quintero to Vidaurri, June 19, 1861.

55 See José Agustín Quintero to R. M. J. Hunter, August 17, 1861, for Quintero's recounting of Vidaurri's offer, and Quintero to Hunter, August 19, 1861, in which he explains, "I called on [Vidaurri] as requested. He said that the world knew he had for years been anxious to establish the Republic of Sierra Madre to be composed of the Mexican States on our boundary, but that the birth of the Southern Confederacy had made him change his mind and he was now in favor of annexation in the Confederate States. There was no hand of union between the frontier states and the Mexican federal government. The institution of peonage had been abolished in the interior and existed only in the frontier states."

Confederate States of America, *Confederate States of America Records*, microfilm reel 32.

56 José Agustín Quintero to William Browne, March 22 [24], 1862, Confederate States of America, *Confederate States of America Records*, microfilm reel 8; emphasis in original.

57 Quintero to Browne, March 22 [24], 1862.

58 José Agustín Quintero to Don Pedro Santacilia, January 29, 1864, in Tamayo, *Benito Juárez*, 593–95.

59 Brock, "José Agustin Quintero," 77.

60 Ferrer, *Insurgent Cuba*, 16.

61 Silva Gruesz, "Subject to the Border," 30–32.

62 Carbonell, *Los poetas de "El laúd del desterrado,"* 27–28. Carbonell reprints only a segment of the poem without providing the poem's original publication history. See appendix for a transcription of the Spanish-language passage that Carbonell reproduces.

63 Carbonell, *Los poetas de "El laúd del desterrado,"* 26. Divanco and Remos y Rubio rely on Carbonell's copy. See Divanco, *El primer periodista*; and Remos y Rubio, *Historia de la literatura cubana*.

64 See Gonzales's March 14, 1851, letter to Lamar in Lamar, *The Papers of Mirabeau Buonaparte Lamar*, vol. 4, part 1, 282–84, and Lamar's April 1851 response in *The Papers of Mirabeau Buonaparte Lamar*, vol. 6, 314.

65 [Quintero], *The Code of Honor*, 21.

66 Silva Gruesz, "Subject to the Border," 32. Brock offers an overview of *The Code*, but Silva Gruesz's analysis remains the only sustained effort to make a case for Quintero's *The Code of Honor* in the context of the Recovering the US Hispanic Literary Heritage project.

67 The 1873 edition of *The Code* held in the American Antiquarian Society's collection is inscribed by Quintero's son, Lamar, with a textual correction in his hand that indicates he had occasion to compare his father's edition of *The Code* to Wilson's.

68 Wilson, *The Code of Honor*, 5. For the history of Wilson's text, the "fire-eater" as a duelist, and Wilson's South Carolina legacy, see Campbell, "Portrait of a Duelist."

69 Lamas, *The Latino Continuum*, 17.

CHAPTER 4. WHEN CUBANS GO SOUTH

1 Mary Chestnut's encounter with Gonzales suggests that the likeness is a point of pride for the Cuban. Her August 23, 1861, entry reads, "Gonzales <<he likes so much to hear of his likeness to General Beauregard>>." Chestnut, *Mary Chestnut's Civil War*, 157.

2 "Ambrosio Jose Gonzales: Death of a Cuban and Confederate Patriot," *The State*, August 2, 1893, 1. At this time, Gonzales's sons, Ambrosio ("Brosie") and Narciso, ran *The State*. De la Cova notes that Ambrose penned the anonymous obituary and suggests that the eldest son, who had been long estranged from his father,

lifted much of the information about Gonzales senior from a piece in *Patria*. See de la Cova, *Cuban Confederate Colonel*, 363, as well as *Patria*, December 31, 1892, for the biography it ran on the then ailing Gonzales.

3 Lonn, *Foreigners in the Confederacy*, 144.

4 Ambrosio Jose Gonzales to Governor Gist, November 19, 1860, Compiled Service Records of Confederate Generals, reel 108, Ambrosio Jose Gonzales.

5 This last point is one of departure from Lazo. "Gonzales is the type of historical actor whose experiences would defy the singularity of an archival concept," says Lazo, though overwhelming evidence points to the singularity of slavery as the keyword that holds together Gonzales's fugitive archive. See Lazo, "Confederates in the Hispanic Attic," 37.

6 Guterl, *American Mediterranean*, 6, 17.

7 Gonzales's life story is not obscure, in large part because of Antonio Rafael de la Cova's detailed and thorough biography of the Cuban Confederate colonel, as he calls him. De la Cova's work is sweeping in the broad historical scene in which he situates Gonzales, and it is meticulous in the way that it uses every available archive on Gonzales and his Cuban Confederate personal, public, and martial life. There is no better authority than de la Cova and his work when it comes to the details of Gonzales's life. However, it is a rare occasion that de la Cova explains or explores Gonzales's relation to slavery and whiteness. See de la Cova, *Cuban Confederate Colonel*. The biographical information related to the Elliott and Gonzáles Family Papers, 1701–1898, housed at the University of North Carolina, Chapel Hill, indicates that William Elliott owned almost a dozen plantations across South Carolina and Georgia, all of which held enslaved people.

8 Lazo, *Writing to Cuba*, 141.

9 Ferrer, *Insurgent Cuba*, 18.

10 Ferrer, "Cuban Slavery," 154.

11 See Lazo, *Writing to Cuba*; and Poyo, *"With All, and for the Good of All"* for foundational works that track the way exiled Creoles crafted forms of Cuban nationalism through Spanish-language print cultures and practices.

12 Rugemer, "Why Civil War?," 16.

13 Ambrosio José Gonzales to Caleb Cushing, March 29, 1849, Cushing Papers; emphasis in original.

14 Ambrosio José Gonzales to U. S. Grant, January 8, 1876, Letters of Application and Recommendation during the Administration of Ulysses S. Grant.

15 See Sinha, *The Counterrevolution of Slavery*, 126–29.

16 "Junta promovedora de los intereses politicos de Cuba," *Washington Republic*, December 10, 1849; emphasis added.

17 Chaffin, *Fatal Glory*, 8.

18 A. J. Gonzales to Mirabeau B. Lamar, March 14, 1851, in Lamar, *The Papers of Mirabeau Buonaparte Lamar*, vol. 4, part 1, 283.

19 See May, *Manifest Destiny's Underworld*, 252.

20 "The Cuban Junta to Governor Quitman," November 20, 1850, in Claiborne, *Life and Correspondence of John A. Quitman*, 385, 386.
21 Quintero, *Apuntes biograficos*, [3].
22 McCardell, *The Idea of a Southern Nation*, 245.
23 Lazo, *Writing to Cuba*, 142.
24 Ambrosio José Gonzales, "Cuban Independence," *Washington Daily Union*, April 13, 1854, 3; emphasis in original.
25 Ambrosio Jose Gonzales to Caleb Cushing, October 20, 1853, Cushing Papers.
26 Ambrosio José Gonzales, "The Cuban Movement—Letter from Gen. Gonzales," *New York Times*, June 23, 1854, 4; see also *New Orleans Picayune*, July 4, 1854, 2; emphasis in original.
27 Unsigned [Ambrosio José Gonzales] to Laurent Sigur, December 14, 1854, box 16, folder 17, Lopez, N.-ALS, 1854 December 14, Keith M. Read Collection.
28 Jones, "William Elliott," 369; de la Cova, *Cuban Confederate Colonel*, 103.
29 Elliott, "A Trip to Cuba," *Russell's Magazine*, October 2, 1857, 60.
30 Elliott, "A Trip to Cuba," *Russell's Magazine*, April 3, 1858, 65.
31 Ambrosio Jose Gonzales, "Cuba—Our Duty to Ourselves," *Washington Daily Union*, May 3, 1854, 3.
32 Quigley, *Shifting Grounds*, 8.
33 Gonzales, *Manifesto on Cuban Affairs*, 4, 5.
34 De la Cova, *Cuban Confederate Colonel*, 134.
35 Walsh, "Radically and Thoroughly Democratic," 201–2.
36 I depart here from Daylet Domínguez's claim that in the *Manifesto* and *Free Press* articles "Gonzales promoted the idea of Cuban annexation not from a regional, Southern, standpoint, but instead by appealing to a notion of US nationalism; one that was imbued with the ideology of republicanism, but also tolerated expansionism and slavery." This is true for the *Manifesto*, but the *Free Press* pieces are steeped in Southern white nationalism of the ilk fueling the rhetoric of secession emerging from South Carolina at the time, where Gonzales penned the pieces. See Domínguez, "Slaveholders in the South," 55.
37 "Cuba," *Detroit Daily Free Press*, November 25, 1858.
38 O'Sullivan, "Annexation," 9.
39 Ambrosio José Gonzales, "Cuba—Introductory Article," *Detroit Daily Free Press*, November 25, 1858; emphasis added.
40 "I am deeply interested in becoming thoroughly acquainted with your, I should say, our, institutions and to practice the English language in connection with diplomatic business to all possible extent." Gonzales to Cushing, March 29, 1849.
41 Gonzales, "Cuba—Introductory Article."
42 De la Cova, *The Confederate Colonel*, 133.
43 Ambrosio José Gonzales, "Cuba: Article III," *Detroit Daily Free Press*, December 1, 1858.
44 Ambrosio José Gonzales, "Cuba: Article IV," *Detroit Daily Free Press*, December 21, 1858; emphasis in original.

45 Gómez, *Manifest Destinies*, 83.
46 Quigley, *Shifting Grounds*, 46.
47 Faust, *The Creation of Confederate Nationalism*, 10.
48 Sinha, *The Counterrevolution of Slavery*, 96.
49 Ambrosio José Gonzales, "Cuba: Article VII," *Detroit Daily Free Press*, December 25, 1858.
50 Boyce, "The Annexation of Cuba," 92.
51 Ayer, "Southern Rights," 18.
52 Hammond, *Speech of Hon. James H. Hammond*, 8–9.
53 Gonzales, "Cuba: Article VII, Continued," *Detroit Daily Free Press*, December 31, 1858; emphasis in original.
54 Hammond, *Speech of Hon. James H. Hammond*, 9.
55 Gonzales, "Cuba: Article VIII," *Detroit Daily Free Press*, January 4, 1859; emphasis added.
56 De la Cova, *Cuban Confederate Colonel*, 140.
57 Ambrosio Jose Gonzales to Jefferson Davis, September 14, 1861, US War Department, *The War of the Rebellion*, series 1, vol. 6, 279, 283.
58 "Lieutenant-Colonel A. J. Gonzales," *Charleston Daily Courier*, June 16, 1862, 2.
59 De la Cova, *Cuban Confederate Colonel*, 153.
60 Hattie Gonzales to Ambrosio J. Gonzales, September 2 [1862], Gonzales Family Papers, transcribed by Antonio de la Cova.
61 *Charleston Courier*, March 14, 1862.
62 *Charleston Mercury*, March 19, 1862.
63 *Charleston Courier*, April 25, 1863.
64 Ambrosio Jose Gonzales to Jefferson Davis, August 25, 1863, Compiled Service Records of Confederate Generals, reel 108, Ambrosio Jose Gonzales.
65 *Charleston Daily Courier*, October 31, 1861; *Charleston Daily Courier*, November 5, 1861.
66 P. G. T. Beauregard to Ambrosio Jose Gonzales, December 10, 1868, Gonzales Family Papers, transcribed by Antonio de la Cova.
67 De la Cova, *Cuban Confederate Colonel*, 287.
68 De la Cova, *Cuban Confederate Colonel*, 256–323.
69 See A. J. Gonzales to Ambrose, February 1, 1891, Gonzales Family Papers, transcribed by Antonio de la Cova.
70 *Preliminary Report of the Commission*, 2, 23.
71 McGarry, *Ghosts of Futures Past*, 51, 14.
72 Gonzales, *Heaven Revealed*, 6, 68.
73 McGarry, *Ghosts of Futures Past*, 133.
74 Gonzales, *Heaven Revealed*, 40, 30, 14; de la Cova, *Cuban Confederate Colonel*, 124.
75 Gonzales, *Heaven Revealed*, 18, 30, 53.
76 Ambrosio José Gonzales, "On to Cuba," *New Orleans Times-Democrat*, March 30, 1884.

77 Ambrosio José Gonzales, "The Cuban Crusade," *New Orleans Times-Democrat*, April 6, 1884.
78 See *Patria*, October 8, 1892; December 31, 1892; January 7, 1893; and August 5, 1893.

CHAPTER 5. FROM UNION OFFICERS TO CUBAN REBELS

1 Dreese, *Torn Families*, 137.
2 See Jova, foreword; Martinez, "Federico Fernández Cavada"; and O. W. Davis, *Sketch of Frederic Fernandez Cavada*.
3 O. W. Davis, *Sketch of Frederic Fernandez Cavada*, 10.
4 O. W. Davis, *Sketch of Frederic Fernandez Cavada*, 11.
5 Poyo, *"With All, and for the Good of All,"* 4.
6 Poyo, *"With All, and for the Good of All,"* 4.
7 I refer to Cavada as "Federico" throughout because it is how he signed as an adult, but I retain the various spellings of his name as it appears in print materials or reference metadata.
8 Adolfo F. Cavada, diary.
9 Adolfo F. Cavada, diary.
10 Adolfo F. Cavada, diary.
11 Adolfo F. Cavada, diary.
12 Adolfo F. Cavada, diary.
13 Adolfo F. Cavada, diary; emphasis in original.
14 Whitman, *Memoranda During the Civil War*, 7.
15 Adolfo F. Cavada, diary.
16 Adolfo F. Cavada, diary.
17 O'Brien and Diefendorf, *General Orders of the War Department*, 160.
18 Walt Whitman's brother, George Washington Whitman, fought with the Fifty-First New York at the Battle of Fredericksburg and was wounded in battle. On December 21, 1862, Whitman visited him and other wounded soldiers at federal camp hospitals in Falmouth, Virginia, outside Fredericksburg shortly after the first battle there.
19 See Foucault's musings on Velázquez's *Las Meninas* (1656) in *The Order of Things*, 1–18.
20 Federico Cavada, diary.
21 Federico Cavada, diary.
22 US War Department, *The War of the Rebellion*, series 1, vol. 27, ch. 39, 503.
23 Collis, *The Case of F. F. Cavada*, 12.
24 "The term 'imagetext' designates composite, synthetic works (or concepts) that combine image and text." Mitchell, *Image Science*, 39.
25 "Libby Life," *Daily National Intelligencer*, June 18, 1864, 3.
26 Federico Cavada, *Libby Life*, 9–10.
27 Dawes, *The Language of War*, 2.
28 Hesseltine, *Civil War Prisons*, 131. The escape was fictionalized in Burchard's juvenile novel, *Rat Hell*, with Cavada perhaps making an appearance as the character Sears, an artist. See Burchard, *Rat Hell*, 36.

29 Federico Cavada, *Libby Life*, 9.
30 Mitchell, *Image Science*, 47.
31 Federico Cavada, *Libby Life*, 33, 32.
32 Federico Cavada, *Libby Life*, 126–27.
33 Federico Cavada, *Libby Life*, 127–28; emphasis in original.
34 Federico Cavada, *Libby Life*, 200.
35 Jova, foreword.
36 "Cuba," *New York Herald*, February 12, 1869, 7.
37 Ferrer, *Insurgent Cuba*, 15.
38 Pérez, *Cuba Between Reform and Revolution*, 83.
39 Ferrer, *Insurgent Cuba*, 9.
40 "War to the Knife and the Knife to the Hilt," *Cincinnati Daily Enquirer*, October 29, 1869.
41 See Ferrer, *Insurgent Cuba*, 24.
42 Pérez, *Cuba Between Reform and Revolution*, 90.
43 *New York Herald Tribune*, October 29, 1869, 4.
44 [Federico Cavada], "The Cave of Bellamar," 826. The piece is unattributed in the November 1870 issue, but the 1886 *Harper's* index names Cavada as the author. He appears as "Gen. F. F. Cavada," "Gen. Frederico F. Cavada," and "F. F. Cavada." See *Index to Harper's New Monthly Magazine*, 49, 109, 737.
45 [Federico Cavada], "The Cave of Bellamar," 828.
46 [Federico Cavada], "The Cave of Bellamar," 833.
47 Earle, *The Return of the Native*, 76.
48 Sellén, *Hatuey, poema dramático*.
49 Federico Cavada, *Ejército libertador de Cuba*.
50 Federico Cavada to wife, June 30, 1871, Fernando Fernández-Cavada Collection. Translation provided by the Cuban Heritage Collection.
51 "From Cuba: The Execution of Cavada and Osorio," *Times Picayune*, July 26, 1871, 2.
52 "Obituary—General Frederico Fernandez Cavada," *Philadelphia Inquirer*, July 12, 1871.
53 Carlos Manuel de Céspedes to Emily Dutton, January 5, 1872, Fernando Fernández-Cavada Collection.
54 Federico Cavada, diary. The poem is transcribed here as it appears in Cavada's diary.
55 Rodrigo Lazo, *Writing to Cuba*, 55.

CONCLUSION

1 Sánchez, "The Latino Nineteenth Century," 1015.
2 Hartman, *Scenes of Subjection*, 101.
3 Hudson's *Latinx Revolutionary Horizons* continues the long line of scholarship taking up the issue of Ruiz de Burton's writings in relation to race, recovery, and relevance for Chicanx and Latinx literary studies. See the essays in Goldman

and de la Luz Montes, *María Amparo Ruiz de Burton*; Aranda, "Contradictory Impulses"; Aranda, "Breaking All the Rules"; González, "Romancing Hegemony"; Szeghi, "The Vanishing Mexicana/o"; Ramirez, "Conquest's Child"; and Contreras, "María Amparo Ruiz de Burton."

4 Lozano, *An American Language*, 21–22.
5 Ruiz de Burton, *Who Would Have Thought It?*, 21; emphasis added.
6 Ruiz de Burton, *Who Would Have Thought It?*, 286, 287.
7 Quoted in Lozano, *An American Language*, 73; emphasis in original.
8 Hudson, *Latinx Revolutionary Horizons*, 5, 12.
9 For a discussion of Ruiz de Burton's conflicted interests in the Francophone notion of the Latin race, see Ruiz de Burton, *Conflicts of Interest*, 193–201.
10 Ruiz de Burton, *Conflicts of Interest*, 301.
11 Ruiz de Burton, *Conflicts of Interest*, 271.
12 See Goldman, "'Who Ever Heard of a Blue-Eyed Mexican?'"; Alemán, "Citizenship Rights and Colonial Whites"; and Hudson, *Latinx Revolutionary Horizons*.
13 See Hanlon for an argument about *Who Would Have Thought It?* as a "form of Confederate literature." In making this case, Hanlon elides the tomes of scholarship on Ruiz de Burton published by Latinx scholars or produced under the auspices of the Recovering the US Hispanic Literary Heritage project. Hanlon, "Confederate Literature," 307.
14 Raymund P. Paredes, "The Evolution of Chicano Literature," 88.
15 Lazo, "Confederates in the Hispanic Attic," 33.
16 I provide an overview of the debates about the veracity of *The Woman in Battle* and its author in Alemán, "Authenticity, Autobiography, and Identity." Confederate General Jubal Early decried the book's publication and, claiming to have met Velazquez, raised doubts about the author's self-proclaimed Cuban identity. William C. Davis reiterated the Confederate general's sentiments in *Inventing Loreta Velasquez*. However, literary scholarship recognizes the fictive play of the book and its authorship. See Hutchison, *Apples and Ashes*.
17 Velazquez, *The Woman in Battle*, 503.
18 Ventura, Kanellos, and Villarroel, "Recovering Our Written Legacy," 29.
19 Velazquez, *The Woman in Battle*, 502.
20 Velazquez, *The Woman in Battle*, 50.
21 Velazquez, *The Woman in Battle*, 44.
22 Sager, "The Multiple Metaphoric Civil Wars," 27.
23 Alemán, "Authenticity, Autobiography, and Identity," xxxiii.
24 Velazquez, *The Woman in Battle*, 42.
25 Bettcher, "Trapped in the Wrong Theory," 382.
26 Boag, "The Trouble with Cross-Dressers," 324.
27 Velazquez, *The Woman in Battle*, 42.
28 Velazquez, *The Woman in Battle*, 130.
29 Halberstam, *Trans**, 4.
30 Galarte, *Brown Trans Figurations*, 131; emphasis in original.

31 This point would stump Davis, whose incredulous attempt to debunk *The Woman in Battle*, Velazquez, and the scholarship on both rings with transphobia. His book on Velazquez "began as an effort to see if her story might have elements of verity," he notes, setting off in the wrong direction for anyone familiar with the Velazquez narrative. "It became a quest to find the *real woman* behind the myth." William C. Davis, *Inventing Loreta Velasquez*, 2; emphasis added.

32 Hutchison, *Apples and Ashes*, 175.

33 Blanco, "Whither Latinidad?," 143.

34 For a biography of the Gonzales brothers, see Ambrose Gonzales's foreword to *In Darkest Cuba*. Also see de la Cova, *Cuban Confederate Colonel*, 367–68.

35 Ambrose E. Gonzales, *The Black Border*, 19.

36 Cooper, *Making Gullah*, 20.

37 Ambrose E. Gonzales, *The Black Border*, 12.

BIBLIOGRAPHY

ARCHIVAL HOLDINGS AND RECORDS COLLECTIONS

Carded Records Showing Military Service of Soldiers Who Fought in Confederate Organizations, Documenting the Period 1861–1865. National Archives and Records Administration, RG 109 (Texas).

Compiled Service Records of Confederate Generals and Staff Officers and Nonregimental Enlisted Men. National Archives and Records Administration, RG 109, reel 108.

Compiled Service Records of Volunteer Union Soldiers Who Served in Organizations from the State of California, 1861–1865. National Archives and Records Administration.

Compiled Service Records of Volunteer Union Soldiers Who Served in Organizations from the Territory of New Mexico, 1861–1865. National Archives and Records Administration.

Confederate States of America. *Confederate States of America Records*. Microfilm reels 5, 8, 9, 32, and 33. Manuscripts/Mixed Material, Manuscript Division, Library of Congress.

Cushing, Caleb. Papers. Manuscript Division, Library of Congress.

de la Guerra Collection. Collection Number DLG. Santa Bárbara Mission Archive-Library, Santa Barbara, CA.

Elliott and Gonzáles Family Papers. Wilson Special Collections Library, University of North Carolina at Chapel Hill.

Fernández-Cavada, Fernando. Fernando Fernández-Cavada Collection, Cuban Heritage Collection. University of Miami Libraries, Coral Gables, FL.

Gay, Colonel John L. Collection of Papers Pertaining to the Armijo Family, MSS-193. Center for Southwest Research and Special Collections, University of New Mexico Libraries.

Gonzales Family Papers, 1861–1893. South Caroliniana Library, University of South Carolina.

Letters of Application and Recommendation during the Administration of Ulysses S. Grant, 1869–1877. National Archives and Records Administration, RG 59, Entry AI 760, "Office of the Chief Clerk: Applications and Recommendations for Public Office, 1797–1901," M968, roll 23, frame 283–286.

Longfellow, Henry Wadsworth. Letters to Henry Wadsworth Longfellow, MS Am 1340.2–1340.7. Houghton Library, Harvard University.

Meketa, Charles and Jacqueline. Papers. Center for Southwest Research and Special Collections, University of New Mexico Libraries.

Read, Keith M. Keith M. Read Collection. Ms921. Hargrett Rare Book and Manuscript Library, University of Georgia Libraries.

Records of US Army Continental Commands, 1821–1920. Letters Sent, December 1852–1891. Fort Union, New Mexico. National Archives and Records Administration, RG 393.

Sherman, William T. Papers. General Correspondence, 1837–1891; Dec. 19, 1849–June 2, 1853. Manuscripts/Mixed Material, Manuscript Division, Library of Congress.

US Naval Records Office. *Official Records of the Union and Confederate Navies in the War of the Rebellion*. Series 3, vol. 3. Washington, DC: Government Printing Office, 1922.

US War Department, Robert N. Scott, et al. *The War of the Rebellion: A Compilation of Official Records of the Union and Confederate Armies*. Series 1, vol. 6. Washington, DC: Government Printing Office, 1882.

US War Department, Robert N. Scott, et al. *The War of the Rebellion: A Compilation of the Official Records of the Union and Confederate Armies*. Series 1, vol. 26, ch. 38, part 1. Washington, DC: Government Printing Office, 1889.

US War Department, Robert N. Scott, et al. *The War of the Rebellion: A Compilation of the Official Records of the Union and Confederate Armies*. Series 1, vol. 27, ch. 39. Washington, DC: Government Printing Office, 1889.

Vallejo Family Papers. Bancroft Library, University of California, Berkeley.

UNPUBLISHED MANUSCRIPTS

Cavada, Adolfo F. Diary. Fernando Fernández-Cavada Collection, Cuban Heritage Collection, University of Miami Libraries, Coral Gables, FL.

Cavada, Federico. Diary. Fernando Fernández-Cavada Collection, Cuban Heritage Collection, University of Miami, Coral Gables, FL.

Chacón, Rafael. "Memorias de Rafael Chacón." Charles and Jacqueline Meketa Papers, Center for Southwest Research and Special Collections, University of New Mexico Libraries.

Quintero, J. A. "Lyric Poetry in Cuba." Manuscript. Boston Public Library, Ms.f.D.33.

Tafolla, Santiago. "Nearing the End of the Trail." Tafolla Family Papers, 1860–1980. Benson Latin American Collection, General Libraries, University of Texas at Austin.

NEWSPAPERS

Bejareño (San Antonio, TX)

Boston Herald (Boston, MA)

Charleston Daily Courier (Charleston, SC)

Charleston Mercury (Charleston, SC)

Cincinnati Daily Enquirer (Cincinnati, OH)

Daily National Intelligencer (Washington, DC)

Daily Picayune (New Orleans, LA)
Daily True Californian (San Francisco, CA)
Detroit Daily Free Press (Detroit, MI)
New Orleans Picayune (New Orleans, LA)
New Orleans Times-Democrat (New Orleans, LA)
New York Herald (New York, NY)
New York Times (New York, NY)
New York Tribune (New York, NY)
Patria (New York, NY)
Philadelphia Inquirer (Philadelphia, PA)
Ranchero (San Antonio, TX)
Santa Fe Weekly Gazette (Santa Fe, NM)
Savannah Morning News (Savannah, GA)
St. Louis Post-Dispatch (St. Louis, MO)
State (Columbia, SC)
Times-Picayune (*Daily Picayune*) (New Orleans, LA)
Washington Daily Union (Washington, DC)
Washington Republic (Washington, DC)

PUBLISHED PRIMARY SOURCES

An Act Amendatory of the Law Relative to Contracts Between Masters and Servants. In *Laws of the Territory of New Mexico Passed by the Legislative Assembly, Session of 1858–9*. Santa Fe, NM, 1859.

Ayer, Lewis M., Jr. "Southern Rights and the Cuban Question: An Address, Delivered at Whippy Swamp, on the Fourth of July, 1855." Charleston, SC, 1855.

Boyce, W. W. "The Annexation of Cuba: Speech of Hon. W. W. Boyce, of South Carolina." January 15, 1855. In *Appendix to the Congressional Globe*. 33rd Congress. 2nd session.

Branch, H. N. *The Mexican Constitution of 1917 Compared with the Constitution of 1857*. American Academy of Political and Social Science, 1917.

[Cavada, F. F.]. "The Cave of Bellamar." *Harper's New Monthly Magazine* 41, no. 216 (November 1870): 826–34.

Cavada, F. F. *Ejército libertador de Cuba: Breve instrucción de guerrilla y guía de los jefes y oficiales en campaña*. Imprenta del Cubano Libre, 1870.

Cavada, F. F. *Libby Life: Experiences of a Prisoner of War in Richmond, VA., 1863–1864*. King and Baird, 1864.

Chacón, Rafael. *Legacy of Honor: The Life of Rafael Chacón, a Nineteenth-Century New Mexican*. Edited by Jacqueline Dorgan Meketa. University of New Mexico Press, 1986.

Claiborne, J. F. H. *Life and Correspondence of John A. Quitman, Major-General, USA, and Governor of the State of Mississippi*. Vol. 2. New York, 1860.

Clay, Henry. "Speech of Henry Clay, at the Lexington Mass Meeting, 13th November 1847." New York, 1847.

Collis, Charles Henry. *The Case of F. F. Cavada*. King and Baird, 1865.

Congressional Globe. 36th Congress, 2nd session. January 21, 1861. Washington, DC, 1861.

de la Guerra, Angustias. "Angustias de la Guerra Ord Journal, 1846–1847." In *Testimonios: Early California Through the Eyes of Women, 1815–1848*, edited and translated by Rose Marie Beebe and Robert M. Senkewicz. University of Oklahoma Press, 2015.

de la Guerra, Angustias. "Occurrences in California as Told to Thomas Savage in Santa Bárbara by Mrs. Ord (Doña Angustias de la Guerra) 1878." In *Testimonios: Early California Through the Eyes of Women, 1815–1848*, edited and translated by Rose Marie Beebe and Robert M. Senkewicz. University of Oklahoma Press, 2015.

de la Guerra, Angustias. "Recuerdos." In *Testimonios: Early California Through the Eyes of Women, 1815–1848*, edited and translated by Rose Marie Beebe and Robert M. Senkewicz. University of Oklahoma Press, 2015.

Elliott, William. "A Trip to Cuba." *Russell's Magazine*, October 2, 1857, 59–63.

Elliott, William. "A Trip to Cuba." *Russell's Magazine*, April 3, 1858, 60–69.

Fletcher, Winfield S., ed. *Territory of New Mexico: Report of the Adjutant General, from January 1, 1891, to December 31, 1892*. Santa Fe, NM, 1893.

Fuller, Margaret. "American Literature: Its Position in the Present Time, and Prospects for the Future." In *Papers on Literature and Art*, part 2. New York, 1846.

Gonzales, A. J. *Heaven Revealed: A Series of Authentic Spirit-Messages, from a Wife to Her Husband, Proving the Sublime Nature of True Spiritualism*. McQueen & Wallace, 1889.

Gonzales, Ambrosio José. *Manifesto on Cuban Affairs Addressed to the People of the United States*. September 1, 1852. Daily Delta, 1853.

Gonzales, Ambrose E. *The Black Border: Gullah Stories of the Carolina Coast* (With a Glossary). The State Company, 1922.

Gonzales, Ambrose E. Foreword to *In Darkest Cuba: Two Months' Service Under Gomez Along the Trocha from the Caribbean to the Bahama Channel*, by N. G. Gonzales. The State Company, 1922.

Greeley, Horace. *The American Conflict: A History of the Great Rebellion in the United States of America, 1860–'65*. Vol. 2. Hartford, CT, 1867.

Hammond, James H. *Speech of Hon. James H. Hammond: Delivered at Barnwell Court House, October 29, 1858*. Washington, DC, 1858.

Hernández, J. E. "El laúd del desterrado." In *El laúd del desterrado*. Edited by Matías Montes-Huidobro. Arte Público Press, 1995.

Lamar, Mirabeau B. *The Papers of Mirabeau Buonaparte Lamar*. Vol. 4. Edited by Harriet Smither. Von Boeckmann-Jones Printers, 1921.

Lamar, Mirabeau B. *The Papers of Mirabeau Buonaparte Lamar*. Vol. 4, part 1. Edited by Charles Adams Gulick Jr. and Winnie Allen. Von Boeckmann-Jones, 1924.

Lamar, Mirabeau B. *Verse Memorials*. New York, 1857.

O'Brien, Thos. M., and Oliver Diefendorf, eds. *General Orders of the War Department*. Vol. 2. New York, 1864.

O'Sullivan, John. "Annexation." *United States Magazine and Democratic Review* 17, no. 1 (July–August 1845): 5–10.

Pino, Facundo, and J. M. Gallegos. "Address of the Legislative Assembly of New Mexico: Manifesto of the Council and House of Representatives to the Inhabitants of the Territory of New Mexico." January 29, 1862.

Preliminary Report of the Commission Appointed by the University of Pennsylvania to Investigate Modern Spiritualism, in Accordance with the Request of the Late Henry Seybert. J. B. Lippincott, 1887.

Quintero, J. A. *Apuntes biograficos del Mayor Jeneral Juan Antonio Quitman.* Sherman, Wharton, 1855.

[Quintero, José Agustín]. *The Code of Honor: Its Rationale and Uses, by the Tests of Common Sense and Good Morals, with the Effects of Its Preventive Remedies.* 2nd ed. E. A. Brandao & Co., 1883.

Quintero, José Agustín. "Review of *Verse Memorials.*" c. 1857. In *The Papers of Mirabeau Buonaparte Lamar.* Vol. 4, edited by Harriet Smither. Von Boeckmann-Jones Printers, 1921.

Richardson, James D., ed. *A Compilation of the Messages and Papers of the Confederacy, Including the Diplomatic Correspondences, 1861–1865.* Vol. 2. United States Publishing, 1906.

Robinson, Alfred. *The Letters of Alfred Robinson to the de la Guerra Family of Santa Barbara, 1834–1873.* Translated by Maynard Geiger. Zamorano Club, 1972.

Ruiz de Burton, María Amparo. *Conflicts of Interest: The Letters of María Amparo Ruiz de Burton.* Edited by Rosaura Sánchez and Beatrice Pita. Arte Público Press, 2001.

Ruiz de Burton, María Amparo. *The Squatter and the Don.* 1885. Edited by Rosaura Sánchez and Beatrice Pita. Arte Público Press, 1992.

Ruiz de Burton, María Amparo. *Who Would Have Thought It?* 1872. Edited by Rosaura Sánchez and Beatrice Pita. Arte Público Press, 1995.

Sellén, Francisco. *Hatuey, poema dramático.* A. Da Costa Gómez, 1891.

Sherman, William T. *Memoirs.* Vol. 1. D. Appleton, 1875.

Tafolla, James Santiago. *A Life Crossing Borders: Memoir of a Mexican-American Confederate/Las memorias de un mexicoamericano en la Confederación.* Edited by Carmen Tafolla and Laura Tafolla. Translated by Fidel L. Tafolla. Arte Público Press, 2010.

Tamayo, Jorge L., ed. *Benito Juárez: Documentos, discursos, y correspondencia.* Vol. 8. 2nd ed. Editorial Libros de México, 1974.

Thompson, Jerry, ed. *Tejanos in Gray: Civil War Letters of Captains Joseph Rafael de la Garza and Manuel Yturri.* Translated by José Roberto Juárez. Texas A&M University Press, 2011.

Velazquez, Loreta Janeta. *The Woman in Battle: The Civil War Narrative of Loreta Janeta Velazquez, Cuban Woman and Confederate Soldier.* University of Wisconsin Press, 2003.

Whitman, Walt. *The Collected Writings of Walt Whitman: Prose Works.* Vol. 1, *Specimen Days.* 1892. Edited by Floyd Stovall. New York University Press, 1963.

Whitman, Walt. *Memoranda During the Civil War*. Edited by Peter Coviello. Oxford University Press, 2004.

Wilson, John Lyde. *The Code of Honor; or Rules for the Government of Principals and Seconds in Duelling*. Charleston, 1838.

SECONDARY SOURCES

Alemán, Jesse. "Authenticity, Autobiography, and Identity: *The Woman in Battle* as a Civil War Narrative." Introduction to *The Woman in Battle*, by Loreta Janeta Velazquez. University of Wisconsin Press, 2003.

Alemán, Jesse. "Citizenship Rights and Colonial Whites: The Cultural Work of María Amparo Ruiz de Burton's Novels." In *Complicating Constructions: Race, Ethnicity, and Hybridity in American Texts*, edited by David S. Goldstein and Audrey B. Thacker. University of Washington Press, 2015.

Alemán, Jesse. "The Invention of Mexican America." In *The Oxford Handbook to Nineteenth-Century American Literature*, edited by Russ Castronovo. Oxford University Press, 2011.

Alemán, Jesse. "Wars of Rebellion: US Hispanic Writers and Their American Civil Wars." *American Literary History* 25, no. 1 (2013): 54–68.

Anzaldúa, Gloria. *Borderlands/La Frontera: The New Mestiza*. Aunt Lute Books, 1987.

Aparicio, Frances R. "Latinidad/es." In *Keywords for Latina/o Studies*, edited by Deborah R. Vargas, Lawrence La Fountain-Stokes, and Nancy Raquel Mirabal. New York University Press, 2017.

Aranda, José F. "Breaking All the Rules: María Amparo Ruiz de Burton Writes a Civil War Novel." In *Recovering the US Hispanic Literary Heritage*, edited by Virginia Sánchez-Korrol. Vol. 3. Arte Público Press, 2000.

Aranda, José F. "Contradictory Impulses: María Amparo Ruiz de Burton, Resistance Theory, and the Politics of Chicano/a Studies." *American Literature* 70, no. 3 (1998): 551–79.

Arenson, Adam. Introduction to *Civil War Wests: Testing the Limits of the United States*, edited by Adam Arenson and Andrew R. Graybill. University of California Press, 2015.

Arenson, Adam, and Andrew R. Graybill, eds. *Civil War Wests: Testing the Limits of the United States*. University of California Press, 2015.

Armitage, David. "Civil Wars, from Beginning to End?" *American Historical Review* 120, no. 5 (2015): 1829–37.

Bache, Richard Meade. *The Life of General George Meade: Commander of the Army of the Potomac*. Henry T. Coates, 1897.

Baumgartner, Alice L. "The Line of Positive Safety: Borders and Boundaries in the Rio Grande Valley, 1848–1880." *Journal of American History* 101, no. 4 (2015): 1106–22.

Benavides, José Luis. "'Californios! Whom Do You Support?': *El Clamor Público*'s Contradictory Role in the Racial Formation Process of Early California." *California History* 84, no. 2 (2006–2007): 54–66.

Bettcher, Talia Mae. "Trapped in the Wrong Theory: Rethinking Trans Oppression and Resistance." *Signs* 39, no. 2 (2014): 383–406.

Blanco, María del Pilar. "Whither Latinidad? The Trajectories of Latin American, Caribbean, and Latina/o Literature." In *The Cambridge History of Latina/o American Literature*, edited by John Morán González and Laura Lomas. Cambridge University Press, 2018.

Boag, Peter "The Trouble with Cross-Dressers: Researching and Writing the History of Sexual and Gender Transgressiveness in the Nineteenth-Century American West." *Oregon Historical Society* 112, no. 3 (2011): 322–39.

Brewster, Michele M. "A Californiana in Two Worlds." *Southern California Quarterly* 102, no. 2 (2020): 101–42.

Brock, Darryl E. "José Agustín Quintero: Cuban Patriot in Confederate Diplomatic Service." In *Cubans in the Confederacy: José Agustín Quintero, Ambrosio José Gonzales, and Loreta Janeta Velazquez*, edited by Phillip Thomas Tucker. McFarland, 2002.

Brooks, James F. *Captives and Cousins: Slavery, Kinship, and Community in the Southwest Borderlands*. University of North Carolina Press, 2002.

Buenger, Walter L. *Secession and the Union in Texas*. University of Texas Press, 1984.

Burchard, Peter. *Rat Hell*. Coward, McCann & Geoghegan, 1971.

Caminero-Santangelo, Marta. *On Latinidad: US Latino Literature and the Construction of Ethnicity*. University Press of Florida, 2007.

Campbell, Richard. "Portrait of a Duelist: John L. Wilson and *The Code of Honor*." *South Carolina Historical Magazine* 119, no. 1 (2018): 4–23.

Carbonell, José Manuel. *Los poetas de "El laúd del desterrado": Quintero, Teurbe Tolón, Santacilia, Turla Castellón, Zenea*. Avisador Comercial, 1930.

Casas, María Raquél. *Married to a Daughter of the Land: Spanish-Mexican Women and Interethnic Marriage in California, 1820–1880*. University of Nevada Press, 2007.

Castañeda, Antonia, and Clara Lomas, eds. *Writing/Righting History: Twenty-Five Years of Recovering the US Hispanic Literary Heritage*. Arte Público Press, 2019.

Chaffin, Tom. *Fatal Glory: Narciso López and the First Clandestine US War Against Cuba*. University Press of Virginia, 1996.

Chávez-García, Mirosilva. *Negotiating Conquest: Gender and Power in California, 1770s to 1880s*. University of Arizona Press, 2004.

Chestnut, Mary. *Mary Chestnut's Civil War*. Edited by C. Vann Woodward. Quality Paperback Book Club, 1995.

Clinton, Catherine, and Nina Sibler, eds. *Divided Houses: Gender and the Civil War*. Oxford University Press, 1992.

Contreras, Alicia. "María Amparo Ruiz de Burton, 'White Slaves,' and Mexican Representation in the American Realist Chronology." *American Literary Realism* 53, no. 2 (2021): 112–16.

Cooper, Melissa L. *Making Gullah: A History of Sapelo Islanders, Race, and the American Imagination*. University of North Carolina Press, 2017.

Coronado, Raúl. *A World Not to Come: A History of Latino Writing and Print Culture*. Harvard University Press, 2013.

Daddysman, James. *The Matamoros Trade: Confederate Commerce, Diplomacy, and Intrigue*. University of Delaware Press, 1984.

Davis, O. W. *Sketch of Frederic Fernandez Cavada, a Native of Cuba*. James B. Chandler, 1871.

Davis, William C. *Inventing Loreta Velasquez: Confederate Soldier Impersonator, Media Celebrity, and Con Artist*. Southern Illinois University Press, 2016.

Dawes, James. *The Language of War: Literature and Culture in the US from the Civil War Through World War II*. Harvard University Press, 2002.

de la Cova, Antonio Rafael. *Cuban Confederate Colonel: The Life of Ambrosio José Gonzales*. University of North Carolina Press, 2003.

de la Teja, Jesús F., ed. *Lone Star Unionism, Dissent, and Resistance: Other Sides of Civil War Texas*. University of Oklahoma Press, 2016.

Divanco, Julian. *El primer periodista y un gran educador*. El Sol, 1955.

Domínguez, Daylet. "Slaveholders in the South: The Networks of Cubans and Southerners in the Age of the Second Slavery." *Atlantic Studies* 18, no. 1 (2021): 51–69.

Downs, Gregory P., and Kate Masur. Introduction to *The World the Civil War Made*, edited by Gregory P. Downs and Kate Masur. University of North Carolina Press, 2015.

Doyle, Donald H., ed. *American Civil Wars: The United States, Latin America, Europe, and the Crises of the 1860s*. University of North Carolina Press, 2017.

Dreese, Michael A. *Torn Families: Death and Kinship at the Battle of Gettysburg*. McFarland, 2007.

Earle, Rebecca. *The Return of the Native: Indians and Myth-Making in Spanish America, 1810–1930*. Duke University Press, 2007.

Echevarría, Roberto González. *Myth and Archive: A Theory of Latin American Narrative*. Cambridge University Press, 1990.

Eiselein, Gregory. "American Self-Fashioning and Problems of Autobiography." In *Teaching the Literatures of Early America*, edited by Carla Mulford. MLA Press, 1999.

Ellis, Richard E. *The Union at Risk: Jacksonian Democracy, States' Rights and the Nullification Crisis*. Oxford University Press, 1987.

Emparan, Maddie Brown. *The Vallejos of California*. Gleeson Library Associates, 1968.

Faust, Drew Gilpin. *The Creation of Confederate Nationalism: Ideology and Identity in the Civil War South*. Louisiana State University Press, 1989.

Faust, Drew Gilpin. *Mothers of Invention: Women of the Slaveholding South in the American Civil War*. University of North Carolina Press, 1996.

Ferrer, Ada. "Cuban Slavery and Atlantic Antislavery." In *Slavery and Antislavery in Spain's Atlantic Empire*, edited by Josep M. Fradera and Christopher Schmidt-Nowara. Berghahn, 2016.

Ferrer, Ada. *Insurgent Cuba: Race, Nation, and Revolution, 1868–1898*. University of North Carolina Press, 1999.

Foley, Neil. *White Scourge: Mexicans, Blacks, and Poor Whites in Texas Cotton Culture*. University of California Press, 1998.

Foster, Travis M. "The Effeminate Man in Nineteenth-Century America." In *Gender in American Literature and Culture*, edited by Jean M. Lutes and Jennifer Travis. Cambridge University Press, 2021.

Foucault, Michel. *The Order of Things: An Archaeology of the Human Sciences*. Routledge Classics, 2002.

Gaddy, David W. "Rochford's Cipher: A Discovery in Confederate Cryptography." *Cryptologia* 16, no. 4 (1992): 347–62.

Galarte, Francisco J. *Brown Trans Figurations: Rethinking Race, Gender, and Sexuality in Chicanx/Latinx Studies*. University of Texas Press, 2021.

Gerke, Amanda Ellen, and Luisa María González Rodríguez. Introduction to *Latinidad at the Crossroads: Insights into Latinx Identity in the Twenty-First Century*, edited by Amanda Ellen Gerke and Luisa María González Rodríguez. Brill Rodopi, 2021.

Glymph, Thavolia. *The Women's Fight: The Civil War's Battles for Home, Freedom, and Nation*. University of North Carolina Press, 2020.

Goldman, Anne E. "'Who Ever Heard of a Blue-Eyed Mexican'?: Satire and Sentimentality in María Amparo Ruiz de Burton's *Who Would Have Thought It?*" In *Recovering the US Hispanic Literary Heritage*, edited by Erlinda Gonzales-Berry and Chuck Tatum. Vol. 2. Arte Público Press, 1995.

Goldman, Anne E., and Amelia de la Luz Montes, eds. *María Amparo Ruiz de Burton: Critical and Pedagogical Perspectives*. University of Nebraska Press, 2004.

Gollar, Walker C. "Jesuit Education and Slavery in Kentucky, 1832–1868." *Register of the Kentucky Historical Society* 108, no. 3 (Summer 2010): 213–49.

Gómez, Laura E. *Manifest Destinies: The Making of the Mexican American Race*. New York University Press, 2007.

Gonzales, Phillip B. *Forced Sacrifice as Ethnic Protest: The Hispano Cause in New Mexico and the Racial Attitude of Confrontation of 1933*. Peter Lang, 2001.

González, John Morán. "Romancing Hegemony: Constructing Racialized Citizenship in María Amparo Ruiz de Burton's *The Squatter and the Don*." In *Recovering the US Hispanic Literary Heritage*, edited by Erlinda Gonzales-Berry and Chuck Tatum. Vol. 2. Arte Público Press, 1996.

González, John Morán, and Laura Lomas. Introduction to *The Cambridge History of Latina/o American Literature*, edited by John Morán González and Laura Lomas. Cambridge University Press, 2018.

Gray, Paul Bryan. *A Clamor for Equality: Emergence and Exile of Californio Activist Francisco P. Ramírez*. Texas Tech University Press, 2012.

Gurza-Lavalle, Gerardo. "Against Slave Power? Slavery and Runaway Slaves in Mexico-United States Relations, 1821–1857." *Mexican Studies/Estudios Mexicanos* 35, no. 2 (2019): 142–70.

Guterl, Matthew Pratt. *American Mediterranean: Southern Slaveholders in the Age of Emancipation*. Harvard University Press, 2008.

Hague, Harlen, and David J. Langum. *Thomas O. Larkin: A Life of Patriotism and Profit in Old California*. University of Oklahoma Press, 1990.

Hahn, Steven. Afterword to *The World the Civil War Made*, edited by Gregory P. Downs and Kate Masur. University of North Carolina Press, 2015.

Hahn, Steven. *A Nation Without Borders: The United States and Its World in an Age of Civil Wars, 1830–1910*. Viking, 2016.

Halberstam, Jack. *Trans*: A Quick and Quirky Account of Gender Variability*. University of California Press, 2018.

Hanlon, Christopher. "Confederate Literature." In *American Literature in Transition, 1851–1877*, edited by Cody Marrs. Cambridge University Press, 2022.

Hartman, Saidiya. *Scenes of Subjection: Terror, Slavery, and Self-Making in Nineteenth-Century America*. Rev. ed. Norton, 2022.

Hartman, Saidiya. "Venus in Two Acts." *Small Axe* 12, no. 2 (2008): 1–14.

Hayes-Bautista, David E. *El Cinco de Mayo: An American Tradition*. University of California Press, 2012.

Hernández, Bernadine Marie. *Border Bodies: Racialized Sexuality, Sexual Capital, and Violence in the Nineteenth-Century Borderlands*. University of North Carolina Press, 2022.

Hesseltine, William Best. *Civil War Prisons: A Study in War Psychology*. 1930. Ohio State University Press, 1998.

Hudson, Renee. *Latinx Revolutionary Horizons: Form and Futurity in the Americas*. Fordham University Press, 2024.

Hutchison, Coleman. *Apples and Ashes: Literature, Nationalism, and the Confederate States of America*. University of Georgia Press, 2012.

Index to Harper's New Monthly Magazine. Vols 1–70, inclusive from June 1850 to June 1885. Harper Brothers, 1886.

Jones, Lewis Pickney. "William Elliott, South Carolina Nonconformist." *Journal of Southern History* 17, no. 3 (1951): 361–81.

Jova, Joseph John. Foreword to *Libby Life: Experiences of a Prisoner of War in Richmond, VA., 1863–64*, by F. F. Cavada. University Press of America, 1985.

Kanellos, Nicolás. "*El Clamor Público*: Resisting the American Empire." *California History* 84, no. 2 (2006–2007): 10–18.

Kemble, Edward C. *A History of California Newspapers, 1848–1858*. Edited by Helen Harding Bretnor. Talisman Press, 1962.

Kiser, William S. *Illusions of Empire: The Civil War and Reconstruction in the US-Mexico Borderlands*. University of Pennsylvania Press, 2022.

Lamas, Carmen E. *The Latino Continuum and the Nineteenth-Century Americas: Literature, Translation, and Historiography*. Oxford University Press, 2021.

Lazo, Rodrigo. "Confederates in the Hispanic Attic: The Archive Against Itself." In *Unsettled States: Nineteenth-Century American Literary Studies*, edited by Dana Luciano and Ivy Wilson. New York University Press, 2014.

Lazo, Rodrigo. Introduction to *The Latino Nineteenth Century*, edited by Rodrigo Lazo and Jesse Alemán. New York University Press, 2016.

Lazo, Rodrigo. *Letters from Filadelfia: Early Latino Literature and the Trans-American Elite*. University of Virginia Press, 2020.

Lazo, Rodrigo. "Migrant Archives: New Routes in and out of American Studies." In *States of Emergency: The Object of American Studies*, edited by Russ Castronovo and Susan Gilman. University of North Carolina Press, 2009.

Lazo, Rodrigo. *Writing to Cuba: Filibustering and Cuban Exiles in the United States*. University of North Carolina Press, 2005.

Lonn, Ella. *Foreigners in the Confederacy*. University of North Carolina Press, 2002.

López, Marissa K. *Chicano Nations: The Hemispheric Origins of Mexican American Literature*. New York University Press, 2011.

Lozano, Rosina. *An American Language: The History of Spanish in the United States*. University of California Press, 2018.

Marbán, Jorge A. *Confederate Patriot, Journalist, and Poet: The Multifaceted Life of José Agustín Quintero*. Friesen Press, 2014.

Martinez, Louis Alfredo. "Federico Fernández Cavada: Loyal to Two Flags." In *Hispanic Presence in the United States*, edited by Frank de Varona. Mnemosyne Publishing, 1993.

Masich, Andrew E. *Civil War in the Southwest Borderlands, 1861–1867*. University of Oklahoma Press, 2017.

May, Robert E. *Manifest Destiny's Underworld: Filibustering in Antebellum America*. University of North Carolina Press, 2002.

McCardell, John. *The Idea of a Southern Nation: Southern Nationalists and Southern Nationalism, 1830–1860*. Norton, 1979.

McGarry, Molly. *Ghosts of Futures Past: Spiritualism and the Cultural Politics of Nineteenth-Century America*. University of California Press, 2008.

Meketa, Jacqueline Dorgan. Introduction to *Legacy of Honor: The Life of Rafael Chacón, a Nineteenth-Century New Mexican*, by Rafael Chacón, edited by Jacqueline Dorgan Meketa. University of New Mexico Press, 1986.

Mitchell, W. J. T. *Image Science: Iconology, Visual Culture, and Media Aesthetics*. University of Chicago Press, 2015.

Montejano, David. *Anglos and Mexicans in the Making of Texas, 1836–1986*. University of Texas Press, 1987.

Mora, Anthony. *Border Dilemmas: Racial and National Uncertainties in New Mexico, 1848–1912*. Duke University Press, 2011.

Mora-Torres, Juan. *The Making of the Mexican Border: The State, Capitalism, and Society in Nuevo León, 1848–1910*. University of Texas Press, 2001.

Moyna, María Irene, and María Eugenia Martín. "'Un Alma Atravesada': Inglés y español en la correspondencia de María Amparo Ruiz de Burton." *Anuario de Lingüística Hispánica* 21–22 (2005–2006): 167–84.

Nelson, Megan Kate. *The Three-Cornered War: The Union, the Confederacy, and Native Peoples in the Fight for the West*. Scribner, 2020.

Nichols, James David. "The Line of Liberty: Runaway Slaves and Fugitive Peons in the Texas-Mexico Borderlands." *Western Historical Quarterly* 44, no. 4 (2013): 413–33.

Nunis, Doyce B., ed. *The San Francisco Vigilance Committee of 1856: Three Views [by] William T. Coleman, William T. Sherman [and] James O'Meara*. Los Angeles Westerners, 1971.

O'Donnell-Rosales, John. *Hispanic Confederates*. 3rd ed. Clearfield, 2006.

Olguín, B. V. "Sangre Mexicana/Corazón Americano: Identity, Ambiguity, and Critique in Mexican-American War Narratives." *American Literary History* 14, no. 1 (2002): 83–114.

Owsley, Frank Lawrence, Sr. *King Cotton Diplomacy: Foreign Relations of the Confederate States of America*. 3rd ed. University of Alabama Press, 2008.

Padilla, Genaro. *My History, Not Yours: The Formation of Mexican American Autobiography*. University of Wisconsin Press, 1993.

Padilla, Yolanda. "*La Crónica*, the Mexican Revolution, and Transnational Critique of the US-Mexico Border." *English Language Notes* 56, no. 2 (2018): 107–20.

Paredes, Américo. *A Texas-Mexican Cancionero: Folksongs of the Lower Border*. University of Texas Press, 1976.

Paredes, Américo. *With His Pistol in His Hand: A Border Ballad and Its Hero*. University of Texas Press, 1958.

Paredes, Raymund P. "The Evolution of Chicano Literature." *MELUS* 5, no. 2 (1978): 71–110.

Pérez, Louis A., Jr. *Cuba and the United States: Ties of Singular Intimacy*. 3rd ed. University of Georgia Press, 2003.

Pérez, Louis A., Jr. *Cuba Between Reform and Revolution*. 5th ed. Oxford University Press, 2015.

Pérez, Louis A., Jr. *Intimations of Modernity: Civil Culture in Nineteenth-Century Cuba*. University of North Carolina Press, 2017.

Pitt, Leonard. *The Decline of the Californios: A Social History of the Spanish-Speaking Californians, 1846–1890*. University of California Press, 1966.

Potter, David M. *The Impending Crisis, 1848–1861*. Harper, 1976.

Poyo, Gerald E. *"With All, and for the Good of All": The Emergence of Popular Nationalism in the Cuban Communities of the United States, 1848–1898*. Duke University Press, 1989.

Prezelski, Tom. *Californio Lancers: The 1st Battalion of Native Cavalry in the Far West, 1863–1866*. Arthur H. Clark, 2015.

Pubols, Louise. *The Father of All: The de la Guerra Family, Power, and Patriarchy in Mexican California*. University of California Press and Henry E. Huntington Library and Art Gallery, 2009.

Quigley, Paul. *Shifting Grounds: Nationalism and the American South, 1848–1865*. Oxford University Press, 2012.

Rable, George C. *Civil Wars: Women and the Crisis of Southern Nationalism*. University of Illinois Press, 1989.

Rael-Gálvez, Estévan. "Identifying Captivity and Capturing Identity: Narratives of American Indian Slavery, Colorado and New Mexico, 1776–1934." PhD diss., University of Michigan, 2002.

Ramirez, Pablo A. "Conquest's Child: Gold, Contracts, and American Imperialism in María Amparo Ruiz de Burton's *Who Would Have Thought It?*" *Arizona Quarterly* 70, no. 4 (2014): 143–65.

Remos y Rubio, Juan J. *Historia de la literatura cubana*. Vol. 2. La Habana, Cuba: Cárdenas y Compañía, 1945.

Reséndez, Andres. "North American Peonage." *Journal of the Civil War Era* 7, no. 4 (2017): 597–619.

Rivera, John-Michael. *The Emergence of Mexican America: Recovering Stories of Mexican Peoplehood in US Culture*. New York University Press, 2006.

Rodríguez, Ricardo J., ed. *Hispanics in the US Civil War: A Compiled List of Men Who Fought for the Confederacy and the Union*. 2 vols. Jar Press, 2010.

Rothera, Evan C. *Civil Wars and Reconstructions in the Americas: The United States, Mexico, and Argentina, 1860s–1880*. Louisiana State University Press, 2022.

Rubio, Darío. *La anarquía del lenguaje en la América Española*. Vol. 2. Mexico, 1925.

Rugemer, Edward B. "Why Civil War? The Politics of Slavery in Comparative Perspective." In *The Civil War as Global Conflict: Transnational Meanings of the American Civil War*, edited by David T. Gleeson and Simon Lewis. University of South Carolina Press, 2014.

Sager, Robin C. "The Multiple Metaphoric Civil Wars of Loreta Janeta Velazquez's *The Woman in Battle*." *Southern Quarterly* 48, no. 1 (2010): 27–45.

Saldívar, Ramón. *The Borderlands of Culture: Américo Paredes and the Transnational Imaginary*. Duke University Press, 2006.

Sánchez, Rosaura. "The Latino Nineteenth Century." Review of *The Latino Nineteenth Century*, edited by Rodrigo Lazo and Jesse Alemán. *Journal of American History* 104, no. 4 (2018): 1014–15.

Schmidt, Kelly L. "Enslavement at St. Joseph College, Bardstown, Kentucky." Slavery, History, Memory, and Reconciliation Project, 2020. www.jesuits.org.

Schmidt-Nowara, Christopher. *Empire and Antislavery: Spain, Cuba, and Puerto Rico, 1833–1874*. University of Pittsburgh Press, 1999.

Scott, Rebecca. *Degrees of Freedom: Louisiana and Cuba After Slavery*. Harvard University Press, 2005.

Shields, John C. *Phillis Wheatley's Poetics of Liberation: Backgrounds and Context*. University of Tennessee Press, 2008.

Silva Gruesz, Kirsten. *Ambassadors of Culture: The Transamerican Origins of Latino Writing*. Princeton University Press, 2002.

Silva Gruesz, Kirsten. "Subject to the Border: The Strange Case of José Agustín Quintero." In *Recovering the US Hispanic Literary Heritage*, edited by Kenya Dworkin y Méndez and Agnes Lugo-Ortiz. Vol. 5. Arte Público Press, 2006.

Sinha, Manisha. *The Counterrevolution of Slavery: Politics and Ideology in Antebellum South Carolina*. University of North Carolina Press, 2000.

Stegmaier, Mark J. "'A Law That Would Make Caligula Blush'?: New Mexico Territory's Unique Slave Code, 1859–1861." *New Mexico Historical Review* 87, no. 2 (2012): 209–42.

Szeghi, Tereza M. "The Vanishing Mexicana/o: (Dis)Locating the Native in Ruiz de Burton's *Who Would Have Thought It?* and *The Squatter and the Don*." *Aztlán* 36, no. 2 (2011): 89–120.

Tafolla, Carmen. Introduction to *A Life Crossing Borders: Memoir of a Mexican-American Confederate/Las memorias de un mexicoamericano en la Confederación*, by Santiago Tafolla, edited by Carmen Tafolla and Laura Tafolla, translated by Fidel L. Tafolla. Arte Público Press, 2010.

Taniguchi, Nancy J. *Dirty Deeds: Land, Violence, and the 1856 San Francisco Vigilance Committee*. University of Oklahoma Press, 2016.

Taylor, Alan. *American Civil Wars: A Continental History, 1850–1873*. Norton, 2024.

Thomas, Lately. *Delmonico's: A Century of Splendor*. Houghton Mifflin, 1967.

Thompson, Jerry D. *A Civil War History of the New Mexico Volunteers and Militia*. University of New Mexico Press, 2015.

Thompson, Jerry D. *Tejano Tiger: José de los Santos Benavides and the Texas-Mexico Borderlands, 1823–1891*. Texas Christian University Press, 2017.

Thompson, Jerry D. *Vaqueros in Blue and Gray*. State House Press, 2000.

Twitchell, Ralph Emerson. *The Leading Facts of New Mexico History*. Vol. 2. Sunstone Press, 2007.

Tyler, Ronnie C. *Santiago Vidaurri and the Southern Confederacy*. Texas State Historical Association, 1973.

Valerio-Jiménez, Omar S. "'Although We Are the Last Soldiers': Citizenship, Ideology, and Tejano Unionism." In *Lone Star Unionism, Dissent, and Resistance: Other Sides of Civil War Texas*, edited by Jesús F. de la Teja. University of Oklahoma Press, 2016.

Varon, Alberto. "Archival Excess in Latinx Print Culture: US National Latinx Literature." *English Language Notes* 56, no. 2 (2018): 67–70.

Varon, Alberto. *Before Chicano: Citizenship and the Making of Mexican American Manhood, 1848–1959*. New York University Press, 2018.

Ventura, Gabriela Baeza, Nicolás Kanellos, and Carolina Villarroel. "Recovering Our Written Legacy: Recounting the Challenge." In *Writing History/Righting History: Twenty-Five Years of Recovering the US Hispanic Literary Heritage*, edited by Antonia Castañeda and Clara Lomas. Arte Público Press, 2019.

Walsh, Justin E. "Radically and Thoroughly Democratic: Wilber F. Storey and the Detroit *Free Press*, 1853 to 1861." *Michigan History* 47, no. 201 (1963): 193–225.

White, Hayden V. "The Burden of History." *History and Theory* 5, no. 2 (1966): 111–34.

Whites, LeeAnn. *The Civil War as a Crisis in Gender: Augusta, Georgia, 1860–1890*. University of Georgia Press, 1995.

Young, Elizabeth. *Disarming the Nation: Women's Writing and the American Civil War*. University of Chicago Press, 1999.

INDEX

Note: Figures are indicated by page numbers in *italics*.

ABOUT THE AUTHOR

JESSE ALEMÁN is Professor of English and a Presidential Teaching Fellow at the University of New Mexico. A scholar of nineteenth-century US Latinx literary and cultural histories, he republished *The Woman in Battle* (2002) and coedited *The Latino Nineteenth Century* (2016). He was a Research Fellow at the Latino Research Institute (University of Texas at Austin) and was named the American Antiquarian Society's 2023–2024 Mellon Distinguished Scholar in Residence.